ALLAH'S
TORCH

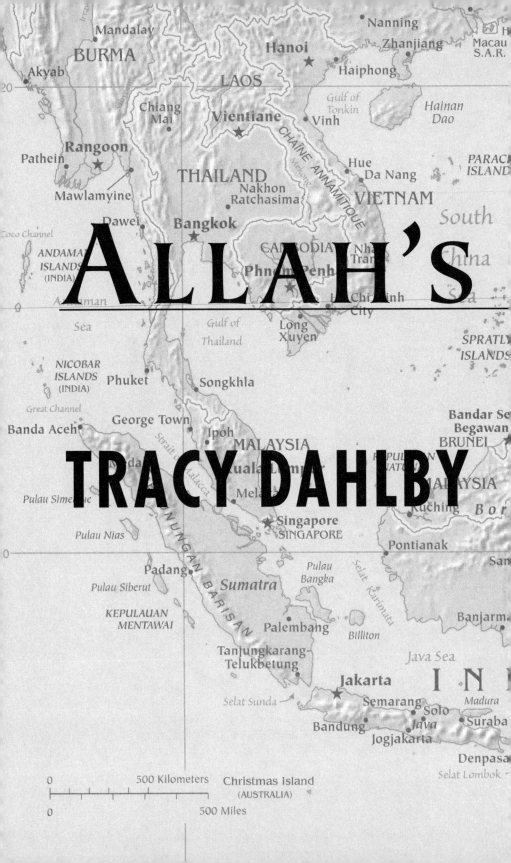

ALLAH'S

TRACY DAHLBY

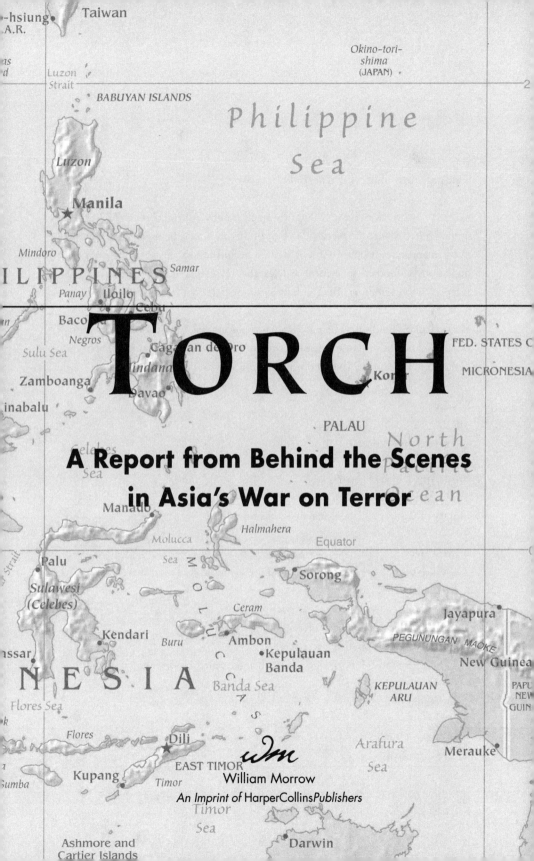

TORCH

A Report from Behind the Scenes in Asia's War on Terror

William Morrow
An Imprint of HarperCollins*Publishers*

Title page map courtesy of *The World Factbook*.

HarperCollins books may be purchased for educational, business, or sales promotional use. For information please write: Special Markets Department, HarperCollins Publishers Inc., 10 East 53rd Street, New York, NY 10022.

FIRST EDITION

Designed by Iva Hacker-Delany

Printed on acid-free paper

Library of Congress Cataloging-in-Publication Data

Dahlby, Tracy.
    Allah's torch : a report from behind the scenes in Asia's war on terror / by Tracy Dahlby.
        p.   cm.
    Includes bibliographical references and index.
    ISBN 0-06-056090-8 (alk. paper)
    1. Terrorism—Indonesia.   2. Islam and terrorism—Indonesia.
3. Anti-Americanism—Indonesia.   4. Dahlby, Tracy.   5. Journalists—Indonesia—Biography.   6. Americans—Indonesia—Biography.   I. Title.

HV6433.I5D34   2004
303.6'25'09598—dc22   2004052554

05   06   07   08   09   DIX/QW   10   9   8   7   6   5   4   3   2   1

For Toshiko

Everything that irritates us about others can lead us to an understanding of ourselves.

—C. G. JUNG

Contents

A Note to Readers

In our ultrasensitive times, a word about the title of this book is in order. *Allah's Torch* is meant to stand, as the alert reader will know, to stand for the light-giving qualities transmitted through Islam, one of the world's great traditions. Like all things great and good, however, that same torch, when hoisted in human hands, can be used either to illuminate the darkness or amplify it. How it's wielded in our world today, and to what end, rests, as I hope the following pages will attest, on the actions and intentions of all of us, Muslim and non-Muslim alike. You should also know that this is a work of personal experience, memory, and opinion, all anchored in firsthand observation; in a small number of cases, it has been necessary to change names and physical details to protect people's privacy. Finally, all journeys are by nature unique. Other travelers will churn up other visions of Indonesia and the dramatic events now shaping its neighborhood in Southeast Asia. This one is mine.

Tracy Dahlby
New York City, 2004

PROLOGUE:
Radical Mystery Tour

February 4, 2003, 4 P.M.

The sky above the sprawling slums of north Jakarta was the color of molten lead and roughly the same temperature as I worked my way deeper and deeper into the dusty mazelike streets. With the U.S. military gearing up to invade Muslim Iraq any week now, it was not the ideal time for a lone American to be roaming the back alleys of Muslim Asia. But there I was, tall and luminously white, inconspicuous as a radar tower, and dogging the heels of my Indonesian friend and interpreter, Norman Wibowo.

Norman had stopped to check the address in his notebook, when a trollish man stepped from behind a small iron gate, smiled at his shoes, and then silently led us down a narrow chute between the crumbling camel-colored buildings and across a dank green courtyard into the compound of Habib Mohamad Rizieq Shihab, one of Indonesia's fieriest anti-American preachers. When I heard the gate clang shut behind us, my pulse began to race.

Rizieq was no Osama bin Laden, mind you. He was

either a selfless holy man or a small-time hood depending on whom you talked to in Jakarta's large and varied Muslim community. At the same time, his private militia, the Islamic Defenders Front, was not the sort of outfit easily confused with the Boy Scouts. In normal times the Defenders had a reputation for waging a hit-and-run campaign against the symbols of American culture by trashing bars and discos, slashing billboards advertising alcohol and slinky lingerie, or by "sweeping"—code for ordering visiting Americans to get the hell out of Indonesia, which they not infrequently did at a trot.

With Iraq on the boil, however, the Defenders had vowed to get really tough. Three months earlier Muslim fanatics had firebombed two popular nightspots on Indonesia's resort island of Bali, murdering 202 people thought to be mainly American tourists but who were, in fact, mainly Australians. Rizieq had played no part in those atrocities. On the other hand, he now was actively recruiting jihadis to fight the American infidel in Iraq, and the betting was that all hell would break loose in Jakarta as soon as the first U.S. bomb fell on Baghdad. Hundreds of anxious foreign residents had already packed their bags and left Indonesia, and the U.S. State Department was warning Americans to stay out.

But I was in of course, and much farther than I wanted to be. Our guide waved Norman and me into a shedlike vestibule, which smelled faintly of damp earth and boiled eggs, and told us to wait. Pretzeling my legs under me on the tattered carpet, I was trying hard not to think about Daniel Pearl, the *Wall Street Journal* reporter who had been beheaded by Islamic thugs in Pakistan in 2002 after following the promise of an interview into a trap, when I suddenly heard footsteps on the path outside.

In the next instant two wiry, unshaven young men had barged through the door and plopped down in front of me. From the way their bulging eyes traveled over my body as if it were a side of beef, I could picture my future, or what was left of it, unfolding with grisly predictability—the quick lunge, the sharp, workmanlike tap to the back of my skull, and the ensuing brisk, incoherent ride to oblivion in the back of a dilapidated van.

But fear isn't always the same as reality, as I have to constantly remind myself, and that didn't happen. Instead, the pair swiveled their heads in unison, gave Norman the same pop-eyed once-over, and then, exchanging faint, knowing smirks, got up and left the room. I looked over at Norman and saw his Adam's apple quiver in the dim light. "Boss," he said, rolling dark eyeballs, "what have you gotten me into?"

Dry-mouthed with fear, the best I could manage was a tight, sheepish grin. Yet I had to admit it was an excellent question: What in God's name *were* we doing here?

The simple answer is that like so many ink-stained Asia hands before me I'd been seduced by Indonesia. Sweeping 3,200 miles from the jungles of New Guinea in the east to the Indian Ocean in the west (the same distance separating Ketchikan from Key West) and four-fifths water, the country is a huge porous sponge of some 13,677 islands, scattered through combing, cobalt blue seas, and as such presents the writer with an irresistibly complex and tantalizing puzzle. Its human registry is magnificently scattered, too. For though Indonesia is nearly ninety percent Muslim, and the world's single largest concentration of believers, its 238 million people are also Christian, Hindu, and Buddhist, and further divide themselves into 300 ethnic groups and speak 300 distinct languages. "Socially," says one Indonesian friend, "it's the United States on steroids."

Heaven knows I'd come to this intriguing arena late enough. Though I'd covered Asia as a journalist for many years, I'd somehow managed to largely skip over Indonesia until November 1999, when my editors at *National Geographic* magazine asked me to go there and see if I could shed any light on where this big, strategically important Jupiter of a country, the geographical pivot of Southeast Asia, was headed. They had certainly picked an historic moment. It was just over a year since a crashing economy and weeks of violent antigovernment rioting had toppled the thirty-two-year rule of former President Suharto, and the country was churning with such comprehensive ethnic and religious strife that even the Indonesians had a hard time keeping track of it. Yet it was a deliriously promising time, too. The strongman's ouster had opened the door for the republic's first democratically elected government in over forty years, and on nearly every street corner peril fought with promise for the country's future. With democratic reform, or *reformasi,* as the Indonesians called it, seemingly on a roll, the betting—or more accurately, the prayer—among the relatively few Americans who paid any attention to the place was that the Indonesians, with their characteristic grit, intelligence, and waggish good humor, just might pull it off.

The optimism was short-lived. With the terror attacks on New York and Washington on September 11, 2001, America's generally rosy view of the planet quickly darkened, and virtually overnight Indonesia was transformed in Western eyes from a game if wobbly new democracy into a den of Islamic terror. Under the circumstances, it was not so wild a nightmare. Vast and virtually lawless, with its endless unpatrolled coastlines and blue volcano-studded redoubts, Indonesia made an ideal hideout for the discriminating terrorist on the lam from the U.S.-led invasion of Afghanistan. Videotapes discovered in the rubble of Al Qaeda hideouts in Central Asia indicated, at least circumstantially, that Osama bin Laden was intent on expanding his franchise operations in Southeast Asia. Early on, and not unreasonably therefore, President George Bush and his advisers identified the area in general and Indonesia in particular as a next important front in GWOT, America's Global War on Terror, and set about trying to persuade the Indonesians, longtime U.S. allies, to join in the fight.

That was where the really tough sledding began. For while we Americans were radically altering our view of them, the Indonesians had been radically altering their view of us. Although the overwhelming majority of Indonesia's Muslims are decent, even-keeled people, and generally about as warlike as Ohio Presbyterians at a church picnic, the U.S.-led air strikes on Al Qaeda and Taliban targets in Afghanistan, with their inevitable collateral killing and wounding of innocent Muslim civilians, had put people in a very sour mood. The reversal in America's popularity was nothing short of breathtaking. (In one typical public opinion survey carried out by the respected Pew Global Attitudes Project, the number of Indonesians expressing friendly feelings toward the U.S. went from seventy-five percent in 2000, higher than any other Muslim country, not to mention France and Canada, to an abysmal fifteen percent three years later.) Meanwhile, even thoughtful Indonesians began to suspect that the CIA may have actually instigated the Bali atrocities to give Islam a black eye.

Given the rising anti-American tone, and viewed from the gauzy distance of the United States, it took little imagination to conclude that it was Indonesia's Islamic fundamentalists, not its democrats, who were hitting their stride. Although in early 2003 Bali still marked the biggest single terror attack anywhere in the world since 9/11, Indonesia had been hit by a string of smaller bombings (churches, car dealerships, fast-food restaurants, even the Jakarta Stock Exchange) attributed, variously, to the country's many interlocking terrorist cells. Growing numbers of nonviolent Islamists openly worked to turn secular Indonesia into a purely Islamic state. Others grandly envisioned *Daulah Islamiyah,* a Muslim superstate that would one day stretch in an unbroken arc from Aceh at Indonesia's westernmost tip to Zamboanga in the Philippines, and along the way sweep in Singapore, Malaysia, and Thailand, and a population of nearly four hundred million people. In Jakarta, meanwhile, the democratically elected government of President Megawati Sukarnoputri seemed frozen in place, caught between U.S. demands that it go after the terrorists in its midst and the view popular with most Indonesian voters that there were no terrorists to go after. And to top it off, pretty much all fundamentalists fundamentally agreed: Once they managed to make *shariah,* the stern Islamic legal code, the law of the land, the poisons of rampant political corruption and godless global consumerism would—*Inshallah,* God willing—burn cleanly away.

That rather stunning shift in mood in a country unknown to most Americans might easily have been ignored but for the inconvenient facts that in our inner-connected world Indonesia's well-being is directly connected to our own continued good health. Stretched out majestically along the floorboards of Asia, it is by far

Southeast Asia's biggest economy and helps anchor, figuratively as well as literally, the dynamo economies of the South China Sea, which in turn account for a cool quarter of the global GNP, and could harbor trillions of dollars in undersea oil and gas deposits. What's more, its encompassing seas boast three of the world's most strategic shipping routes, the Malacca, Sunda, and Lombok straits—blue, zigzagging slots that carry over half the commercial shipping on the planet. Trouble there would inevitably mean fewer low-priced sneakers, hand towels, backyard barbecues, and other essential Asian imports down at the local Wal-Mart; somewhat more seriously, it might also crimp the flow of Middle Eastern oil to places like Japan and send world stock markets into a dangerous swoon.

And of course that was precisely the point—if the world's biggest Muslim country suddenly became Fundamentalist Central, or merely fundamentally dysfunctional as a nation, like Pakistan or Afghanistan, to name only two, then where in the world would that leave the rest of us?

That is what I wanted to know, and to be honest I was surprised and chagrined that I didn't already know it. Thanks to my *Geographic* assignment, I'd spent months traveling the country from stem to stern, plunging myself, however briefly, into some of its many pockets of turmoil. Not unreasonably, I suppose, I prided myself on knowing a little bit about the place. Now suddenly, after 9/11 and the surprise attacks on the World Trade Center and the Pentagon, it appeared I'd missed the story completely, which is to say Indonesia's alleged big-time connection with Osama bin Laden and worldwide Islamic revolution. Plenty of others far more knowledgeable than I—scholars, diplomats, and spies—had missed it, too, mind you. But the fact remained: I'd missed it.

Luckily, I knew what I had to do. As soon as I could figure out how to pay for an independent reporting trip, I'd leave my newly terrorized but comfortable island of Manhattan to revisit the chronically turbulent islands of Indonesia. My plan was to build on what I knew while looking for new clues as to how Indonesia's troubles might be connected to what had happened in my own backyard through the vehicle of militant Islam. I'd explore its teeming cities, eat its fiery curries, tramp the dusty village roads, and visit the mosques and religious boarding schools that were said to be incubators of anti-Western hatred. How deeply had Al Qaeda sunk its roots in Indonesia? What was the nature of its kinship with local militant groups? If my luck held, I would return with a clearer picture of who or what we were up against and what we really meant when we talked about a war on terror.

It had seemed like an excellent idea at the time. Then, in the way one thing quickly leads to another, Norman and I had slipped into that airless little room at the back of Rizieq's headquarters, and were sitting there exchanging worried glances, when a grim-faced young man, thin as a cadaver in his embroidered white tunic and skullcap, came in to announce, "The imam will see you now."

Norman, up and nimble, was at the door in a flash. Turning to see what was keeping me, he said, as if I really had any choice in the matter, "Hey, Boss, you don't want to miss the fun, do you?"

PART ONE

PART ONE

1

Holy War

The moon was shining over the harbor at Makassar, the storied old spice port nine hundred miles east of Jakarta, when Norman and I stood in the steamy night, staring up at the huge steel flanks of the interisland passenger liner the *M. V. Bukit Siguntang*. With its upper decks wrapped around a large single funnel, and bathed in a garish yellow light from intertwining floodlights, the vessel resembled a giant wedding cake from hell. Dozens of embarking passengers, shoving and yelling, and using their luggage as battering rams, fought for a foothold on the rickety gangway. Every now and then, pairs of gimlet-eyed cops in maroon berets and camouflage would yank some poor devil out of the mob, probe his deteriorating cardboard box with the snout of a machine gun, and haul him off into the shadows.

Alarmed by the chaos, I grabbed Norman by the arm, and said, "Remember, pal, we're here for a look—but that is all. If anything, and I mean *anything,* seems dangerously out of whack, we're off the ship immediately. *Comprendo?"*

Norman nodded in agreement, but from the way his eyes dilated with excitement I could tell he wasn't really listening. In the next instant he raced ahead to the base of the gangway, waved for me to join him, and then suddenly disappeared into the levitating mob like a man being sucked up into the bowels of an alien spacecraft.

I froze. Without Norman I was absolutely and forever sunk—just a confused, ignorant *bule,* or "white face," stranded on a dock in the middle of nowhere. And so I took a deep breath, walked forward on legs of concrete, and burrowed into the scrum. Halfway up the ramp a blunt object struck me square in the forehead—*thunk!*—and my skull rang like a brass bowl. When the ringing stopped, I was inside the belly of the ship.

It was dark and strange in there, the underpowered fluorescent tubes casting everything in a sickly greenish hue—the long rows of wooden bunks, the surging crowd, the sea of oily bobbing heads. But when I finally managed to locate Norman in the mob and we reached the broad lobby outside the first-class cabins, there was something far more sinister to worry about. All around us now, hunkered down on dirty strips of cardboard or old pieces of straw matting, were large numbers of very unhappy-looking young men.

Mostly in their late teens or early twenties, and eerily silent to a man, they had the look of shipwreck survivors clinging to the wreckage. Those not rocking on their haunches, mumbling noiselessly over dog-eared copies of the Koran, stared fixedly into the middle distance. And unless I very badly missed my guess, I knew that we were staring into the face of a shadowy new Islamic terror brigade calling itself the Laskar Jihad, or Holy War Army.

I can't say we hadn't been forewarned. The Jihad's founder and spiritual leader, a man named Jaffar Umar Thalib, had vowed for weeks now to hurl his holy warriors at eastern Indonesia's far Molucca Islands, which happened to be our destination, too. Jaffar held the view, shared by many local Islamists, that a United Nations–sponsored independence referendum in predominantly Christian East Timor in 1999 had been part of an evil scheme hatched by then-president Bill Clinton (who was identified in militant propaganda as head of something called the "American Church") and his fellow capitalist cronies to break up Indonesia by creating a Christian republic in its distant watery gut.

It was to thwart that alleged plot that Jaffar had publicly proclaimed the establishment of the Jihad in January 2000 from his base in Central Java. And now, four months later, he boasted a strike force of ten thousand fighters, the largest of a small but dangerous constellation of radical Islamic organizations using reformasi freedoms jujitsu-style to undermine democratic society by raising private armies. Jaffar's call to adventure in defense of Islam was particularly popular with the alienated young men from Java's impoverished tobacco- and coffee-farming belts, and delicious paranoia made the glory of dying *shahid*—a martyr for Islam—all the sweeter.

In Jakarta, meanwhile, Jaffar's threats of holy way had duly alarmed President Abdurrahman Wahid, a moderate Muslim cleric and Indonesia's first democratically elected leader since 1955. But when Wahid sent an order for Jaffar's arrest through constitutional channels, to both his armed forces chief of staff and his civilian defense minister, he was promptly ignored. Indonesia's military didn't cotton to Wahid's reformist plans to curb its vast powers, and so in the great wormy can of Indonesian politics, the Laskar Jihad had become—as an authoritative report published by the Brussels-based International Crisis Group, later put it—"the greatest symbol of the government's impotence."

Jakarta is an inordinately gossipy place, and word on the street had run that Jaffar was looking for a way to inject three thousand jihadis into the Moluccas to begin cleansing them of their one million Indonesian Christians. And now, judging from the squatters on the decks of the *Bukit Siguntang,* the Laskar Jihad had found its opening—and, as luck would have it, Norman and I had found the Jihad.

"Sweet Jesus," I gasped, as we dove inside our tiny, cell-like stateroom and locked the door. The sly, sharklike grins we'd encountered while picking our way across the jihadis' cardboard archipelago had encouraged my stomach to contract into something roughly the size of a baseball. But this was no time to panic; I needed to think. Sitting down on one of a pair of grimy bunks, I said to Norman, as calmly as I could muster, "Why don't you pop up to the bridge and see what the hell the captain thinks is going on around here."

"Sure thing, Boss," said Norman. Firing off a snappy salute, he was out the door in a flash, and glad to be gone, I wager. Norman really was an excellent traveling companion, full of rakish good humor or fire-and-fight as the situation required, but I was very upset with him just then and he knew it. Riding into a holy war with a bunch of wild-eyed jihadis wasn't the trip he'd promised me. Far from it. What he'd promised was a rare glimpse of an untrammeled tropical paradise, a place of soaring green vistas and sparkling white sands—a place called the Banda Islands.

The Bandas, thirteen jots of volcanic rock located in a stretch of far ocean between the Java and Arafura seas, north of Australia and west of New Guinea, were interesting for a variety of reasons. It was there in 1512 that sailors, swabbing in the squadron of the Portuguese explorer Antonio de Abreu, had followed an alluring fragrance smack into the fabled islands to discover an incredibly large treasure hidden in a deceptively small package—the golden, walnut-sized fruit *Myristica fragrans,* otherwise known as the common nutmeg.

It is hard to fathom today just how popular the nutmeg was in Europe in those benighted days. More than three hundred years before the invention of anything remotely resembling either modern refrigeration or miracle drugs, the humble fruit, dried and grated, was prized (correctly) for keeping meat from rotting, and (wrongly but understandably) as a poultice for warding off the Plague, a.k.a. the Black Death, which had wiped out a full third of Europe's population and was still at its deadly work. In addition, the nutmeg's use as a tranquilizer, sleeping potion, and a medieval form of Viagra led to a stiffening demand that set its price in the bourses at Rotterdam, London, and Paris on a par with silver and gold.

And that was when it was available at all. Up to the time of Abreu's discovery, the nutmeg had arrived in Europe as if by magic—traveling from the Orient by caravan through the bazaars of Central Asia, passing through many hands, exact point of origin unknown. When the Turks conquered Constantinople in 1453, effectively cutting off Europe's fix, it was collective nutmeg withdrawal that helped propel Europe into its vaunted Age of Exploration. Christopher Columbus had been searching for a sea link to the "spiceries" of the East when he'd had the rum luck to bang into North America. When the luckier Abreu found his way into the Bandas two decades later, the tiny archipelago, the only known source of nutmeg on earth, quickly became a focal point of the global economy. As author Giles Milton notes in his riveting history *Nathaniel's Nutmeg,* the shipyards of Portugal, Spain, England, and Holland went into "a flurry of activity that sparked what would later become known as the spice race, a desperate and protracted struggle for control of one of the smallest groups of islands in the world."

With nutmeg now selling FOB Europe at fantastical markups northward of 30,000 percent, the European spice hunters, and the merchant princes who backed them, were only too happy to make their money the old-fashioned way, which is to say through murder and theft. After outmaneuvering both Portugal and Spain, Holland seized the Bandas in 1621, and set about "pacifying" the native population. According to one historical account, the Dutch briskly killed or displaced 14,400 of the 15,000 Bandanese islanders.[1] Less successful in uprooting the well-armed British, who had managed to grab the harp-shaped island of Run, the most prolific natural nutmeg factory of them all, the methodical Hollanders eventually struck a deal. Under the Treaty of Breda, signed in 1667, the English gave up their stake in the Bandas in return for New Amsterdam, a larger but comparatively unpromising Dutch trading post on the same chilly northern island where I now happened to live— Manhattan.

---

1. For this and other fascinating details see Kal Muller's excellent guidebook, *Spice Islands: Exotic Eastern Indonesia* (Lincolnwood, IL: Passport Books, 1993).

Manhattan?!

"We can actually go there?" I asked Norman when he'd first told me about the remotely magical Bandas and then managed to persuade me he wasn't pulling my leg. We were sitting in the elegant lobby of the Regent Hotel in Jakarta at the time, having coffee at the base of its grand staircase, as Norman fixed an appraising Javanese eye on our curvaceous waitress, who sashayed among the tables in her tight-fitting sarong. But he was excited about the Bandas, too.

"Yes, Boss," he said, his nostrils flaring as if already processing the sweet scent of island spices. "That's where we'll see the real old-time Indonesia!"

I was smitten. From that relaxed and cozy vantage point, the thought of visiting a sun-splashed backwater whose jungles had grown up around one of history's great geographical ironies struck me as wildly seductive. Looking back on it now, I guess I should have been more alert to the fact that Norman had never actually set foot in the Bandas, either. But though like most journalistic hacks (and here I exclude the increasingly chirpy anchors who play journalists on TV) I am a deep and terrible skeptic, I trusted Norman to the highest degree possible. First, he was impressively overqualified for the work he was doing with me. He'd graduated from a job as a photographer for *Tempo* magazine, Indonesia's top newsweekly, to run his own successful photo studio in Jakarta. Tall for an Indonesian, with a long, angular nose, high cheekbones, and a head of wavy black hair, he'd even played the romantic lead in a film, by a rising young Indonesian director, about young love at bay amid the spooky ruins of court life in the old Javanese capital of Surakarta.

When the same Asian economic crisis that drove former President Suharto from office also forced Norman, like many of Indonesia's bright and ambitious young people, to scramble for ways of earning hard currency, he'd hired himself out as a local fixer for visiting foreign photographers and film crews. And there was nobody better at it than Norman. Having studied in the United States, he was a veritable multitasking, globalized, digitized marvel, who was incessantly juggling dueling Palm Pilots, lining up interviews on one of two cell phones, sometimes both, and was intimately plugged into the steady flow of gossip on which Indonesia's capital thrived. In addition, Norman had a grasp of loyalty rare in young men in today's world. That was because generations of Javanese ancestors on his father's side had lifted swords to defend the mystical kings of Old Java. ("Wibowo is not my real name," he once confided to me; his real name was inscribed on the hilt of a *kris,* or Javanese dagger, buried in a secret vault in old Surakarta. "But if I told it to you, I'd have to kill you.") In short, Norman represented the ideal global man—in touch with both the brave new rhythms of life in a high-tech, interconnected world and the sacred cultural bedrock.

Thus I had taken Norman at his word, and his word on the Banda Islands was that they were loaded with the kind of unsullied charm you look for in a tropical paradise, complete with a towering volcano and abandoned Dutch forts with ghostly cannon pointed out on sleepy turquoise lagoons. And unlike much of the rest of Indonesia now, there wasn't a single McDonald's, 7-Eleven, or KFC within many a far mile.

In fairness to Norman, he did suggest it might be a little tricky actually getting to the Bandas. That was because they were, geographically speaking, a subset of the Moluccas' much larger, California-shaped archipelago, also known as the Spice Islands, and the Indonesian government had at least technically banned Western journalists from traveling to the area because, as Norman had explained, there was this "fighting and stuff" going on there between Christians and Muslims. I know people generally assume that anybody who writes for the *National Geographic* is automatically some kind of whiz at map study. But that is not the case with me. To be honest, I had only the haziest notion of where the Bandas were actually located, and I was so eager now to part the palm fronds and see the islands for myself that I didn't give their precise location much thought. In fairness to me, it is my distinct memory that Norman never actually used the phrase "war zone" in describing our travel plans.

Instead, he stressed that the Bandas were the ideal place to catch a glimpse of Indonesia's colorful past—"Indonesian history in a nutmeg shell," as he put it; the place that had originally inspired the

Dutch, in their lust for spices, to cobble together an entire country, the Dutch East Indies, which was mainly designed for pumping out the area's vast natural wealth, its coffee and cloves, tea and palm oil, and of course the lucrative nutmeg and its valuable cousin, mace, the spice grated from the nutmeg's sun-dried outer husk.

Norman also stressed that the Bandas were a convenient window on today's Indonesia. Having escaped the general fighting in the wider Moluccas, the islands had taken in thousands of refugees from more murderous areas. From talking to them, he theorized, we could piece together a picture of the ambient religious war but vicariously, like observing flashes of lightning on a distant horizon, while we kept tabs on Banda's large and rollicking dolphin population, sunned ourselves under the volcano's green cone, and ate our way through the twenty-seven local varieties of bananas said to grow among the nutmeg groves on gentle island slopes. As for the government's travel ban, Norman suggested we simply ignore it.

Then a few days later, in the zany way things can sometimes happen in Indonesia, I boarded a flight in Jakarta and promptly evicted a man who had mistakenly deposited himself in my assigned seat. The interloper turned out to be none other than Des Alwi, a very big wheel in the Moluccas, and top banana, so to speak, in the Bandas. *Ketua orlima,* the islands' elected leader, as well as their traditional high chief, he owned the best hotel in the Bandas, one of the best in Ambon, the regional hub, and was considered the great impresario of business and tourism in the whole beautiful, beleaguered area.

"People call him king or sultan," said Norman, but the title was less important than the simple fact that, if you had any business in the Bandas, Des Alwi was the man to see. And it wasn't hard to see why. For one thing, Des was utterly charming. Very relaxed for a king, he spoke his English in a thick, rolling accent, and had a voice as rich and creamy as a mango pudding. When our flight landed in Makassar, so-called Gateway to the Spice Islands, I apologized for my boorish behavior on the plane, but Des waved it off with a big fleshy paw. He said, "Tracy, if you want to know about Indonesia, Banda is the very place. You *must* come visit me."

Then in a confidential tone, as if to sweeten the deal, Des said, "I have built a new shark pool next to my hotel, Tracy." His eyes twinkling with merriment, he suggested it was a tourist attraction but also a solution—"if there are any tourists we don't like, you see." As he chortled at his joke, his face dissolved into a series of smiling concentric folds.

"Come see me in Banda, Tracy," he repeated, his bushy eyebrows arching dramatically. "Have Norman call me, and we will set it up—one, two, three!"

Having watched one too many Clark Gable, soldier-of-fortune movies as a kid, I immediately felt the old tug of high adventure. With visions of visiting a tropical paradise dancing in my head, war canoes zipping across garlanded seas to greet the returning king and his honored bule guest, I said to Norman, "Okay, let's fit in a trip to the Bandas, if you're reasonably sure we can do it without getting killed. Ha, ha!"

2

UNBOTTLED LIGHTNING

The trouble in the Moluccas started on January 19, 1999, when a pair of Muslim youths, Usman and Salim, are said to have boarded a minibus in the leafy provincial capital of Ambon and tried to rob the driver, Yopy, a Christian, at the point of a big curved knife called a *pisau badik*. Yopy went for a bigger knife, a machete, and chased his would-be assailants into a Muslim market nearby.[1]

Rumors flew—Muslims were attacking Christians and vice versa. (In an alternate version of the story, popular among Muslims, Yopy played the villain.) A few hours later, as eyewitnesses remembered it, the first columns of smoke were climbing over the city's green hills, neat white houses, and its forest of TV satellite dishes. Then in no time at all, greater Ambon, a place of 350,000 souls, former center of the spice trade, proud of its status as an

---

1. Two of the best sources of reporting on events in Ambon and the conflict in the Moluccas, which the international media covered sporadically, are the meticulous briefings put out by Human Rights Watch and the International Crisis Group, which can be found, respectively, at www.hrw.org and www.icg.org.

up-and-coming regional center, a city with good restaurants, tidy hotels, ATMs, Internet cafés, cinemas, and a university with a world-class fisheries institute, had started its astonishingly brisk descent into hell.

Having literally torn itself to pieces, Ambon existed now as a cluster of barricaded communities where Christians and Muslims lived separate lives, each with their own schools, hospitals, and supermarkets. In between lay corridors of scorched earth and rubble, haunted by sappers and snipers, and coursing with a peristaltic violence that periodically surged into a new round of arson attacks on churches, mosques, commercial buildings, and private homes. Ninety percent of the buildings in Ambon had been destroyed. On the surface, it was a jaw-dropping mystery—the Ambonese themselves were at a loss to explain how a routine stickup could lead to such cascading violence.

Not all that surprisingly, though, the answer lay buried in the tangled coils of local history. The Europeans, in their eagerness to extract the area's spices, had injected the Moluccas with a passion for Christianity ("Cannonballs off the port bow, Bibles off the stern," as the old saying went), as Arab traders had earlier seen fit to sow the seeds of Islam. With the population of Ambon (both the city and its encompassing island) more or less equally divided between Christians and Muslims since the late 1500s, the two communities had long basked in a reputation for interfaith neighborliness that was the envy of Indonesia's feistier neighborhoods.

Below the charming surface, however, life in Ambon was never as blissful as the foreign guidebooks or the Indonesian media let on. Ambonese society was in fact chronically edgy, and the edge had always gone to the Christians. In colonial times the Dutch looked kindly on their co-religionists when it came to doling out limited schooling and civil service jobs. Christians became the teachers, the police constables, and the clerks and quill-drivers down at the local colonial office, while Muslims scooped the trash and picked the papayas. When Indonesia finally won its independence from Holland in 1949, and gave the Dutch the long-awaited boot, members of the Christian political elite suddenly had serious second thoughts. Taking a hard look at the founders of the republic in far-off Jakarta, most of whom were Muslim, they decided, all things considered, they'd prefer to live in something they called the Christian Republic of the South Moluccas. A vigorous thumping by Jakarta's security forces brought the separatists back into line, but not before the renegades had put many a Muslim in an early grave, torched many a Muslim village, and scored many a Muslim heart with grief and grievance.

Slowly, the tables turned. By the early 1970s, Christians were in fact under siege—not by wild-eyed Muslim fanatics, however, but by the bogeyman of demographics. Forced out of the surrounding islands to look for work, desperately poor Muslims ventured into Ambon, put down roots, and thus tipped the population balance in favor of the progeny of the Prophet. Leading the way were the Bugis, the very race of seafarers whose piratical ancestors had proved so discombobulating to early European travelers that they in fact contributed the word "bogeyman" to the English language. The Bugis now struck fear into local hearts, not with the blade or the hook, however, but by settling in economically depressed neighborhoods where they proceeded to procreate the daylights out of the Christians.

The Christians responded with the usual favor of viewing the Muslim newcomers as oversexed, subhuman interlopers and set about denouncing their neighborhoods as incubators of crime and squalor. When Suharto's government belatedly moved to level the playing field for the migrants with affirmative action policies in the 1990s, many Christians, now directly challenged for their prized civil service jobs, looked at the upwardly mobile Muslims and saw the fruiting of their old paranoia.

Looked at another way, the story of Ambon was just another chapter in the old, complicated saga of Indonesia itself. The archipelago's mad ethnic and cultural chemistry (matched only in modern times by the old Soviet Union) was converted into a political entity four hundred years ago when those enterprising Dutch joined together scattered bits of geology belonging to Australia, Asia, and the Pacific Islands into a geographical container whose volatile ingredients they then kept under control by virtue of their superior technology, mainly musket and cannon, and a long-running and highly successful divide-and-conquer strategy that kept the empire's sultans, rajahs, and tribal chieftains too busy fighting one another to fight the Dutch. (It was a familiar trick among European colonialists—as Norman Mailer has put it, "Let the madmen duke it out, then jump the one or two who are left.")

After independence Indonesia's founding fathers sought to make up for the sins of the Dutch by showcasing their country's many "summits of culture," and pressed the ringing national slogan of "unity in diversity." But behind the scenes they relied on a modified Dutch formula—a blend of charm, cunning, and military muscle—to keep the country's feral forces in check. And nobody was better at ordering the chaos than General Suharto. As a rising Army officer, Suharto (who like many Indonesians uses only the one name) fought to expel the Dutch from the main island of Java. Then in the 1950s, he helped out Sukarno, the republic's first president, by crushing a variety of popular uprisings around the country. When the puckish, womanizing Sukarno lost control in the midsixties (a scalding time remembered as the Year of Living Dangerously, after a line from a Sukarno speech, and immortalized in a shrewdly beautiful novel of the same title by Christopher J. Koch, as well as an excellent 1982 Peter Weir film starring Mel Gibson), Suharto corked the bottle with a crackdown that cost a million lives or more, and made the not infrequently brutal Dutch look genial by comparison.

His own stupendously sinful record on human rights notwithstanding, Suharto went on to translate two oil booms into impressive economic and social gains, lifting much of his big country above the poverty line, and fueling aspirations among many ordinary Indonesians for a democratic voice. But despite Indonesia's connections with the International Monetary Fund and other progressive global organizations, Suharto insisted on dragging his country into the modern world by ruling it like one of the feudal kings of Old Java. From his gilded palace in Jakarta, he cemented fealty by doling out patronage or cracking skulls, as the situation required, all the while projecting the flat enigmatic smile that earned him the nickname the "Smiling General."

What emerged over the years was a vast kleptocracy by which Suharto and his cronies siphoned billions of dollars out of Indonesia's provinces, with their mighty stores of timber, gold, oil, and gas—and created a vast sucking sound that was music to the ears of what Indonesians referred to as "progress" or the Suharto *mafiya*, depending on which end of the money hose you happened to be on. And because most Indonesians were kept well away from the nozzle, the Smiling General used his military to keep the grumbling to a minimum. Suharto's Java, always the center of Indonesia's administrative web, with two-thirds of the country's population, became even more central as the cash flowed in, and resentments against "Javanese imperialism" simmered and grew in the fleeced provincial islands.

Then beginning in 1997, the Asian economic crisis hit the foundations of Suharto's elaborate Ponzi scheme like a tsunami. Overnight the value of Indonesia's currency, the rupiah, plummeted, and its economy experienced the biggest single one-country free fall since the Great Depression of the 1930s. When Suharto was finally forced to resign on May 22, 1998, his many warlords, assistant warlords, hangers-on, and a few out-and-out psychopaths were scrambling to preserve their stakes, and Indonesia, from Aceh in the far west to Irian Jaya in the far east, had devolved into a sort of murderous, equal-opportunity jumble.

Viewed in that light, it was the conflict in the romantic old Spice Islands that set an appalling new standard for how bad and bloody things could get when people really put their hearts and minds into it. First, the stain of violence allegedly set off by that failed bus station heist in Ambon just kept on spreading out, island by idyllic island, until anywhere from three thousand to thirty thousand people were dead, depending on whose numbers (none of them particularly reliable) you believed. Victims met their ends in horrifyingly Neolithic ways—burned alive in their homes, blown apart by homemade grenades, or dispatched by machetes, long knives, spears, arrows, or slingshots. Small wonder then that an estimated five hundred thousand people, equivalent to the entire population of Portland, Oregon, had fled their homes to mill frantically around the islands, looking for a safe place to alight. There were some dark places in Indonesia, all right, but if you were looking for a worst-case vision of what the entire country might become if the post-Suharto experiments at democratic *reformasi* collapsed in a steaming heap, it was the storied, romantic Spice Islands.

I was not totally ignorant of the situation. As the weeks rolled by, and Norman worked out the details for visiting Des Alwi's kingdom in the Bandas, I caught up on my homework, reading scattered press reports on the troubles in the Moluccas. Having belatedly unfurled a map long ago provided me by my thoughtful editors at the *Geographic,* I now knew that the Bandas, which resembled a little bell attached to the bottom of the anchor-shaped Spice Islands, were centered on a spot approximately 4° S, 129°E, and therefore well inside the danger zone. For all that, though, Des had assured us that traveling to the Bandas was entirely safe. And according to Norman, nobody had a better feel for Indonesia, its endless contradictions, or the mystery of how all its moving parts were organically linked, than Des Alwi.

I'd only met Des that once on the tarmac in Makassar, and so my faith in him was less certifiably religious. But as everyone knows, travel of any sort requires a leap of faith, the willingness to put yourself in trust to those who know the territory better than you, and so I was satisfied that accompanying the king was the kind of travelers insurance you couldn't find on any Web site at any price. I mean, who in his right mind, Muslim radical, Christian renegade, or freelance vigilante, would mess with the king of the Banda Islands?

Then two weeks before our scheduled departure, Des threw us a curveball. The king and I were standing on the front steps of the Regent Hotel, squinting into the intense Jakarta sunshine, when, big and bearish, his black *peci* cap tilted at a rakish angle, he said, "Tracy, I have been called away on urgent business to Europe, so very unfortunately I cannot go with you to Banda. But don't worry. I am sending my daughter Tanya to accompany you. You'll be okay."

You'll be okay? That isn't exactly the ringing endorsement one looks for when one is headed into a war zone. Whatever feelings of confidence I'd had about the trip rested entirely on traveling in the protective company of the king. Frankly, being fobbed off on a young woman I'd never even laid eyes on sounded a good deal less than *okay* to me.

But Tanya in the flesh turned out to be a lot of fun, and highly resourceful, too. In her midthirties, she was a tiny woman, with ruddy medallion cheeks, a shrewd, sweet smile, and the fizzing energy of a very small nuclear reactor. When the interisland passenger ship into the Spice Islands from Makassar suddenly seemed too risky for travel because of the potential presence of Jaffar's jihadis, Tanya made an alternate plan. We'd fly from Jakarta to Makassar on a commercial jet as planned, but instead of taking the ship, we'd simply switch planes and fly on to Ambon.

When I expressed my concern about flying into the eye of the fighting, Tanya said, "No worries, Pak Tracy. I've got a friend in the Navy in Ambon who can fly us to Banda on a Navy plane. The military shares the runway with the airlines at Ambon, so we can fly in and out without ever leaving the airport. It's faster and safer that way, yah?"

I confess that given the mounting risk I now had nearly zero enthusiasm for seeing the Bandas by any means, ship, plane, or time machine. But I'm a sucker for personal initiative, and in the face of Tanya's unstoppable zest, I went ahead and agreed to pay two thousand dollars in crisp American bills for her Navy flyboys to drop us into the Bandas and then pick us up again when we were ready to come home.

It was shortly thereafter that the flaws in Tanya's plan began to emerge. The morning of our departure, for example, the Navy in its wisdom announced its intention to throw up a total military embargo around the Spice Islands to prevent the Laskar Jihad from going in and causing trouble after hundreds of jihadis had already been allowed to go in and do just that. I was ready to pull the plug on the whole loony escapade when Norman and I met Tanya in front of the check-in counters in the dim, cavernous interior of Jakarta's Soekarno-Hatta International Airport.

Tanya had just got off the phone with Captain X, her prized military contact in Ambon and a high-ranking local commander. According to the captain, approximately two thousand Laskar Jihad troopers had boarded the good ship *Bukit Siguntang* in the East Java port of Surabaya the previous day, and were currently steaming toward a stopover in Makassar, where they would arrive by late afternoon. As Captain X delicately phrased it over the telephone to Tanya, taking the ship under such circumstances would be suicide.

But not to worry, he'd said. The Navy ships wouldn't be in position to enforce the embargo for at least another twelve hours. That gave our little crew just enough time to hop into the islands before the curtain rang down, and the good captain would take us from there. When we tried to buy our air tickets for Ambon, however, we were told the airport there had suddenly shut down for security reasons. Absurd, said Captain X, when Tanya got him on her cell phone again. He could see the planes taking off and landing from his office window. The airlines people in Jakarta must be confused!

To further complicate matters, Norman, for reasons as mysterious to me as they were incredible, insisted on arguing strongly in favor of taking the ship. But Tanya wouldn't hear of it. "Forget the stupid ship!" she said, with surprising vehemence. And so under the potted palms on the departure concourse we were experiencing a quintessential Indonesian moment, full of conflict and indecision, when Norman drew me aside. "Boss, I don't trust this captain guy," he said, rolling his eyes. "I'm getting the vibes."

That brings us to a central fixture in Norman's Javanese worldview, which was his faith in the so-called Anchor of Java, the mythical opening to the spirit world that is said to exist at a precise point on a rugged plate of land among the blue volcanoes of West Java called the Diyeng Plateau, which in turn lies between the old rival court cities of Surakarta, or Solo, as it is now generally called, and Jogjakarta. Norman often referred to receiving signals from the Anchor, which he jokingly portrayed as a sort of psychic conning tower. But I knew he was only ever half-joking, and now I'd had it with his spooky, paranormal hoodoo.

"No wonder people in this part of the world put so much stock in the supernatural," I blurted out angrily. "Being clairvoyant is your only hope of figuring out what the hell is going on around here."

"Boss, trust me," he said soothingly. "I really think the ship will be okay."

"How can you possibly say that, Norman," I cried, finding his persistence beyond belief. "Why on earth would the military talk about stopping the ship if it didn't spell big trouble?"

He said, "How do we know the military *is* going to stop the ship?"

I was flabbergasted. "Because Captain X said so, that's why," I said, as if nothing could be plainer. "Why would he say the ship wouldn't be let in if he didn't have solid intelligence?" (I submit this as a sample of the antique thinking that allowed Dick Cheney, Donald Rumsfeld, and other Bush administration "strategists" to persuade the American people they had solid intelligence that would lead them straight to Saddam Hussein's weapons of mass destruction.)

Norman regarded me expressionlessly for a moment, and then brightened, as if replying to a question on a TV game show.

"Money?" he said.

Waffling and unable to agree, Tanya and Norman pressed me to fly up to Makassar to investigate further. When we got there we discovered that the airport in Ambon was in fact shut down tighter than a proverbial drum. Pretty much to humor Norman I agreed to go take a look at the ship, but only on the clear understanding that if there was a single jihadi on board, we'd fly straight back to Jakarta saying we'd tried our best. And since we'd already been told on good authority that the ship was loaded to the gunwales with jihadis, I knew there wasn't a chance in hell that we'd be taking that ship.

As a veteran newshound you pride yourself on developing a keen eye for the nasty logistical surprises that can befoul any trip. What I'd overlooked in concocting all my various nightmare scenarios, however, was the simple fact the pier that night in Makassar was in such chaos that, before I fully realized what was happening, a tidal wave of bodies had literally sloshed us into the bowels of the ship, depositing Norman and me in our stateroom, Tanya in hers, and then effectively acted as a stopper in a drain, preventing us from reversing course.

And so it was I found myself sitting on a greasy bunk in that tiny sweltering cabin, nearly catatonic with fright, as disturbing visions began to flicker through my head. Accused of working as Christian spies, humanitarian aid workers had been viciously harassed in the Moluccas in recent months. At least two had been killed. And now the last remaining foreigners were being airlifted out of Ambon as I was headed in. Under the circumstances, it wasn't all that hard to picture the ship exploding in riot before we got to the islands, the islands exploding in riot once the Laskar Jihad got there, or me, bule gate-crasher, watching goggle-eyed as I was gutted like a pompano and tossed over the side into the horrible night sea.

Thus I was entertaining unmanly thoughts of jumping ship when Norman returned from his information-gathering mission to the bridge. Stepping in briskly from the harsh light and noise of the companionway, he did a neat little pirouette, and bolted the flimsy sheet-metal door behind him. "Bad news, Boss," he said, his eyes widening dramatically. "The captain confirms—it's the Jihad."

No big surprise there. The more disturbing news from my point of view, however, was the fact that the captain had heard nothing at all about any Navy embargo and was sticking like a barnacle to his schedule—Ambon in two and a half days, the Bandas in three.

"Holy crap, Norman," I blurted out, more as an indictment than needless repetition of fact. "We're on a ship headed for a holy war!"

"Looks that way, Boss," he said nonchalantly.

His attitude was indescribably irksome. "And just how would you propose we survive a trip with all these jihadis on board?" I asked.

"Try to remain inconspicuous?"

Inconspicuous? "For chrissakes, Norman," I yelled, jabbing a thumb toward the companionway and the jihadis, "we're both Christian!"

Well, Christian enough, anyhow. Norman's reputation as something of a ladies' man in Jakarta's ferny coffeehouses notwithstanding, he'd attended one of the city's top Catholic prep schools, and the national ID card he carried in his wallet clearly identified him as *kristen*. And of course any bule traveling in this neck of the woods was automatically Christian, whether he liked it or not—those four unhappy centuries of life under the Bible-thumping, nutmeg-hoarding Dutch masters had long since seen to that.

Frowning in thought, as if considering our burden of faith for the first time, Norman said at length, "Okay, so that part doesn't look so good."

Grimacing, I glanced down at my watch. It was ten to eight. That gave us ten minutes before the ship sailed. The embarking mob had thinned out sufficiently now that if we hurried, and kept our elbows up, we could still make a run for it, down the gangplank and back up the hill over the harbor to a lovely little Mediterranean-style resort hotel I fancied. I was contemplating a nice bedtime gelato and the prospect of stretching out between clean sheets when Norman said, "Look, Boss, I really don't think they want to kill *us*."

"That's extremely reassuring that you think so," I muttered.

"I'm serious, Boss. Listen, if these Jihad characters kill us, then embargo or no embargo the authorities will stop the ship before it ever gets to Ambon, right?"

"I can't believe we're having this conversation . . ."

"In that case," said Norman, "they never get the chance to kill the people they really want to kill, who are all in Ambon!"

Norman beamed, as if he had just won the Nobel Prize in theoretical physics. When I ignored him, he encouraged me to "look on the bright side."

"And where would that be?"

"The captain says that if things get, you know, really touchy, he'll let us sleep up on the bridge and bolt the doors. That's what they did last time."

"Last time?"

Norman's eyes darted warily, realizing he'd gone one sentence too far. "Well, uh, I guess there was a riot on the ship a couple of months ago . . ."

"A what?"

"A riot—but just a little one." A band of Muslim youths had

wanted to slit the throats of the entire crew, who happened to be Christian, or something like that. "Sorry, Boss, I didn't have time to get all the details. The captain was busy getting ready to leave port and stuff."

That did it. I grabbed at the handle of my duffel bag, and said, "Okay, we're getting the hell off this ship right now . . ."

"Boss, Boss," said Norman, as if trying to reason with a frightened four-year-old, "you want to write about Indonesia, don't you? Well, this"—he revolved his chin, indicating our sauna-box of a stateroom and the ship housing it—"is the best way to see Indonesia, the real Indonesia."

I stared at him in disbelief. "Need I point out that it's pretty hard to write anything about Indonesia, or anything else for that matter, if you happen to be dead?"

"Don't get huffy now, Boss," Norman scolded. "You can't see the real Indonesia from the lobby of your five-star hotel in Jakarta, now can you?"

That really hurt. Worse, Norman had grasped the essence of the journalistic endeavor I was doing my best to ignore, which is: If you don't go, you'll never know. And so it was decided, although journalism had very little to do with the decision. Of all the stupidities embedded in human nature the one we often fear most is the prospect of losing face in the eyes of those whom we like and respect. And quite simply, I didn't like the idea of appearing to come off looking like the Great White Chicken in front of either Norman or Tanya.

"Okay, we go," I said. "But just offhand, what do you suppose the chances are we'll still be alive when we reach paradise?"

Norman received the news with perfect Javanese aplomb, but from the way his eyes glittered I could tell he was overjoyed. "Boss, you won't regret it," he said with conviction. "Now you're going to see the real Indonesia."

"That's what I'm afraid of," I said. Then all at once the ship's horn let out a low, mournful blast, and the hair on the back of my neck stood to attention. A few seconds later the huge steel hull groaned and shuddered, pulling hard to starboard, as if being dragged to sea by a giant magnet. The *Bukit Siguntang,* with Norman and me on board, was finally and inescapably lurching toward the lion's den.

By the time I'd drifted off to sleep that night, having pondered that ridiculously fragile little door separating us from the tender mercies of fourteenth-century fire-and-brimstone Islam, I had more or less convinced myself that the chances were excellent that I'd wake up dead.

3

UNHAPPY CAMPERS

The next morning I surprised myself by waking up not only alive but feeling remarkably refreshed. The hypnotic effect of big engines thrumming way down in the ship's core had lulled me into a fast dreamless slumber, and now yawning and stretching, I pulled back the nubbly curtains over our porthole for my first glimpse of the seas east of Makassar. It was absolutely gorgeous! The sun, already high and fierce, was shining in a sky the pale blue color of a robin's egg and dazzling a sea dark and weighty as a pool of India ink. "This was the East of the ancient navigators," I thought, remembering a line from Conrad I'd long ago committed to memory—"so old, so mysterious, resplendent and somber, living and unchanged, full of danger and promise."

I was feeling a surge of the old romance that had pulled me out to have a look at Asia as a young man, and all that sunlight put me in such an exuberant mood that when I spied a large cockroach perched on the edge of Norman's mattress, dwarfed by the looming massif of his still-sleeping form, I playfully picked up a book and hurled it sidearm at the intruder. I hit Norman instead.

"Agghhhhh!" spluttered Norman, sitting bolt upright. Then with frightening speed, he hopped into the corner of his bunk and, squatting on his haunches, regarded me with the opaque, unseeing eyes of a gargoyle.

"Holy mother, I've shocked the man into some kind of irreversible trance," I was thinking, horrified, when Norman calmly blinked his eyes, and smiled. "Boss, you really ought to be more careful about how you treat a poor Javanese," he said. "We're very delicate emotionally, you know. I might have gone amok."

With that he leaped to the floor, rolled up a newspaper, and shouted, "Behold the sword of Old Java, Boss." He was whacking at a newly arrived patrol of roaches, demonstrating his impressive repertoire of Bruce Lee moves, when there came a loud knock on the door.

Instinctively, I jumped back, suddenly remembering all those cruel-looking jihadis lined up in the passageway from the night before. Norman meanwhile, in keeping with his proactive nature, sprang forward, quietly reaching for his camping tool, a complicated piece of equipment he'd asked me to buy for him in the States. With its many blades and corkscrews it looked like a miniature Jaws of Life.

"Who is it?" he asked as he put his ear to the door, brandishing his weapon. After a long silence, during which I closed my mouth so my heart wouldn't fly out of my throat, a low, raspy voice said in English, "It's the Jihad. We're here to cut your throats!"

"Tan-*yah!*" scolded Norman as he unbolted the door to reveal the princess of the islands, doubling over with laughter, while the ambient jihadis craned their necks, trying to get a peek inside the den of the infidels.

Stepping inside, Tanya promptly slammed the door on the inquiring faces, and commenced her reconnaissance report. The news was grim. After settling in her cabin the night before, and in keeping with her gregarious nature, Tanya said she'd decided "to go chill" in the nonalcoholic cabaret offered nightly in the ship's dining room. Hardly was she seated, however, than some hothead started a scuffle because he *thought* he'd caught the chanteuse in the deadly sin of singing a "Christian" song.

I couldn't believe my ears. "You mean like 'White Christmas'?" I asked, while I reeled inwardly at the ethereal looniness of a situation in which 2,700 passengers flirt with a watery grave because the lounge singer picks the wrong repertoire.

No, Tanya said, it wasn't that simple. The offending signal had been so subtle even she hadn't clicked to it. Broadly speaking, though, the mere singing of a song made popular by an artist *thought* to be Christian (or Muslim if you were on a Christian ship, of course) was grounds enough to trigger murderous riot.

"Scary, yah?" said Tanya in wide-eyed conclusion. Then instantly brightening, she added, "But breakfast in the dining room is good, yah? Pretty tight with the pastries, though, I must say." She followed this with a burst of whooshing, maniacal laughter as she edged out the door. "Enjoy, boys. I'm going up to the bridge to say hello to the captain—and see if he's armed. Ha, ha, ha. See you there if we all make it, yah?"

When Norman and I stepped into the corridor a few minutes later, no fewer than fifty jihadi heads snapped in my direction, and I was absolutely positive I'd be a goner before I could make it the fifty yards to the breakfast rolls. But it was then, while I involuntarily glanced down at the holy warriors to avoid trampling any toes, that I couldn't believe my eyes. In the light of morning, these men, who'd seemed like such ferocious killers the night before, now looked uniformly fatigued, and unless I was woefully mistaken, more than a little frightened. Rimmed in scraggly teenage whiskers, their expressions seemed to reflect not so much the desire to terrorize as the boyish innocence of the first-time traveler.

This was the face of Islamic terror? Had I been a medical man, judging from all the hollow cheeks and rheumy eyes, I'd have been inclined to diagnose pervasive malnutrition. (A senior Laskar Jihad Official would later boast to an interviewer that the group could send one jihadi into battle in the Moluccas for the equivalent of $13.20, which quite obviously did not include either healthful rounds of tennis on the afterdeck, had there been such a thing, or access to the all-you-can-eat buffet.)

From the strictly humanitarian point of view, you had to feel for these kids, all jammed into the ship like a million bees in a cigar box. But I wasn't about to let down my guard. Everybody knows there is nothing more dangerous than a collection of youthful psychologies aimed and fired in the wrong direction, and as Norman and I tiptoed our way across the cardboard floes to breakfast, you didn't have to be a shrewd observer of the human condition to see that these young fellows were the original made-to-order blank slates—words, thoughts, and orders to act to be supplied by their esteemed leaders.

Looking back on this moment over the smoky hump of 9/11, I now realize that it was then I got my very first inkling that our struggle against Islamic terror was in one important respect a basic numbers game. Let's do the math. First, you take Indonesia where, according to United Nations estimates, roughly ninety million people live in abject poverty. Add in, conservatively speaking, another two hundred million or so dirt-poor kids from places like Saudi Arabia, Egypt, and Morocco. Bust up all the militant organizations across the Muslim world you want—arrest or kill all the identifiable leaders, Al Qaeda, Taliban, or from the dozens of smaller, less exalted terror outfits—and you've still got a virtually endless supply of disenfranchised kids with no real jobs, few diversions, and loads of anger in their hearts.

The other thing we've learned since 9/11 of course is that radical Islam appeals not just to the downtrodden but to the educated and upwardly mobile as well. And it is especially this latter group of able communicators which absorbs and propagates the galvanizing ideas for global jihad. What ideas? Millions of idealistic Muslim kids the world over, including those under the wing of the likes of Jaffar Umar Thalib, are smitten with the writings of intellectual heroes of whom few of us in the West have ever heard. And by the time Norman and I were riding among the jihadis, one Sunni Muslim writer in particular, an Egyptian, was enjoying a roaring posthumous comeback among the predominantly Indonesian Sunnis. His name was Sayyid Qutb.

Though hanged by the government of Egyptian strongman Gamal Abdel Nasser in 1966 for in essence thinking dangerous thoughts, Qutb (pronounced *kuh-tahb*) not only is said to have become Osama bin Laden's theoretician of choice but is currently as popular a figure with young and restless Muslims, I am told, as Oprah or Deepak Chopra is with self-questing American TV viewers. I'd hasten to add, however, that Qutb's worldview was much less perkily upbeat. That is because he set out to explain the central question that sits like a chunk of hot lava at the heart of Islamic angst. To wit, where, historically speaking, had Muslim civilization hopped the tracks?

It was and is an excellent question. After all, by its golden age in the fourteenth century, Islamdom represented one of humankind's true high-water marks. It had set the basis for the development of modern mathematics, kick-started the scientific revolution, rolled ahead such enlightened thinkers as Avicenna and Averroës, and was hard at work refining the fields of architecture, interior design, and poetry. And then, bafflingly, things screeched to a halt, while over the next few centuries Western technique and technology literally left Islamic society in the dust. Inquiring minds like Qutb wanted to know why.

His answer was ingenious, if a little cranky (which can happen if you are forced, as Qutb was, to pen your thoughts in a moldering jail cell during ten ghastly years of confinement and torture). Qutb argued that the Muslim world had divorced itself from *tawhid,* the all-important unity with God, and that rebellion against God's sovereignty had engendered "humiliation and backwardness." Meanwhile the West had been up to its devilish tricks. Greedy Europeans had essentially engaged in a long-running heist of Islam's original discoveries, exploiting their overwhelming power for manipulating and transforming the material world. In the process, however, our Western forebears, by definition Christian, pagan, and deviant, paid a heavy price by separating themselves even farther from God than had erring Muslims. And because the marauding, godless, anxiety-ridden Europeans could no longer live easily in their own skins, they had to try and drive Muslims away from their true faith as well. Thus in Qutb's view, as author Paul Berman writes, the "Europeans inflicted their 'hideous schizophrenia' on peoples and cultures in every corner of the globe. That was the source of modern misery . . . the sense of drift, the purposelessness, the craving for false pleasures."[1]

Not surprisingly, perhaps, it was post–World War II America that personally taught Qutb a thing or two about the perils of earthly pleasures. Before joining Egypt's Muslim Brotherhood in the early fifties (the same group that later nurtured Ayman al-Zawahiri, Osama's chief deputy and Al Qaeda's reputed mastermind), Qutb spent two years in the U.S. on assignment for the Egyptian Ministry of Education studying American schools—"an experience in cross-cultural living," educator Ted Thornton has observed wryly, "that did not go well." Generally appalled by the freedom of sexual expression he found stateside, Qutb was blanched to his moral core one fateful Sunday night in Greeley, Colorado, when, invited to visit a sock hop put on by a local church group, he witnessed fully clothed bobby-soxers gyrating, shockingly, to the sounds of "Baby It's Cold Outside." Back in Cairo, the traumatized Qutb set about vigorously developing the puritanical concept of *jahiliyaa,* or "pagan ignorance and rebellion against God."[2]

Less quaintly, Qutb was upset by the racism he had witnessed in pre-civil-rights America. In the country's appalling treatment of its black citizens the Egyptian saw a meanness of spirit that helped persuade him that by hook or by crook the "Crusaders" and "Zionists," for reasons perhaps as deeply Freudian as they were wickedly political and economic, were determined to dominate Muslim lands, and then to methodically wipe Islam from the face of the earth. Not unreasonably, from his point of view, Qutb argued that the Muslim

1. Paul Berman, "The Philosopher of Islamic Terror," *New York Times Magazine,* March 23, 2003. Also see, *Occidentalism: The West in the Eyes of Its Enemies* (New York: The Penguin Press, 2004), by Ian Buruma and Avishai Margalit.
2. See Ted Thornton's useful and user-friendly History of the Middle East Database at www.nmhschool.org.

world's only defense against such unprincipled enemies was to impose a sort of wartime discipline on its societies by restoring God's sovereignty through selfless jihad and the rule of Islamic law. And while for many of us in the West shariah is synonymous with unacceptably harsh punishments (the loss of limbs and digits for thievery, or death by stoning for an extramarital fling), Paul Berman points out that for Qutb it "meant freedom of conscience . . . from modern schizophrenia."

Now a half-century later the kids on board the *Bukit Siguntang* were at least theoretically riding the ideas of Islamic utopia into battle at Ambon. From the looks of them, however, you really had to wonder if all that many knew exactly what they were getting themselves into. Frankly, I came to suspect that, not unlike the doughboys who left the family farm in Wisconsin or Somerset to hustle off to Flanders fields and the carnage of trench warfare in World War I (or the young in any war, for that matter), these kids were rallying in support of a vaguely shining idea bigger than themselves, dreams of exalted glory, and hoping for a crackling good adventure into the bargain.

Apparently, though, at least some of them didn't want to be there at all. "[T]asked to fight Christians," a study for the Center for Defense Intelligence in Washington, D.C., would eventually point out, "many volunteers have said they felt deceived because they had joined to assist in humanitarian activities. When they sought to return home, leaders threatened to kill members who refused to fight against Christians."

The dining room was a big, busy rectangle running the full width of the ship, filled with darting, mustachioed waiters in threadbare red tunics, and alive with the sounds of clinking utensils and passenger chatter. The moment I walked in, however, the place went as deadly quiet as the saloon in a Western movie when Memphis Slim, the black-hearted gunslinger, parts the swinging doors. Amid a chorus of astonished whispers of "Bule! Bule!," Norman and I settled at a table in the first-class section, prompting a slim, goggle-eyed man already sitting there to grow considerably more goggle-eyed, bolt down his coffee, and scurry away. One table over, meanwhile, a tarty-looking young woman with long showgirl legs only partially obscured by a black-leather miniskirt stole a glance at me and then snickered stealthily into her palm. Repressing a powerful urge to turn her in to the religious police for exposing a scandalous stretch of upper thigh, and of course for laughing at me, I said to Norman, "I take it not many Europeans travel this route these days."

"Very few Vikings," Norman confirmed absentmindedly as he scanned the room for potential troublemakers. After squinting in the direction of the long tables lined up under the big picture windows, which looked radioactive in the hot white sea glare, he added happily: "But no Jihad, either, Boss, at least for now."

Holy warriors or no, I still felt wildly uncomfortable, and so I kept my eyeballs glued on the table d'hôte, which struck me as quite elaborate for a terror cruise. There were several kinds of white fish, fried and poached, a small mountain of hard-boiled eggs, a platter of chicken sausages, stacks of toast, squares of butter wrapped in foil, and a selection of marmalades made from rambutan, jackfruit, and other tropical delicacies. I had absolutely no appetite of course, but to put a brave face on things, I grabbed a piece of plain white bread, slathered it with a thin yellowish substance that smelled of oranges but tasted of cheese, and chewed unenthusiastically.

Meanwhile Norman heaped his plate with victuals and dug in with the determination of a high school wrestler trying to eat his way into the next higher weight classification. Then, looking up between forkfuls and glancing around the room, he said, "Wow."

"Wow, what?" I said.

"Lots of police on this ship, Boss. That guy in the corner, for example." Norman elevated his chin toward a pudgy man with a pair of quick, calculating eyes, who was sitting with his back to the far wall and sizing up every new face to come through the swinging doors. "He's deputy police chief of Jakarta."

Waggling his fork at a group of hard-looking men who hovered near the exit in camouflage battle dress with machine guns slung over their shoulders, Norman said, "Wow, military security, too. I guess the authorities are taking this Laskar Jihad thing seriously."

"No shit, Sherlock," I said, not even slightly reassured by the tight security arrangements. In my limited experience the presence of so much armed muscle only amplifies the larger dangers against which it might have to be hurled. My other concern was this: Knowing what we knew about the military's alleged role in helping to stir the pot in the Moluccas, how could we now be sure that at least some of those charged with protecting us from the Jihad were not in fact in cahoots with the Jihad?

Norman complimented me on an excellent question to which he said there was no answer. Then, having made our situation sound as ominous as possible, he gulped down his sweet tea and stood up. "Let's go, Boss," he said brightly. "Maybe we can make it to the bridge without getting murdered."

We pushed our way through the swinging doors and out onto the polished teakwood deck, which swept forward in a gentle curve rising toward the bow. There were people everywhere here, too— mostly refugees who, uprooted from their homes in the troubled islands, were squatting, standing, lying down, and generally looking unhappy, while beyond them the Java Sea, deceptively calm, glistened with sunlight all the way to the horizon. When I elevated my eyebrows toward a group of young men slouched menacingly against the gunwales, Norman identified them as prime candidates for a regular constituency of freelance thieves and shakedown artists who plied the passenger lines hereabouts. "Christians," he whispered in further explanation, but not the Mother Teresa type, Boss."

To say I did not like the vibes I was picking up on deck would be a ridiculous understatement. And so I scrambled behind Norman, as if roped to him in a chain gang, while he pressed ahead, chin up, torso erect, masking his own nervousness behind his regal Javanese coolness. My notes are a little sketchy here, given that I was encountering a series of stares of such smoldering intensity that I thought my hair might catch on fire. But if memory serves, it was then and from the far end of the deck that I could see a white blur moving toward us at some speed. Drawing nearer, the shape separated into the figures of three men, bodies bent forward, their snowy robes flowing out behind, as big hairy calves pounded angrily against the wooden deck.

"The guys from the plane!" said Norman.

"Shhhhh," I said. "They'll hear you!" But Norman was right. While waiting on the tarmac during a stopover in Surabaya the previous day, Tanya had been showing me her Hajja's veil, a souvenir from one of her two pilgrimages to the holy shrine at Mecca.(Tanya, like Des, was technically Muslim, though her late mother had been a Christian.) Tying it behind her ears and giving her head a coquettish tilt, she was promising to disown me should we ever get ourselves into a tight spot with the radicals, when this same trio walked down the aisle in their desert gear and plunked down in the seats opposite.

"Ooooh, look!" Tanya had said, jabbing her finger and speaking in a voice loud enough to be heard all the way to the cockpit. "It's the Jihad, yah?!"

Hearing the operative word, the men turned their heads in unison and regarded us with looks not so much hostile as clinical, as if they were encountering an alien life form. (How an emotionally frozen Viking sitting sandwiched between a madly burbling princess and a Palm Pilot–toting poster boy for the globalized lifestyle with a modified Elvis coif could have stood out in any way is beyond me.) Two of the men were tall and gaunt. The third man was a short, stocky fellow with a smiling, boyish face but a pair of feral-looking eyes that told me he was no callow youth.

On the other hand, if somebody had told me at that precise moment that I was sitting less than a dozen feet from the Islamic warlord Jaffar Umar Thalib, who the New York Times would two years later identify as "arguably the most feared militant in the most populous Muslim nation on earth," I would have told them to stop pulling my leg—or more likely I suppose, I'd have unbuckled my seatbelt and quietly hightailed it for the terminal.

At that point, however, not even those astute observers of the Jakarta scene, Tanya or Norman, could have picked Jaffar out of a parade or a police lineup. All things considered, it may have been just as well that I would only later piece together a portrait of the thirty-nine-year-old cleric. Typical of Southeast Asia's radical Muslim brotherhood, Jaffar had rallied to the defense of the Islamic heartlands in the 1980s by joining the fight to end the Soviet occupation of Afghanistan. It was there, and while attending a militant "prep" school in neighboring Pakistan, that he studied the unforgiving Wahabi brand of Islam and met fellow holy-warrior-in-training Osama bin Laden. Jaffar would later insist that bin Laden was neither much of a Muslim—"an arrogant," "spiritually empty man," weak on his Koranic ABCs, he told one interviewer—nor a particularly gifted soldier.[3]

Nonetheless, there were some worrying similarities. The two men were bound together not only by their shared experiences as anti-Soviet guerrillas, but by an unwavering belief in pressing the worldwide Islamic community to return to the pure *salafi* form of Islam—at the point of a scimitar or rocket-propelled grenade launcher, if necessary. And while the Muslim world's many moderate thinkers pressed the principle of the Greater Jihad, the never-ending, Zenlike process whereby the individual uses life's challenges as grist to refine both spirit and mind, Jaffar and Osama were quite prepared to make a great bloody thing out of the so-called Lesser Jihad, taking the fight to the infidels, as a means of achieving their political ends.

Interestingly, though perhaps coincidentally, Osama and Jaffar were also both of Yemeni ancestry. More to the point, Jaffar, like many of Indonesia's strictest fundamentalists, was *hadrami,* meaning an Indonesian of Arab descent. While approximately eighty percent of Indonesians are of Malay stock, and fifteen percent Melanesian, roughly as many as five percent trace bloodlines to the Middle East, and as a group tended to foster ties with the sterner forms of Islam. Like Osama, Jaffar did not believe in democracy, political parties, women's rights, capitalism, or Save the Whales. According to his blueprint, Indonesia would be ruled by Allah's law, the shariah—not

---

3. Andrew Marshall, "The Threat of Jaffar," *New York Times Magazine,* March 10, 2002.

the laws of men—and a board of Islamic wise men would be responsible for picking presidents and deciding policy.

A day would come when, long after Jaffar had reached a startling prominence in national politics, Eko Prasetyo, a human rights activist and scholar who had broken with his own fundamentalist past, would tell me that, above all things, Jaffar believed in the glory of jihad, the "active act of fighting and dying *shahid,* a martyr."

On the plane the only thing that had been obvious, from the way the two taller men smiled and nodded deferentially, was that the chunky third man had the power over them. And now on the high seas, it was this very same fellow taking the lead as the trio stomped the deck, going somewhere in a big hurry and—thank God for small favors, I thought—completely ignoring Norman and me.

"Not the happy campers, Boss," observed Norman.

And we found out why soon enough. Climbing the twisting stairway to the bridge deck, Norman and I followed the sound of Tanya's penetrating laughter through two steel-plated outer hatches, and then onto the bridge itself—a modern, light-filled wheel room that, in contrast to the passenger decks below, had the clean, orderly appearance of a well-run, seagoing vessel. When we walked in, Tanya was seated in a big swivel chair, her feet dangling off the floor, and talking to a tough-looking man in a crisp white uniform shirt whose gold bars identified him as the ship's chief officer.

When she saw us she cried, "Those three guys from the plane . . ."

"We saw them . . .," I said.

"Well, they're the leaders of the Laskar Jihad all right and very pissed off, yah," said Tanya. "They think Pontoh here has given them the wrong times for their prayers. Oh my God, right?"

"Yes, they accuse me, Andre Pontoh!" said the man in uniform. Eyes wide with drama, he spoke in an ebullient, tommy-gun stutter, and as Norman and Tanya took turns translating, he explained that the Jihad bigwigs had stormed the bridge earlier that morning, demanding justice.

I gulped inwardly. Everybody knows devout Muslims, required to bow in the direction of Mecca five times a day, are understandably very particular about getting their prayer times exactly right. In our current unhappy circumstances, it went without saying, any mix-ups in that department could bear some decidedly unhealthy consequences.

"I tell you, these guys are nothing but a bunch of hicks," Pontoh fumed. "They come from these Islamic schools that teach only the Koran—no scientific knowledge whatsoever! Don't they know that the earth revolves around the sun and time changes as you change your position?!"

The irony of the thing was that, knowing how sensitive the jihadis were likely to be, Pontoh had painstakingly calculated the prayer schedule, using his global ship's almanac as a guide. But arguing his case with the three imams on the basis of some infidel book had been like talking to a chill wind.

As I watched Pontoh throw his hands up in frustration, I liked him immediately. Part of it was his raspy bullhorn of a voice, his lively way of telling a story, and the way his arms shot out at all angles to illustrate whatever point he was trying to make at the time. But it was in his flat, slightly crumpled nose that I detected the sign of a man who knew how to handle himself in a rough situation, and I decided then I would stick as closely to Pontoh as I possibly could from there on out.

"You'd be a fool not to take this stuff seriously," Pontoh went on, recalling another incident that had occurred eight months earlier, a few weeks after the people of nearby East Timor had voted to secede from Indonesia. The U.N.-sponsored plebiscite marked the beginning of the end of a period of world-class brutality, which had started in 1975 when Indonesia illegally annexed the former Portuguese colony with the tacit approval of then-president Gerald Ford and his secretary of state, Henry Kissinger. Suharto's military, underwritten financially by the United States of America, had gone on to seal the deal by killing as many as two hundred thousand people—a third of the tiny half-island's entire population.[4]

---

4. See William Burr and Michael L. Evans, eds., *East Timor Revisited: Ford, Kissinger and the Indonesian Invasion, 1975* (Washington, D.C.: National Security Archive Electronic Briefing Book No. 67), available at www.gwu.edu/~nsarchi.

But the long-awaited vote, which many in the West saw as a stirring blow for the freedom of an oppressed people, was viewed by
many Indonesians as an attempt by the great bule powers, mainly
Australia, which headed the international peacekeeping force, to
throw their weight around and put Indonesia in its place. However
irrational that response appeared on its face, it was a powerful
reminder of how, for former colonial subjects, the idea of white foreigners dabbling in their affairs had ripped the scabs off some very
old and deep sores. Muslim militants had gone a step farther with
their claims that the infidels were angling to set up a Christian
republic in league with the Spice Islands' Jesus-worshipers. It was a
highly emotional time, accelerating tensions all across the country,
and a few weeks later, in September 1999, the ripples hit the *Bukit
Siguntang.*

A scuffle broke out in steerage, Pontoh recalled. A couple of
punches were possibly thrown. One disputant was Muslim, the
other a Christian, but it wasn't a religious quarrel, at least not at first.
The combatants were separated and that was that. But of course it
wasn't. The Muslims got to stewing among themselves and decided
the Christians had been let off too lightly.

"And their 'proof' was right here on this bridge," said Pontoh.
Despite the fact that the *Bukit Siguntang* had been officially declared
a Muslim ship, the Pelni shipping line had maintained in force its
traditional practice of promoting mainly Christians to the officer
ranks. "All of the ship's officers at the time, including me, Andre
Pontoh, were Christian!

"Next thing we knew those Muslim kids had all lined up all
along the windows here," said Pontoh, jabbing a finger at the big
panes of glass encasing the bridge. It wasn't long before the rioters
were pointing at the crew and chanting "Obet! Obet!"—the local
equivalent of the N-word for Christians. "They ran their fingers
across their throats," said Pontoh, hopping up and down on his seat
as if it were an electric frying pan, while he demonstrated a slicing
motion just above his Adam's apple.

Pontoh had bolted the door to the bridge and prepared the crew for imminent attack, while he pondered the possibility of the wholesale slaughter of all the Christians on board, including himself. He suggested that if I wanted it straight with the bark off, the rioters weren't any different from the kids down there in the passageways right now, "except of course they were ready to kill us!"

"What happened next?" I asked Pontoh, with growing self-interest as I realized how ludicrous it was to think we could save ourselves from a full-scale riot by hiding out on the bridge. Dumbfounded, the chief officer emitted a mirthless, stuttering laugh and said, "Why, we pulled the shades!"

Pontoh looked over at Tanya, his eyes wide in mock surprise, and they both went into hysterics, Tanya's roller-coaster giggle swooping and dipping and gaining momentum as it mingled with Pontoh's staccato croak. Recovering, the chief officer said, "If you want to know the truth, that's the man who saved us right over there!"

Pontoh lowered the angle of his chin to indicate a smiling, avuncular character in a baseball cap who had been sitting at a nearby table, quietly listening to our conversation. Tanya introduced him as Abdurrachman Khoe, one of Des's old friends from Ambon. On that tumultuous day, Pontoh said, Khoe had hoisted the ship's microphone to urge calm, and then walked the decks, talking the young hotheads down. It hadn't been easy. This was a Muslim ship, they'd argued—purity of faith demanded that Muslims serve fellow Muslims! The Christians be damned!

"Yes," said Khoe, remembering the incident with a self-effacing laugh, "that's when I told them, 'Look here now, the cook is a Christian, too. Kill him and you starve.' " The pithy logic of the stomach was something that poor farm boys understood only too well. The riot quickly ended, and the ship sailed on to Ambon without further incident.

I wondered out loud what had given Khoe the clout necessary to bargain with the angry Muslims, and Tanya informed me that this affable man, so subdued and mild where Pontoh was peppery and outspoken, was none other than a senior official of the main mosque in Ambon that would be playing host to the Laskar Jihad! I was flabbergasted. Dressed in his faded blue windbreaker, Khoe had the look of a friendly high school janitor from Queens—somebody you'd see in the stands at Yankee Stadium quietly enjoying a ball game on a sunny afternoon.

Human nature really is terrible when you get right down to it, but I confess that as I inspected Khoe's face more closely now I couldn't help but notice how his eyes had suddenly positioned themselves closer together and taken on a decidedly shifty aspect. Starchily, but still struggling to maintain some shred of objectivity, I asked the transmogrified Khoe what the Laskar Jihad intended to do in Ambon.

Khoe replied with a smile and a friendly flap of the hand. He stated accurately, as the record would indeed show, that physical attacks on Muslim villagers and mosque-goers in the Christian-dominated city had escalated in recent weeks. Even so, he swore, thrusting a forefinger heavenward, that the Jihad was bent not on vengeance but on a purely social mission to aid Ambon's beleaguered Muslims.

I didn't believe him. I thought then that he was either fooling himself or varnishing the truth, and in any event, and for reasons we'll get to a little later, the Jihad's humanitarian cover would be quickly blown as soon as Jaffar's boy troopers disembarked at Ambon. Sensing the tension. I think, Pontoh broke in to ask me if I wanted him to show me around the ship, and off we went.

Tramping the decks in the high, blazing sunshine, Pontoh, Tanya, Norman, Khoe, and I traversed the very top of the *Bukit Siguntang*'s wedding-cake superstructure, while Norman clicked off a series of commemorative snapshots. We then descended straight down, many levels, to the engine room, and ended the tour in the ship's galley.

There a tall, lanky young man in a bloody butcher's jacket emerged from the meat locker brandishing a large cleaver in his right hand—the galley supervisor. With his wild spiky hair and long sideburns he looked like a cross between fifties movie idol James Dean and a bewitched fairy tale character. Waving his cleaver at me, he said gruffly, "So what do you like to eat?"

My eyes ran swiftly to a large vat of tofu nearby. "Well, I like tofu," I stuttered uncertainly as the galley supervisor glowered in thought.

"Okay then," he said, cracking a wolfish grin, "I'll make a nice tofu dish for you!"

4

MIKE

The tofu appeared at lunch, expertly braised and sautéed with snow peas in a delicious garlic sauce. But while Norman and Tanya and Pontoh ate with gusto, my attention was riveted on the several dozen young men who had suddenly filed into the dining room and took up pews at those long, rectangular tables against the far bulkheads— the Jihad's junior-executive class, as Norman identified them. Self-assured in freshly laundered gray tunics and baggy pants, these fellows were indeed a different kettle of fish from the ragged teenagers riding the cardboard out in the passageways. In fact, they very much reminded me of the political cadres I'd met in China in the old days before the Chinese joyously all but chucked the idealistic rigors of Mao Zedong's Communist kingdom for local access to Starbucks, Wal-Mart, and Pizza Hut.

How quickly times change, I thought. It seemed like only yesterday (because, historically speaking, it *was* only yesterday) that the fall of the old Soviet Union and the rise and subsequent fizzle of the Japanese economic threat in the 1980s had paved the way for China to become

America's No. 1 geopolitical rival. But all you had to do was travel in China nowadays, as I'd recently done, and you could tell the Chinese were going to be big disappointments in the enemy department. Basically, we—Chinese and Americans—wanted the same things out of life: nice, mainly apolitical families, a little electronic gadgetry to fool with, and a tract house in the suburbs with a sports utility vehicle in the driveway. Our respective governments might occasionally try and screw things up, and trade sharp elbows over trade or security issues, but chances were good we'd find a way to solve our differences without scuttling the global economy that made our mutual dreams possible.

But the Islamic revolution as evidenced on board the *Bukit Siguntang* was still in its volatile formative stage. And while its cadre, the "fish swimming in the sea" of the masses of the people, as Mao said famously of his vanguard class, were enjoying the table d'hôte the Jihad "masses" grubbed from a communal pot down in steerage. The thing of it is, though, the junior execs didn't seem to be enjoying their material perks in the least. Heads bowed, eyes fixed on their plates, they ate in monkish silence, all the while exuding a sort of low-grade hostility that by comparison made the old-time Communists seem as lighthearted as a bunch of stand-up comics.

Whether long-overdue economic and social development in the Muslim world would eventually "drain the swamp," as the experts liked to say, by providing young Muslims with better education and jobs, more convivial lifestyles, and a greater measure of personal dignity very much remained to be seen.[1] Sizing up the lunchroom crowd, though, you could clearly see that for the time being we were operating on fundamentally different tracks—the Western free-market model with its cheering, if not infrequently ruthless, philosophy of go forth and conquer, the Jihad on an opposite formula: sacrifice and submit—to God and his hierarchy on earth. (For did not Sayyid Qutb himself observe that "[in] God's

---

1. For those interested in investigating human conditions in the Muslim world, have a look at the comprehensive Arab Human Development Report put out annually by the United Nations and available on line at www.undp.org.

market the only commodity in demand is the commodity of faith"?) It would be, for now and sometime to come, as the author Benjamin Barber presciently forecast in his 1995 book of the same title, a case of "Jihad vs. McWorld."

As we sat there eating our lunch, the sun persisted in wheeling in the sky overhead, despite the wishes of the jihadi leadership, and was turning the big dining room windows into panels of trembling blue light, when the three imams came bombing in, hairy calves still pounding away. "Whoa, they're still pissed about something," said Tanya as we all watched the harrumphing figures take up seats a few tables away in first class.

The fussbudget behavior of the clerics only confirmed Tanya's judgment that I'd best restrain my reporterly instincts, and hold off trying to speak directly with the jihadis or their leaders until we saw whether my presence waved any red flags before the rambunctious mullahs. With rumors about Christian spying and skullduggery circulating freely, it was a hard argument to refute. And so reluctantly (but not that reluctantly), I agreed for the time being to keep my mouth shut.

Meanwhile brave Tanya, clutching that protective Hajja's veil of hers, had taken to testing the reportorial waters on her own—and quickly discovered that the jihadis, being good team men, did not, like team men everywhere, give up much beyond the agreed-on script.

"You going to Ambon?" she had asked randomly, singling out one or another of the boys hunkered down in the passageways.

"No," would come the inevitable reply, "I'm going to visit my relatives in Ceram"—a big island due west of Ambon that Tanya knew well and about which the boys' ignorance appeared nearly absolute.

"All your friends here, they're going to Ceram, too?"

"Friends? Uh, I'm not with those other guys."

"If you believe any of that," observed Tanya over our tofu, in her slightly dated American slang, "there's a bridge in Brooklyn I'd like to sell you, yah?"

A day eventually arrived when I'd have better luck speaking

freely with people who associated themselves with the top of Laskar Jihad's leadership pyramid.This included a particularly lively session in a Jakarta TV studio one afternoon with a man named Eggi Sudjana. Despite Eggi's credentials as a lawyer and labor organizer, who headed his own small Islamist action group, the Indonesian Muslim Workers Brotherhood, senior Western diplomats had warned me that, in their view, he was little more than a freebooting troublemaker.They blamed Eggi for stirring up riots in early 1999 in heavily Islamic Lombok Island (located off the eastern tip of Bali and a place the travel brochures billed quaintly as the "Land of a Thousand Mosques") before going on, they said, to move mysteriously behind the scenes in the embattled Moluccas.

Given the buildup, I was feeling nervous about meeting Eggi face-to-face, but I relaxed when things quickly took on that screwball quality that was to mark so many of my encounters in Indonesia. In keeping with his reputed man-of-mystery profile, Eggi had insisted we rendezvous at the Jakarta headquarters of RTCI, a large private television network.When I walked into a conference room where Eggi was waiting, however, it was clear that his choice of venue had less to do with me than with a certain TV actress of his acquaintance.

"We were in drama club together in high school," Eggi explained enthusiastically as he introduced me to his friend, a woman at the slightly fleshy, pulchritudinous tipping point of middle age, who smiled coquettishly through her pancake makeup. In case I'd missed his point, Eggi added, grinning suavely, "I go away to Hajj in Mecca tomorrow!"

Eggi was an ebullient man who made his points in tortured English, gamely and with the help of big meaty fingers. For starters, he vehemently and categorically denied charges that he was in any way linked to terrorism. "Laskar Jihad was established because in Ambon many Muslims were killed," he said, adding with lawyerly logic, *"therefore,* I must fight!"

Why did he suppose some people thought he might be a terrorist? I asked.

"I am famous demonstration!" he replied, obscurely but with a vigor that made his meaning clear enough. "I not agree with government and I [organize labor] strikes! *Therefore,* many people like you and government have stigma for me, for fundamentalism. This is no *gooood!*"

"I can't speak for any government," I said, correcting him gingerly. "But I don't have a stigma for you. I just want to hear what you have to say."

Eggi raised his head, which seemed huge, with deep-set eye sockets and a mop of curly black hair—a bull ready to charge. He then broke into a big lopsided grin that reminded me, strangely, of an old high school classmate, a lovable hood manqué named Frank. "Okay, okay," said Eggi, "not you!"

But what I had to understand, he said in effect, was that with him, it was all Islam, all the time—he was ready to aggressively confront anybody who wanted to prevent shariah "to become rule of the game in Indonesia." What right did people have to deny him his religious convictions?

So people who linked him with terrorism were just confused, was that it? I asked.

"Not confused!" he bellowed. "They just make trouble for me and fundamentalism." His main enemies, other than the United States, which he said had placed him on its terrorist watch list and denied him entry ("Not fair!"), were the two largest mainstream Muslim lay organizations in Indonesia, Nahdlatul Ulama and Mohammadiya. Claiming a combined membership of over fifty million Muslims, they adamantly opposed the wholesale imposition of shariah, and were, *"therefore,"* Eggi said, playing dirty.

"In Italy," Eggi opined, "many people are Catholic at the Vatican, and so the Catholic system becomes the rule of the game for the state. Why then, when I want Islam to become rule of game in Indonesia, your people get angry?"

But Italy was a democracy, not a theocracy, and the Vatican was something else again, I suggested.

"No problem," said Eggi, quickly changing the subject to avoid getting mired in the details. "Your government has a hidden agenda in Indonesia!"

"So you think the U.S. is waging a disinformation campaign to label people like you terrorists?"

"Yes!" Eggi smiled truculently. "And this is very much insulting to me and the *unmat,* the [Muslim] community."

Things were getting edgy again, and when Eggi's cell phone erupted, shouting, *"Allllaaaaah"* in a resonant tenor's voice, I confess I jumped a little in my seat. Eggi laughed heartily, his big head and chest heaving with mirth. Don't worry, he said, the call to prayer was just the sound effect he'd programmed into his phone instead of the standard ring.

Watching this voluble man stride around the room, yukking it up with whomever was phoning him, I thought again of Frank, and how you'd love to hang out at the local drive-in with him, swapping jokes and talking tough, and getting a little thrill out of the hint of danger. The difference here of course was that back at the hamburger stand the danger was pretend and we knew it.

And when Eggi rang off, he left me with a chilling thought: "Knowledge is important," he said, his deep-set eyes glowering, and *therefore* he had agreed to talk with me. "But when we don't have knowledge we have the gun!"

Headed for holy war, our companions in the dining room were not nearly so jovial as Eggi. But at least they had no guns. Pontoh had personally assured me that repeated security sweeps of the passenger and cargo areas had turned up only the odd rusty blade or machete. I'd also learned something useful about myself. With the ship on edge, I quickly determined that the difference between being seized by near-paralyzing bouts of fear or experiencing some degree of emotional comfort depended almost wholly on where I happened to be at the time, exactly who I happened to be looking at, and, more important, who was looking at me. And so I made it a point to spend as much time as I possibly could hanging out up on the bridge staring blankly out to sea.

It wasn't necessarily any safer up there, mind you. That point had been amply driven home after that shipboard riot the previous

September when the Pelni shipping company had in its wisdom assigned the *Bukit Siguntang* its current captain, F. A. Harahap, a Muslim, on the theory that a Muslim master could more easily keep his co-religionists in line. But Harahap had hardly reported for duty when a gang of a hundred radical Islamists held him captive on his own bridge, and perhaps as a consequence, I thought, I had yet to see him topside.

No, it wasn't the promise of safety that drew me to the bridge so much as the relaxed family atmosphere up there. When you get right down to it, the crew of the *Bukit Siguntang* was really just a pocket-sized version of the whole marvelously strange country—one big, gregarious, if occasionally disputatious, family. On a fairly typical afternoon later in our journey through the Moluccas, the bridge lineup included the ship's third officer, a shy young woman with protruding teeth and a tight but ill-cut khaki uniform, who hailed from Manado, and a big mincing farm boy from West Java who was dressed in a snappy, old-fashioned blue sailor's middy. Both of their faces lighted up like neon when I told them, through Norman, that I hailed from New York.

"New York! Wow!" cried West Java Man, curiosity trumping his natural Javanese reserve. "How much does it cost to rent a flat over there?" When I gave him a lowball figure of fifteen hundred dollars a month, his jaw dropped in amazement.

"How could anything cost that much?" he said. It was a perfectly logical question for somebody who, I'm guessing, would have been lucky to make the equivalent of fifty dollars a month.

"Don't be silly," said a middle-aged man who was standing at the nearby chart table fiddling with a map and a compass. A squat, balding character with a pugnacious smile and the rolling gait of a friendly bulldog, he said, "Here, I'll give you a lesson in economics."

"Now you take the price of a prostitute," said Bulldog, searching for an everyday example he thought any young able-bodied sailor would understand. The woman with the teeth clucked her tongue and shot Bulldog a disgusted glance.

"Okay, forget prostitutes," he said. "Let's take a bottle of beer." Bulldog then launched into an explanation of the economics of

supply and demand as it related to the theory of cost-of-living dif-
ferentials with such verve and confusion that I began to question my
own shaky grasp of the subject. Within three minutes he'd wrestled
himself into complete verbal submission. Stopping in midsentence,
Bulldog furrowed his brow, scratched an ear in thought, and then
turned to me and asked, "Okay, so who do you think is the best
prizefighter who ever lived—Muhammad Ali?"

The afternoon was floating by very pleasantly, all things considered, when West Java Man asked to be excused. It was time, he said,
to announce the afternoon prayers over the ship's public address system. After Pontoh's run-in with the angry imams, the crew had been
warned against the slightest miscue. "Gentle passengers, your kind
attention please," the sailor intoned smoothly over a big old-
fashioned crooner's mike that sat atop the ship's control panel. He
then dropped his voice a half-octave, rendering it even mellower:
"The time for prayer is upon us."

He went on, "Honored guests, to locate the Holy City of Mecca
you will kindly stand facing the back of the ship." By now his voice
was dripping with honey and honorifics, in a way the Javanese consider the height of classy speech. "If it pleases, turn fifteen degrees to
your left. And now, with God's blessing, let us begin . . ."

Carefully placing the microphone back in its stand, West Java
Man reached over and flipped the switch on an electronic boom
box, and the muezzin, in prerecorded form, sang out, *"Allah . . . u
akbar . . . Allahhhh . . . u akbar!"*—"God is great!"

The lovely, haunting Arabesque tapestry of the call to prayer rose
and fell and rose again as it gushed from the ship's loudspeakers. And
let me tell you, my friends, there was a great feeling of romance
attached to hearing this performance in such an exotic setting, and
gooseflesh rose on my infidel forearms in spite of the gummy heat.

"La ilaha illa Allah, Muhammad rasul Allah"—"There is no god
but God, and Muhammad is his Messenger."

His work done, West Java Man smiled, flicked off the tape player,
and we resumed our discussion of prizefighters. Quickly, though, all
five of us gathered around the ship's console fell into a kind of collective reverie, staring out the big windows where the lowering sun

imposed a sort of magical, burnished calm on the surface of the waters. Then, as not infrequently happens, this slow and lovely moment induced in me a feeling of that peculiarly American guilt—that I should be up and doing something constructive.

And so I got to thinking it couldn't really hurt if I sought out not any militants as might have been on deck then, but some of the refugees. Heaven knows, the ship going and coming was loaded with them, and I could add to my collection of eyewitness accounts. Norman would have to translate of course, but when I looked around, he had quietly slipped out the door. Instantly I became very annoyed. Nothing irked me more than having him disappear just when I needed him, and so I called out, "Norman!"

When there was no reply, I rose from my chair, and tried again: "Norman! Where the hell are you?!"

Nothing. Now my blood really began to boil. "Goddammit, Norman!" I shouted. "Come here, man! I need you!"

I repeated words to that effect three or four more times for good measure and then stormed around the bridge deck in a state of high bule dudgeon, opening doors, sticking my head into the sleeping area, the toilet, and so on. Eventually, I discovered Norman sitting in the radio room, smiling to himself as he idly checked out the ship's electronic gear.

"Hello, Boss."

"For chrissakes, man, get out here and help me out!"

"Okay, Boss, but, jeez, don't get so huffy," said Norman. We were just about to hit the decks for action, when Tanya bolted through the door, looking disheveled and frightened.

Let me point out here that the Higher Power, in His or Her infinite wisdom, has gifted me with a loud, booming voice, which over the years has taken on a sound suggesting that my vocal chords have been given a good going-over with paint-grade sandpaper. And according to Tanya it was in this same resonant voice that she'd heard me say, distinctly, "Norman, goddammit, man, get over here!"

She then added pointedly, "They heard you all over the ship."

I suddenly felt my cheeks grow very hot as I stammered out, "Me? All over the ship?"

Tanya nodded, and then of course it hit me: Wrapped up in our conversation about Muhammad Ali, the prostitute-pricing index, and other fascinating topics, West Java Man had forgotten to switch off the mike after he'd issued the call to prayer.

"Oh shit," said Norman as the gravity of my offense sank in.

"My God, they'll be cutting your throat for sure now," said Tanya, chasing the observation with her trademark laugh, the roller-coaster cars making an especially quick ascent, pausing a split second on the precipice, then whooshing down and around the curves with spine-tingling abandon. Then, seeing my horrified expression, she stopped abruptly and said, "Sorry, man . . . Maybe you should go hide out in your cabin for a while, yah?"

That struck me as excellent advice. You didn't have to be a crack detective to deduce that the deep voice speaking out of turn from the bridge, *in English,* crashing in on the holiest of Muslim moments, while invoking, angrily, the name of the Christian deity, belonged wholly and unmistakably to the lone bule on board. It was only a matter of time, I reasoned, before an irate mob arrived on the bridge hunting for the foul blasphemer.

"Come on, Norman, let's blow," I said, and we hightailed it down the twisty steps from the bridge, out across the sweep of the main deck, oblivious to any thug or groups of thugs who might cast eyes on us now, and ducked back inside the first-class lobby near our cabin. As we did so I could see Pontoh standing outside the tiny steward's office, his arms flailing. "Weaklings! Cowards! Idiots!" he yelled as two junior stewards, limp as dishrags, cowered under his Neptune-like wrath.

Seeing us, Pontoh intermitted his bombast and cheerfully waved us over, whereupon Norman filled him in on my open-mike problem. Listening intently, Pontoh glowered, and then smiled. He said something in Indonesian to Norman, who smiled, then glowered, and said in English, "Oh, okay." Then without further explanation Norman flew off down the corridor leaving me standing there with Pontoh.

Never for a moment considering it an impediment to communication that neither of us spoke the other's language, Pontoh promptly unleashed a burst of indignant, rapid-fire Indonesian that seemed to end with a question. The chief officer had worked himself up into a mild fury when a man in combat fatigues sauntered into the office. A dark and stocky fellow with a jaunty, almost Parisian spring in his step, he had a .45-caliber pistol strapped to his hip and on his head the maroon beret of Kopassus, the Army's redoubtable Special Forces branch.

The man smiled amiably at Pontoh from under a huge walrus mustache, but the smile vanished when he saw me. His jaw dropped open, and he proceeded to look me up and down, as if too much dried nutmeg (a popular Spice Islands snack and regarded as a mild hallucinogen) had thrown up a fantastic bule apparition. Barking angrily at Pontoh, the commando jabbed a stubby finger at my chest and, judging by intonation and body language, the conversation went something like this:

Commando: "What in blazes is *he* doing here?"

Pontoh: "It's okay. He's with us."

Commando: "What do you mean 'okay'? A bule? On this ship? Are you out of your frigging mind? He's a sitting duck."

To drive his message home, the cop leveled his index fingers at me like a pair of twin tommy guns. He then put his lips together and spluttered, "Ffftt! Ffftt! Ffftt!"—mimicking the sound of bullets being pumped into my body. I went completely, immediately, and stark ravingly numb. But Pontoh, his steel-plated personality intact, shrugged off the cop's words with a flap of his hand, as if to say, "Take that weak stuff down the street!"

The commando stood there for a long moment, his legs wide apart, hands on his hips, while he continued to look me over from head to foot and back again, as if fixing my image in his mind while he still had the chance. Then at length, he muttered sardonically, "Okay," and walked away, shaking his head.

Oh Christ, I thought, I *really* am a goner now. Without waiting for Norman to return, I rushed to our cabin on wobbly legs, turned my key in the lock with shaky fingers, and then closed the door behind me. Sitting down in a heap on my bunk, I was overwhelmed with a kind of fear-induced nostalgia. As if viewing myself from a disembodied position somewhere near the malfunctioning air-conditioning vent in the middle of the ceiling, I saw a bulky, aging specimen trapped at a far corner of the globe, a man who had wasted his life clodhopping around Asia while his friends from high school and college had led sensible lives—going on to law or medical schools, learning to teach, paying down multiple mortgages, raising families. O, Youth! O, Humanity!

I had completely caved into my desperate melancholy when Norman entered the room at top speed, and then halted abruptly when he saw me sitting on my bunk in my morose condition. Ever the keen observer, he said, "Looking a little depressed there, Boss."

I glared at him, but from the absence of return fire he could tell I was still mortified by my potentially lethal gum-flapping spree. "Why was that Special Forces guy so freaked out by me being on the ship?" I asked him brokenly. "What does he know that we don't?"

"Don't really know, Boss, but I'll check into it if you want."

In Norman's Javanese code, "I'll check into it" meant let's just give it a rest and see what happens, okay? And since I really didn't want to know the answer either, I didn't push.

"I wouldn't take this thing so hard, Boss," said Norman sympathetically. "I mean, basically I don't think these fundamentalist guys are all that well organized."

Coming events, in Indonesia and much closer to home in the world, would prove Norman stunningly wrong in that assessment of course, but given the circumstances it was exactly the right thing to say at the time.

5

MURDERERS AND THIEVES

Look, Boss, rubber bullets!" said Norman.

It was the morning of our arrival in the Banda Islands, and I was standing at the bridge windows looking out to sea, which sparkled like polished chrome under luminous gray skies. Norman had positioned himself a few feet away, and was at the moment reverently fingering a cartridge handed him by a shy, doe-eyed Javanese cop who rested the butt end of his automatic rifle against the spokes of the old-fashioned ship's wheel.

"Yes, Boss," Norman went on without encouragement, rolling the brass casing in his fingers. "The first three bullets are rubber. The fourth one is the so-called money bullet. That gives rioters a chance to stop rioting before somebody gets shot."

"Absolutely fascinating, Norman," I said, my tongue planted firmly in my cheek. But I was in fact in an exceptionally jolly mood this morning. Not only had I passed another night in safety but as of five A.M., when we'd put in at Ambon, the *Bukit Siguntang* was irrevocably jihadi-free, or so I'd judged from the muffled commotion in the corridor signaling the Laskar Jihad's departure. I'd have been even more elated, I suppose, had I known that Jaffar Umar Thalib, soon to be the media's pick for the hardest-working warlord in Islamdom after Osama bin Laden, had decamped at the head of what a final accurate tally put at six hundred troopers. (In fact, it would be some months before I unfolded my morning newspaper in New York and, spluttering on my coffee and bagel, saw those familiar feral eyes staring back at me from a news photo clearly identifying Jaffar as the source of large mischief in eastern Indonesia. We'd have further business with Jaffar but not for a while.)

As it was, I'd risen in the dusky predawn to observe embattled Ambon through our porthole and I was astonished at how remarkably tranquil everything looked. The sun was just beginning to lift over green and pleasant hills, edging tiers of boxy white buildings in orange and gold, and bouncing mellow light off satellite dishes that grew like mushrooms from the flat roofs. It was hard to believe that this was the infamous hellhole of the Moluccas, but Ambon's split psyche was, in fact, dangerously at work. As a "Muslim" ship, we'd been obliged to put in at the city's Muslim pier, while containers of frozen fish for the ship's galley were, appropriately enough, Christian, and on this morning had been held up at one of the Muslim barricades. News of the mix-up made me suddenly very glad that the recent uptick in fighting had foiled Des's big plans to send me into the city on an educational dawn patrol with the local Navy commandos.

Pontoh, on the other hand, was taking the case of the missing fish very personally, pacing the bridge like a noisy tiger and muttering to himself, when Tanya burst through the door. Her hair wet and shimmering from her morning shower, she flew to the windows. Pointing a finger at a vague loaf-shaped hump on the blue-gray meniscus of the sea, she cried happily, "There's Banda!"

Through binoculars, I could in fact pick out two smaller masses at the edge of sea and sky, and I don't mind telling you that I felt as if we were approaching some prehistoric land at the extremities of the earth. It was just that kind of ghostly, premonitory scene. Overhead, the sun was trying hard to burn through the smoky pallor that had engulfed the ship, the product of shifting winds and uncontrolled wildfires endemic to Indonesia's giant hardwood forests on Borneo and Sumatra, and the air smelled faintly of smoked salmon.

I confess I felt a shiver of excitement just then as I watched the magical nutmeg islands rise slowly in the offing. I looked around me. There was Pontoh, poster boy for the two-fisted life of the sea, and the boyish-girlish Javanese cop, languidly fingering his trigger guard. ("Some of these guys look like girls," Norman had assured me, "but they're tough as nails underneath.") And of course there was Tanya, honorary princess of the islands. All of them stood by, looking silently, hopefully, dreamily ahead, enchanted by the spell of the sea.

"This is the East . . ." I heard that refrain from Conrad begin playing itself in my head again, "And these are the men." The words belonged to Marlow, the author's master narrator, in conjuring up the memory of his first voyage to such exotic parts in the story "Youth." And damned if I, or the eternal adolescent in me, didn't feel as if I'd encountered an important essence, the sense that I was somehow always meant to be exactly where I was now, even if I had absolutely no business being there.

It was Tanya who broke the spell. "I sent the dolphins an e-mail to tell them you were coming, Pak Tracy," she said, looking toward her slowly enlarging island kingdom as her giggle soared and dipped. "But I don't know whether they got it, yah?"

I laughed good-naturedly at Tanya's joke in keeping with my overall mood, and then I slipped out on deck for a breath of fresh air and a little privacy. I was standing there at the rail, enjoying the otherworldly flash and sheen of the sea, the bracing rush of ozone, and the antics of Pontoh's large white cockatiel, Jakob, who commanded this area of the ship, when Norman's Javanese cop came shuffling fast along the narrow deck, with Norman hot on his heels.

"Come on, Boss," said Norman excitedly. "We're going to see the prisoners!"

"What prisoners?"

"The ones who killed that nutmeg planter guy on Banda."

It took me a moment, but then I remembered the case quite clearly. I'd only recently read a riveting account of the crime written by my friend and former colleague on the *Far Eastern Economic Review* John McBeth, who was now the newsweekly's esteemed Jakarta bureau chief. On the night of April 20, 1999, five members of the Van den Broeke family, one of the last traceable descendants of the Dutch *perkeniers,* or nutmeg planters, had been summarily butchered in their home on Banda Besar, the largest of the nutmeg islands. Quick on the scene, Des found one of the Van den Broeke sons gurgling through a slashed throat, but had somehow managed to save his life.

What I had overlooked—until now, that is—was the connection between the grisly event and the outbreak of violence in Ambon that, as John succinctly put it, had "island-hopped across the Banda Sea—until it reached paradise." It was in fact a revenge killing. The Van den Broekes, for all intents and purposes local Bandanese whose marbled origins included a remote Dutch link to the high days of the spice trade, had been murdered in retaliation for an incident that had occurred earlier the same day on nearby Hatta Island, in which a Christian had killed a Muslim teenager.

Muslim refugees who, as John noted, had "witnessed wholesale killings in Ambon at the hands of Christian mobs," and fled to the Bandas for their lives, appeared to have targeted the Van den Broekes, if for no other reason than the dangerous hint of Christianity and foreignness conveyed by this thoroughly local family's surname. And now, with paradise coming up fast on the horizon, I was troubled by my failure to put two and two together, and the further unwelcome clue that the Bandas were not the quiet eye of the typhoon in the Moluccas I had been led to believe.

The Javanese cop led the way to the brig, which was located a short distance away along the side of the ship. An open hatchway exposed a dark, pungent hole and fifteen men squatting on their haunches. Gaunt and bony, they had the submissive posture of scared animals and a lazy fear swimming behind reddened eyes. The man closest to the door stopped picking his nose when he saw me and smiled obsequiously. The Java cop told me through Norman that the men had been convicted at trial in Ambon and were now being returned to Banda to serve out their sentences.

"Banda has a prison?" I asked. (I might just as easily have said, "Ambon has a court?")

Norman rolled his eyeballs, suggesting whatever penal facilities the Bandas boasted were very likely to give new meaning to the phrase "minimum security." The man at the door smiled dreamily and went back to excavating his nostrils.

"What do think, Boss?" said Norman, who appeared to be as fascinated with the Banda desperadoes as he had been mesmerized earlier by the rubber bullets.

"Macabre," I replied. The word had become an inside joke with Norman, who had taken a shine to it when I first used it on him in Jakarta. He had cocked his head and repeated it over and over, savoring its dark mystery on his tongue, before observing, "Very handy word for Indonesia these days, Boss."

"Definitely macabre, Boss," Norman now said, adding with a mischievous sparkle in his eye, "Wait till Tanya hears about this."

It was time for lunch. Norman peeled off on one of his existential errands, leaving me to make it to the dining room on my own—but who the hell cared? With the jihadis safely off the ship, I was feeling relaxed and a little cocky. Suddenly famished, too. And so I hurried down to our regular table, which was still empty, and sat down. I was unfolding my napkin, getting ready to dig in, when I was suddenly overcome with that uncanny, self-conscious feeling you get when you sense you're being watched.

When I swiveled my head to see who might be sizing me up, my heart gave a loud thump—I could barely believe my eyes! There, sitting at their regular table against the far wall, were roughly a dozen jihadi junior executives! Holy mama, I thought, as one of the men raised his head and fixed me with a dead-level gaze.

Blanching, I looked away fast, and then pretended to be wholeheartedly absorbed in the menu, while my mind raced to process this unsettling mystery. If the jihadis had been so all-fired eager to wage holy war in Ambon, I thought, what were some of them still doing on the ship six hours out of port? Were my eyes playing tricks on me? When the steward came by, proffering the rice caddy so I could help myself, I used the opportunity to steal another glance across the room.

That was a mistake, as I immediately caught the eye of the same jihadi who had been staring at me before. But it was also a revelation because I could clearly see, to my further astonishment, that this man wasn't even Indonesian! In contrast to the hairless, sallow features of his Malay counterparts, he had a bushy black beard gushing from a face as free of pigment as mine. And unless he was sitting on a telephone book, he was a full head taller than any of his lunch mates. He could be Pakistani, I thought—possibly Afghani—but clearly South or Central Asian, and most definitely not Indonesian. What on earth, I thought, would non-Indonesian jihadis be doing on the *Bukit Siguntang?*

You can see how laughably naive I was in those innocent days before 9/11. The woods out east were in fact full of these guys, and had we (and by "we" I mean the international media as well as U.S. intelligence) been paying more attention, we'd just possibly have gotten a better hop on a deadly link between attempted Islamic revolution in eastern Indonesia and a network that Al Qaeda had begun quietly putting together in the region in the late 1980s. That effort got under way, it is now generally acknowledged, when Osama bin Laden's brother-in-law, Mohammed Jamal Khalifa, set up a string of Islamic charities and front companies in Malaysia and the Philippines. Within five years, the Al Qaeda–sponsored financial network had grown into a complex of terror training camps on the southern Philippine island of Mindanao, where Philippine intelligence officials estimated hundreds of Indonesians were among the several thousand jihadis who received guerrilla training from Al Qaeda instructors between 1996 and 2001.[1]

For those of you interested in the hidden interactions of other

---

1. For further study, see *Inside Al Qaeda: Global Network of Terror* (New York: Columbia University Press, 2002), by Rohan Gunaratna; also, the encyclopedic *Militant Islam in Southeast Asia: Crucible of Terror* (Boulder, CO: Lynne Rienner, 2003), by Zachary Abuza, gives a detailed account of training camp activity.

important militant groups operating in and around Indonesia, be patient—we'll get into that in more detail a little later. Suffice it to say for now that while there was ample evidence kicking around in the days before 9/11 that a terrorist infrastructure was a-building in Southeast Asia, it was largely ignored by the government of the United States. Why? First of all, America's senior diplomats, soldiers, spies, and foreign policy pundits were in the main still focused, anachronistically, on China as the biggest challenge to America's dominant position in Asia.

Moreover, Southeast Asia, with its traditionally moderate form of Islam safely contained inside mainly quiescent multicultural societies like Singapore, Malaysia, and Suharto's Indonesia, was the last place even old Asia hands were suspecting a serious challenge by a resurgent, in-your-face Islam. Finally, officials in Washington harbored what Asian diplomats generally regarded as a chronic cultural bias against investing much credence in what the wags condescendingly called "third-world intelligence."

Let me give you an example. In talking with highly placed regional intelligence officials, I would later learn that certain governments in Southeast Asia had repeatedly tried to alert first the Clinton White House, then the Bush administration, as well as the Australian government, to the growing dangers posed by an obscure terrorist group called Jemaah Islamiyah, the outfit to be eventually fingered for the Bali bombings in October 2002. Senior Asian officials were sufficiently alarmed about JI's activities in the summer of 2001 to travel to Washington with a private warning for the Clinton administration. "We wanted to talk about [the threat of] political Islam in Southeast Asia," one source told me. "The Americans thought we wanted to talk about China! We told the Australians that Jemaah Islamiyah is out to get you. They laughed at us."

But who was I to talk? Looking back on that revelatory moment in the ship's canteen certainly brings me a pang of newsman's regret. I can't help but think that had I been smarter, more courageous, done my homework better—something—I might have done a better job of figuring out exactly who my lunch companions were and how they fit into the overall picture. As it was, isolated on a ship in far waters, I could feel my blood pressure rise dramatically with the sudden reappearance of a danger I'd thought was safely behind me.

Still, not even fear can kill curiosity completely, and so I managed to summon the guts to take another peek at the far side of the dining room. Sure enough, the man who wasn't supposed to be there was staring at me as relentlessly as before. His eyes burned darkly in that hirsute face of his, and if looks could kill, I decided, my head would have been bobbing in the soup that very minute. I was averting my eyes, and making an unconvincing effort to appear nonchalant by shakily lifting a cube of tofu to my mouth, when a sudden tremor rocked my table. Somebody, I knew, had sat himself down in the chair opposite me, and with aggressive heaviness.

Involuntarily looking up, I found myself gazing at a frightening apparition who might have been mistaken for the Incredible Hulk's dangerous tropical cousin. He had a pitted, scowling face in a head that was large and flat like a mallet. Rising above his flowery Aloha shirt was a neck thick and ribbed as a tree stump. Around the stump were looped a variety of gold and silver chains, at least one of them ending in a Christian cross the size of a small hamburger spatula.

That really was the last emotional straw. I was seriously considering falling to my knees and begging for mercy when the Hulk, scowling more intensely now, pointed in a jerky rhythmic fashion, first to the cross, then to what appeared to be a series of old stab wounds on his arms. He then grinned horribly, exposing a glittering collection of silver fillings. "My name Rudi," he thundered in fractured English, thumping his chest with a meaty fist.

"Aha," I said.

Rudi smiled back, flashing more silver teeth. "Security!" he bellowed, continuing to beat his mighty rib cage like a drum. "Me, security!"

"Ah, very interesting," I replied lamely.

I had lowered my head and was praying strenuously for deliverance when Tanya breezed in and sat down. In no time at all she was able to establish that Rudi worked for Médecins Sans Frontières, the

French equivalent of Doctors Without Borders. The doctors had worked local refugee camps in Ambon, providing medical care, and Rudi had provided security for the doctors, until the situation had grown so patently hairy the medicos were forced to evacuate. Thus Rudi was a free man for a bit, and was heading home to visit his family on one of the outer islands.

Relieved at Tanya's report, I wondered out loud about where Rudi had acquired his impressive collection of scars. "Scary, yah?" said Tanya, in a hushed, appreciative burble, and then added, "I'm going to invite him to drop by the hotel for a coffee when we get to Banda. You never know when you might need some good security, yah?"

I was seriously considering entering that remark in the Understatement of the Year contest when Norman flew in and took his seat, smiling coyly.

"Hey, man, how's it hanging?" said Tanya. With corresponding good cheer, Norman told Tanya of his journalistic coup—how he'd persuaded the young Javanese cop to show us the nutmeg murderers.

Tanya stared at him, aghast, the blood draining from her face. "Oh my God," she said. "You didn't tell them I was on the ship, did you?"

Of course not, said Norman, but what if he had?

"Because it was Des who got those guys arrested!" she cried. After discovering local authorities were reluctant to get involved in the Van den Broeke killings, fearing an investigation might stir up further trouble, the king of the Bandas had demanded that justice be done.

Tanya now looked as depressed and anxious as I had felt for the past three days. "As soon as this ship docks, I'm outta here!" she said, following it up with a whooping little laugh. But from the way it quickly faded, I could tell her heart really wasn't in it.

6

PARADISE

Shortly before two P.M., on May 13, 2000, Captain F. A. Harahap, master of the *Bukit Siguntang,* stood on the bridge, barking orders as he steered his ship through the narrow slot separating the wild blue Banda Sea from the tiny turquoise harbor at Bandanaira, the islands' only real town. The elusive captain had revealed himself to be not quite so mysterious after all. In the flesh he was a lean, silver-haired grandpa, with foxy, hooded eyes and a blunt, wry manner, who told me when we'd finally met that—not surprising given current events—he was very much looking forward to his retirement a few months hence.

"Quarter starboard engine," cried Harahap as the big volcano Gunung Api closed in on our right, a massive green wall gliding by the windows at an accelerating clip. Meanwhile gumdrop-shaped Karaka, or Crab Island, rushed up startlingly close off the port bow, its vertiginous jungle suddenly seeming to suspend itself over the ship. Among the green and tangled vines you could see birds of all sizes and types flapping excitedly and bickering complaints as we pressed in on their wild kingdom.

Positioning himself directly behind the captain, Pontoh silently flicked his fingers in a series of quick counterorders as he watched the ship pass through the tight opening, flinching and gesticulating like a bowler relying on body language to keep his ball from spinning into the gutter. Not unlike Indonesia as a whole, it wasn't entirely clear who was really in charge.

"There's the hotel," cried Tanya, pointing to a Dutch colonial–style building separated from the harbor by a rolling greensward anchored by a gnarled and spreading banyan tree. When the ship had nearly slowed to a stop, a big weighted hawser went sailing out over the water as if shot from a cannon, and plunked down on the big lawn. Two men ran from the hotel and chased the anacondalike rope around the yard until they'd succeeded in tethering it to a metal capstan buried near the tree.

"Okay, so much for sightseeing, yah?" said Tanya, cackling mirthlessly. "Let's get the hell off the ship before those criminals see us!"

We disembarked. Walking briskly, Tanya led us to the base of the gangway, where we were met by three sturdy men, Alwi retainers, who tugged the bills of their baseball caps as if at forelocks and grabbed our bags. Then like some exotic retinue, tiny princess of the islands in front, lumbering bule giant in the middle, Rudi Security, smiling from ear to ear, flexing scarred forearms, bringing up the rear, we proceeded through the cyclone fencing that separated the landing area from the main town, and turned left down a narrow alley to the hotel. The whole trip took less than five minutes.

The hotel was laid out in the shape of a modified horseshoe— fifty rooms built around a central veranda facing the lagoon. One of the hotel boys hauled my duffel bag up the stairs to the second-floor balcony, and showed me to a tidy corner room smelling of freshly laundered sheets. After our confinement on the *Bukit Siguntang,* this was heavenly bliss—like stepping into a suite at the Plaza Hotel in New York City. There was a soft double bed, an air conditioner that worked, and in the bathroom a *mandi,* the cistern of cool, clean water Indonesians ladle over their bodies when they want a bath. According to Tanya, this very bed had been occupied, at different times, by the likes of Mick Jagger, Jacques Cousteau, and Sarah Ferguson. The mind briefly boggled, and then I joined the others downstairs on the veranda.

But here I have to say—having come all that way, having tiptoed among the jihadis and all—nobody seemed to be all that thrilled to finally be in paradise. We sat around a table spread with a yellow oilcloth in a sort of funeral silence, vacantly watching the sun dazzle the waters of the lagoon while, a short distance across the bay, the green immensity of Gunung Api, conical slopes rushing up to make its uneven point, brooded over all. Uncharacteristically quiet, Tanya looked as dispirited as I felt, and I felt alternately wrung out, bamboozled, frightened, confused, and of course stupid, for having let myself get swept out into a situation far beyond either my understanding or control. Norman, far removed from the Anchor of Java now, sat looking dazed and occult. Even Rudi, waiting for his coffee, well mannered as a Sunday school pupil, seemed unnaturally subdued.

Adding to our imported gloom was Tanya's younger brother, Ramon, who lived at the hotel and oversaw Des's local interests. A round, heavy man with dark eyes flashing in a handsome, melancholy face, he broke the wax casing from a big round of Gouda cheese Tanya had brought him from Jakarta and stuffed his mouth with a large, asymmetrical chunk.

Desperate to break the tropical ice, if only to reaffirm my continued existence with the sound of my own voice, I turned in the direction of the smacking sounds, and said, "That cheese seems to agree with you, Ramon."

Ramon shot me a wary glance. "You get bloody tired of eating fish and bananas every day of the week, I can tell you that," said the squire snappishly.

Well, so much for island hospitality, I thought. As I turned my head around and squinted sullenly seaward, I realized with a little stab in my gut that the situation here was not nearly as bucolic or peaceful as Des had advertised.

Somewhat belatedly in my opinion, Tanya happily confirmed that such was exactly the case. Her moods seemed to shift as quickly as the local weather—bleak one minute, sunny the next—and now that the subject was trouble, she grew cheerfully animated as she reeled off some enlightening facts. Norman and I, it turned out, were the first guests—"Suckers, I mean, er, guests, ha, ha, ha," was how she'd put it, I recall—to stay at the Alwis' hotel in nearly two years. But at least there was still a hotel here to stay in; Des's sister hotel in Ambon had recently been burned down!

"I beg your pardon?" I said.

"Yes, right down to the ground, and Des had just installed a new swimming pool, too," said Tanya, chortling gleefully. "But don't worry, Pak Tracy—they always burn our buildings last, yah?!"

Tanya then grew gloomy again, confirming that the real trouble in the Bandas had all started that one horrible day, April 20, 1999, when the Muslim kid had been knifed on nearby Hatta Island. When the boy's brother brought the corpse here to Naira, the main island, that same afternoon, the situation had quickly unspooled. Muslim mobs, including some of the 3,500 refugees who'd escaped Christian atrocities in Ambon, went on a rampage, torching twenty-eight Christian homes, and destroying the two local churches. As Naira danced with flames, the Van den Broekes had been cut down by machete on big Banda Besar, the hooked tail of which we could now see across the bay.

"Des found the Van den Broeke boy right over there," Tanya said, elevating her chin toward the sliver of white sand you could see at the bottom of the descending nutmeg groves, and slid a forefinger under her chin, "with his throat cut."

I gulped, suddenly uncomfortably conscious of the workings of my Adam's apple, as Tanya went on: "You know what one of these thugs had the guts to tell me? 'Be grateful we purified your island, Tanya.' Can you imagine, yah?"

I was imagining, vividly, when Tanya's tales of Grand Guignol inspired Ramon to intermit his snacking, and say, "Right there is where Des saved the Christians." He jabbed his cheesy fingers toward an adjacent archway behind which was visible the quaint little cobblestone alley we'd walked from the pier. During that same hellish day of fires and knifings, Ramon said, nearly four hundred frightened Christians had streamed into the hotel, seeking protection from the ketua orlima, Papa Des. ("That was the first time the hotel was fully booked, Tracy!" Des told me, when he went over the details with me later in Jakarta.) Des had just returned from investigating the killings on Banda Besar that night when the lane behind the hotel suddenly filled with two thousand angry Muslims. Armed with torches and blades, they shouted, "We want the Christians! Send them out!"

Instead Des sent out a medical doctor he'd brought with him from Jakarta to attend ailing islanders. An observant Muslim wise in the study of the Holy Koran, the good doctor stepped into the alley to remind the surging mob of the Prophet's injunction—anybody fleeing danger, regardless of his or her religion or creed, had to be offered sanctuary and protection. The scriptures decreed it. That was God's law.

But the fine words raised only catcalls from the crowd. "Nooo!" voices shouted. "Give up the Christians! Now!"

"That's when I got fed up," Des would say. Placing his Hajji's prayer cap on his head, and draping his shoulders with his Hajji's prayer shawl, he grabbed a rifle one of Suharto's generals had given him to shoot wild boar, and went out to face down the rabble. Blocking the entrance, legs widely apart, Des was the very picture of kingly resolve. "If you want enter this hotel, it's over my dead body!" he cried, brandishing his weapon. "I've got twenty-four bullets here. Who wants one?"

"By the way," Des averred in retelling the story, his eyes twinkling, "I also told them it would look very funny if the papers ran the story that Des Alwi, sultan of Banda, had died defending the Christians against his fellow Muslims, you know." The agitators got the point and dispersed, but the danger lingered. The next afternoon the Navy sent in a warship on Des's instructions to evacuate all Christians who wanted to go to Ambon. Two days later Des, no longer safe in his own domain, left the islands in tears.

Though Ramon's account was brief and to the point, I could easily picture Des standing in the doorway in his impressive getup, bristling in defiance, for though he was a promoter extraordinaire, he was also an old-school romantic, long ago infected with the charismatic idea of Indonesia's nationhood—plus, as both unofficial king and the elected head of his people, he had a strongly felt moral and fiduciary duty to protect them all, Christian or Muslim, without fear or favor.

Des had by all accounts handled the situation exceedingly well, which only served to buttress the original point I'd made back in Jakarta: If the king wasn't around, who would protect *us*? Having been in the Bandas for about thirty minutes now, I was all at once consumed with the overwhelming impulse to get off the island and back to civilization just as fast as humanly possible. But how? In a few minutes the *Bukit Siguntang* would weigh anchor, and continue its swing out into the farthest islands, before circling back to Naira on its return voyage to Makassar the following week.

Luckily, Tanya and I were broadcasting on the same mental wavelength. "Maybe I should try and call Captain X in Ambon and just see if his boys aren't too busy fighting the war to come and rescue us, yah?"

"Excellent plan," I said empathically. "Let's do it."

But when Tanya tried phoning, all the hotel lines were busy—and of course we were now well beyond the reach of cell phones. While we waited for our communications challenges to sort out, Tanya suggested we take a little island tour. And so, as Rudi waved goodbye and went off to rejoin the ship, Tanya, Norman, and I piled into Des's shiny black SUV, one of a handful of roadworthy cars on the island, and were soon driving the narrow, gravelly streets, winding up and around the steep ridges above the harbor, the sparkling tropical sea on the left, and, on the cliff side, green flowering trees clinging tenaciously to dark volcanic rock.

Our first stop was Des's museum—a refurbished Dutch mansion where rusty arquebuses and Delft-style crockery decorated with charming little windmills occupied glass cases in a musty, lifeless parlor. We passed an outdoor market where Mick Jagger, one of the most recognizable people in the celebrity culture of the planet, had strolled anonymously in less troubled times. "Nobody knew who he was, yah?" said Tanya. "Finally, one Bandanese guy looked up at him and said, 'Hey, Brown Sugar!' "

As we continued across the island, I could see that Norman had got at least one thing right about the Bandas—there was nary a McDonald's or KFC to clutter the landscape. No sooner had the dusty little shops given way to lush green jungle interspersed with tin-roofed houses, weed-choked yards, and dilapidated autos than Tanya's melancholy seemed to evaporate, and she waved to curious onlookers as if from atop a float in the Pasadena Rose Parade.

But Tanya's renewed cheerfulness, and all those dark, moist, eerily quiet shadows, only deepened my own primal misgivings. This, I hasten to add, was not her fault at all, but the workings of a mood that inevitably descends on me in the tropics. It is one of those personal mysteries that never cease to amaze you: While still at home I get myself all jazzed up about the prospect of glimpsing the places we've all been conditioned to think of as earthly paradise only to become automatically and deeply troubled when I actually find myself there, staring paradise in its face.

Part of it, I think, is simply due to the changeability of weather I spoke of earlier—glorious one minute, black or raining the next— nothing solid to hang on to. But there's something buried deeper in the cave of the psyche, too, that gets activated by all those green and dripping glades. I don't know exactly how to describe it except as a sort of malign watchfulness, or a ghost story told in a whispering voice in broad daylight. In any event, I find it very unsettling. (A quick study of tropical cultures will, I believe, support my theory that sunshine breeds a unique form of darkness.)

In the Bandas of course this natural spookiness was amplified by evidence of fresh man-made terror. Fire had demolished the island's redbrick Catholic church. A few blocks away the barnlike shell of the Dutch Protestant church had survived intact, but inside the wooden pews had been ripped from their moorings and scattered around like a shipwreck. Wading through the several hundred years of yellowed documents that littered the floor, I bent down and plucked a sheet at random—an expense ledger from 1743 written in the precise, flowing script of a long-gone Dutch bookkeeper.

History was literally around every corner on the small island. Driving the interior road, we passed the site of an imposing Dutch mansion where only the big, blocky foundation stones remained. Weeds grew luxuriantly in a scorched quadrangle that I reckoned must have been the ballroom, and I could easily picture the flaxen-haired daughters of old pipe-sucking perkeniers swirling around marble floors dancing a cotillion. In fact, however, the planter's lifestyle here was generally about as glamorous as the gout. According to Willard A. Hanna, in his illuminating history *Indonesian Banda,* the transplanted Europeans were prone to a long list of horrifying conditions, including "beriberi, dysentery, dropsy . . . an appalling variety and frequency of infections and skin afflictions, recurrent plagues of cholera and smallpox," and, no big surprise in Hanna's view, "a woeful susceptibility to hypochondria."

The perkeniers were also chronic deadbeats—the result of debts piled up in competitive spending on mansions that featured, along with their acres of marble, "crystal chandeliers . . . fine mirrors in gilt frames, massive tables, and chairs of highly polished, beautifully grained wood." Then there was the flagging Dutch libido to consider. Mainly poorly educated, crapulous, self-indulgent young men, the nutmeg *nouveau riche,* it turns out, were also chronically lonely guys, since, as Hanna points out, "few Dutch women migrated to Banda . . . [but for] orphans, paupers, and prostitutes . . . notoriously lacking in beauty, charm, or even refinement." Marriage to local women was outlawed and trysts, when discovered, were punished by the lash. This led the inventive Dutchmen to pioneer the practice "of purchasing, baptizing, and adopting attractive young slave girls, who, having been somewhat Christianized and domesticated, might win the governor's approbation for a wedding license."

By far the most depressing stop on our grand tour, however, was Des's vaunted shark pen. Located next to the hotel, it resembled a long, very untidy swimming pool separated from the lagoon by a low blue wall. Peering into the brackish waters, I counted three or four small sharks, three or four feet long, knifing listlessly through the complicated ooze, when it hit me that I was in fact inspecting an important symbol of Des's master plan for the future of the Bandas—a future that so far at least had patently not worked.

• • •

The future was already plenty murky by the time Des was born in the Bandas in late 1920s. The Dutch still ruled Indonesia's colonial roost, but the glory days of nutmeg had long since fizzled; the curious little fruit was now grown in places as far-flung as Grenada in the Caribbean, oversupply had led to a collapse in world prices, and Naira had slouched into existence as a seedy, end-of-the-line Dutch resort, intermittently hit by destructive earthquakes and the rare but highly memorable eruption of Gunung Api. A once-booming local industry for producing the mother-of-pearl used in the making of fancy buttons for Europe was also headed for oblivion. Bakelite, an early form of plastic developed during World War I, had gone into commercial use by then, and Des's maternal grandfather, Said Baadilla, once touted as the Pearl King of the Spice Islands, and their richest citizen, had lost his considerable fortune.

By 1936, Des was just another little island boy, living far from the glamour and intrigue of the Dutch capital in Batavia, as Jakarta was then called, when one day, as he later told me, "I was just horsing around with some friends on the big dock in the harbor at Bandanaira you know, when I saw two gentlemen get off a Dutch steamer."

Though nattily attired in white linen suits, the two men were pale as a couple of ghosts. "When people looked like that," said Des, "you knew they always came from the Dutch concentration camps on New Guinea."

What really roused the little boy's curiosity, though, were the eight steamer trunks the men had between them, filled to the brim with books—there weren't so many books in all of the Bandas! And when the Dutch port controller refused to help the pale travelers transport their portable library ("Let the rats carry their own goods!" he sneered), Des scurried to lend a hand.

As Des guided the magnificos to the house of another exile just across the narrow island, Dr. Tjipto Mangunkusumo, a nationalist thinker also in hot water with the Dutch, he read the names of the men off the sides of their trunks—Mohammad Hatta and Sutan

Sjahrir. And thus, in that fluky way things can happen in Indonesia, Des had inadvertently hitched his canoe to a nationalist tidal wave, for the two men he'd befriended, along with a third, Sukarno, were the top nationalist leaders of their day, and about to become the founding fathers of modern Indonesia.

As the months rolled by, Des showed the two men the best places to swim, and because they swam like intellectuals, he coached them on improving their strokes. In return ("Probably to keep him from bothering them," Norman observed), they lent Des some of their books to read, and personally introduced him to the breathtaking romance of Indonesia—the idea that this crazy quilt of a country put together by the profit-seeking Dutch was in fact a real, honest-to-goodness nation-in-waiting, with a real, if richly marbled past, and thus a common, if mind-boggling complex, national identity.

In 1942, the Japanese invaded Indonesia and threw what Dutch they could catch into appalling prison camps. Released from their internal exile, Hatta and Sjahrir returned to Jakarta, where Sukarno soon joined them. While Sukarno and Hatta agreed to set up a nationalist government under the soldiers from Nippon, whom Indonesians generally regarded as fellow Asians and liberators, it was agreed that Sjahrir would, as historian M.C. Ricklefs notes, "stay aloof and build an 'underground' network . . . and would attempt to make contact with the Allies." Meanwhile, the Japanese quickly proved themselves to be even bossier and more brutal than the Dutch, and the popular enthusiasm quickly faded. Informally adopted by Sjahrir, Des was attending radio broadcast school in Jakarta when he joined the anti-Japanese underground. Eventually picked up by the Kempetai, Imperial Japan's fearsome secret police, Des told his captor, a Sergeant-Major Suzuki, that he was Hatta's "nephew" (Hatta was then serving as vice president of the puppet regime) and to please go check. "Okay," said Suzuki, "but if you're not telling the truth, you won't come out of here alive."

"My timing was good," said Des. Hatta vouched for his young protégé, the Kempetai let Des go, and the very next day, August 15, 1945, the Japanese surrendered to the Allied forces. Two days later

Sukarno and Hatta declared Indonesia's independence at Sukarno's residence in Jakarta. Des took a mortar fragment in the leg in the Battle of Surabaya, as he fought to keep the Dutch from reclaiming their colony, and then Sjahrir sent him to London to continue his education. In the 1950s, Des served as a diplomat in London and Paris. In 1959, when the autocratic Sukarno simultaneously swerved left (wooing the Communist Party of Indonesia, the PKI) and right (shutting down Indonesia's parliament), Des did a turn as a revolutionary, joining in the anti-Sukarno Permesta Rebellion.

When the uprising failed, and Sukarno sidelined his protectors, Hatta and Sjahrir, Des went into hiding, first in Hong Kong, and then in Kuala Lumpur. When Suharto sidelined Sukarno in 1966, Des was restored to his place in Indonesia's rambunctious pecking order, where he once again displayed his gift for impeccable timing. He gained points with General Suharto by solving a diplomatic crisis with neighboring Malaysia that Sukarno had stirred up by threatening to invade. (The Malaysian prime minister happened to be an old classmate from London.) He set up a factory in Malaysia to build transistor radios in the high days of transistor radios and sold imported cars to Suharto's growing elite in Jakarta. He produced popular films, and as foreign tourists began to discover the untrammeled natural beauty of the Moluccas, he opened his hotels in Ambon and Bandanaira. In the mid-1990s, Des persuaded Suharto, a sometime fishing partner, to provide government money to resuscitate nutmeg cultivation in the Bandas.

Then Des trained his eyes on the loftiest goal of all—transforming his beautiful beleaguered islands into a vacation hideaway for the world's rich and famous. Using his high and panoramic connections, Des managed to lure in a "host of the famous and the near-famous," as he put it, and was working on a deal to lease three DeHavilland Otter seaplanes to ferry VIPs from Ambon, the regional air traffic hub, to the airstrip on Naira, when Ambon exploded in violence.

Now, a little over a year later, Des's big dreams lay in ruins. Ebullient as ever at age seventy-two, but frustrated and depressed by all the turmoil, Des was struggling to keep the Bandas afloat by sheer force of his considerable will. And that of course is where I had humbly entered the picture; with tourism dead and the area written off as a war zone, a little publicity from a magazine like the *National Geographic,* read and respected by millions worldwide, couldn't possibly hurt. Thus had I swallowed greedily on the Bandas and felt neither barb nor shaft.

Evening had fallen, and the waters of the bay took on a vast silver-brown sheen, like tarnished pewter, when Tanya ordered the boys to crank up Des's speedboat and take us for a spin. Freed from the green gloom of the jungle, I was feeling immeasurably better as we inscribed a wide circle around the massive base of Gunung Api. Up close, the volcano's giant cone was broad and muscular, an immense vibrating beacon, carpeted in low bushlike vegetation that glimmered in the failing light. Legend has it that Joseph Conrad chanced upon the harbor at Bandanaira during his seafaring days, eventually appropriating the locale for *Victory,* the old bule master's novel of love, greed, and murder under the whispering palms. Lord knows, the setting was perfect.

"Oooh, and here's where my grandfather hid out from the Japanese during the war," said Tanya, pointing to a wide-mouthed cave at the base of the volcano. Occupying the islands in 1942, the Japanese were a considerable pain, but generally more popular in the Bandas than elsewhere in Indonesia; in contrast to the meddling Dutch, they mostly left the Bandanese in peace, except of course when it came time to round up bodies for slave labor. Three years later came the liberating Americans, bombing Naira from the air. "They thought it was a Japanese radio station, yah?" said Tanya. But lo and behold, the intelligence was flawed—the Japanese had already fled, taking their weapons of medium destruction with them. Thus the Americans entered Bandanese history, remembered largely for a misplaced bomb that killed a hundred happy islanders at a wedding party.

When we pulled around the backside of the volcano and reentered the main harbor, a Japanese fish-processing ship was riding at anchor at the neck of the lagoon and we pulled alongside. While Norman hopped aboard to negotiate the price of a tuna for our dinner with the Bandanese deckhands, I learned a little more about Tanya's history. Born in Singapore during Des's self-imposed exile, she'd grown up mainly in Malaysia. After graduating from film school at the University of California at Berkeley, she lived it up in New York for a time, working in documentary films, dreaming about a glamorous, creative career. Then Papa Des called her home to help out in the family businesses.

Des got more than he'd bargained for. After growing up as de facto princess in exile, Tanya plunged into acquainting herself with the Bandas with her typical verve, only to be appalled by what was being allowed to happen to the natural environment. Out of economic desperation, local fishermen were routinely dynamiting the area's coral reefs to get at more of the pricey reef-dwelling species prized by Chinese restaurants from Singapore to Hong Kong. (Over the past twenty-five years the practice, encouraged by big regional fishing conglomerates, has helped kill off as many as half the coral reefs in Southeast Asia, seriously threatening one of the world's last great natural protein factories.)

Tanya vowed to put a stop to the destruction. And so when Des chided her for wasting time on coral instead of corralling tourists, she simply ignored him. Joking and cajoling her way into the presence of cabinet ministers in Jakarta, she managed to get the offending companies' fishing permits summarily revoked in a matter of weeks. Then, going to work on Des, Tanya argued in favor of concentrating on ecotourism; by luring in fewer but wealthier customers, happy to spend the big bucks for a rare glimpse of paradise in the raw, the Alwis could minimize human traffic while maximizing the islands' biggest draw—their stunning natural beauty. Thus did Tanya's efforts help convert the traditional leader of the Bandas into an ardent, high-profile environmentalist, proud of the fact, as he later told me, "They've named a species of table coral after me, Tracy. You can look it up—*Acropora des alwi.*"

Sitting there in Des's taut little sea rig, listening to Tanya tell her story, as we watched the men on the big tuna boat hose the squamous tangle of guts from the decks, I suddenly realized how badly I had underestimated this impressive woman. Despite her occasionally cuckoo-bird manner, she was no flighty airhead—not by a long shot. I could see now that her dithering effervescence was in fact a weapon Tanya employed with purpose and precision to disarm the unwary before she zeroed in for a friendly kill.

It was also apparent that Tanya, her father, and others like them, who were trying to build for the future and provide for their neighbors, represented the best natural antidote to Indonesia's epidemic of violence. The depth of the wounds, and the fact that the government in Jakarta was so much at a loss to help out, only made the enterprise seem all the more heroic.

Having concluded his protracted negotiations, Norman hoisted up a bright-eyed tuna the size of a small torpedo so I could take a snapshot, and then we shot off across the waters for the hotel. Possibly delirious from all the oxygen molecules kicking around out there in the lagoon, I decided right then and there to forgive the Alwis for having put the genial con on me. (Or, more precisely, I should say, for enabling me to con myself.) Who knew how our risky little fling in paradise would turn out, I thought, as we made a beeline for the big banyan tree in front of the hotel, and the whole broad fandango of the island sunset spread out before us in streaks of yellow and white and orange—but all at once I felt tremendously heartened. I had arrived at the belief, which I maintain to this day, that the Alwis were, in addition to their undeniable charm, people of courage and intelligence, and my affection for them permanently deepened.

7

FROGS

Oh my God!" said Tanya. "The phones are dead!"

I'd just come from my evening mandi, feeling marvelously refreshed after ladling water over my head and shoulders that felt cold as Pluto, to find Tanya pacing the veranda in the evening cool and biting her lip. She'd been trying to get through to Captain X, but either a telephone relay station had burned out somewhere along the line, as not infrequently happened or—more likely in our present case, Tanya feared—the Laskar Jihad had landed in Ambon and the situation was not well in hand. When fighting flared, the military was in the habit of intentionally cutting the phone service to confuse the combatants.

My own worries quickly crawled from the shadows again as Tanya said, "Ooooh," and started thinking out loud: What if the situation in Ambon went to all hell as a result of the Laskar Jihad? What if the Navy belatedly put its embargo in place and the *Bukit Siguntang* couldn't get back this way to pick us up? What if Captain X's pilots were too busy fighting to fly to the rescue? What if, what if, what if . . . ?

The plain truth of our situation was that we had absolutely nothing to go on. This was despite the fact that Ramon's large-screen TV filled one end of the veranda with the grinning faces of CNN anchors, who chatted amiably via satellite dish about such essential items as the eternal American presidential campaign, Hollywood's latest celebrity hangnail, and reports from a still-booming, dot.com-delirious Wall Street. Had we been privy to the wire services, which still attempt to report the news as news and not entertainment, we'd have read some unnerving bulletins about the situation in Ambon just then:

VIOLENCE FUELED BY ARRIVAL OF 2,000 HARD-LINE MUSLIMS.

INDONESIAN TROOPS ORDERED TO SHOOT SNIPERS ON SIGHT.

AMBON'S AIRPORT CLOSED . . . BOMB EXPLOSIONS AND THE RATTLE OF GUNFIRE ECHO THROUGH CITY.

Meanwhile actual events on the ground in Ambon were quickly putting the lie to claims that the Laskar Jihad was there on anything remotely resembling a humanitarian mission. As the story would later break, the arrival of Jaffar Umar Thalib and his boys not only sparked new fighting, but sharply boosted casualties, particularly among the now badly outnumbered Christian fighters. As the weeks rolled by, and the tide of battle swung to him, Jaffar set about destroying Christian hamlets in order to save them for Islam. (For a child of the Vietnam War generation there was an eerie echo of the infamous maxim that villages had to be destroyed in order to save them from the godless Communists.) In a place called Waai, for example, Jaffar was said to have stood in the aftermath, rejoicing that a great historical crime had at last been corrected. Waai had converted to Christianity in 1670.

When I later had the chance to review eyewitness accounts of the violence, I was mystified. If all those sweepings of the *Bukit Siguntang* had turned up no significant weapons, as Pontoh had confirmed, then how could the militants have possibly seized the initiative so quickly? Evidence would eventually turn up to show that nine containers of weapons had come by a separate ship to Ambon, where they were picked up by jihadis on the docks under the watchful eye of the military. According to an International Crisis

Group report, Army units were later seen "providing covering fire for . . . attacks on Christian neighborhoods."

I'd done enough reporting from Indonesia to know that the military, the Tentara Nasional Indonesia, or TNI, differs vastly from its American counterpart. Credited with ridding the country of the Dutch, TNI had started out after independence as Indonesia's proudest institution—at times, it was the only reliable, sometimes the only *functioning* instrument of government. And therein lay the problem. All that power and public respect had given TNI incredible latitude; it operated as both a military-industrial complex and a political party with a guaranteed number of seats in parliament. And since under Suharto all filaments of money and power eventually traced back to the wily puppet master, the military had inevitably become his chief enforcer.

Thus historically, one path to power for ambitious military men had lain in quietly provoking conflict among rival ethnic or religious groups in outlying areas, and then stepping in to save the day by declaring an emergency, while money and favors changed hands under the table. It was the old story of the cunning arsonist, matchbox tucked safely into his pocket, rushing forward to take credit for putting out the fire.

And so it was for good reason that fingers immediately pointed at military finagling in the Moluccas. Citing Western intelligence sources, the Center for Defense Intelligence in Washington would eventually surmise: "Laskar Jihad was actually founded with covert backing of military hardliners who wished to destabilize" Wahid's reformist government. Proof of this had by then come to light in the form of some $9.3 million that had allegedly found its way out of the military's combat budget and into the pockets of the Jihad.

One good thing about a situation of no news is that it allows you to enjoy your dinner in peace. And on this night dinner was a breezy island delight. Candles flickered on the sideboard as the shy kitchen ladies padded across the veranda, fetching one succulent dish after another. There was a crunchy salad featuring local roots and vegetables and topped off with shavings of *kanari,* the Java almond (plucked from trees the perkeniers had long ago planted around the nutmeg groves to protect them from the ravages of sun and wind). There was a spicy fish curry, and a large bowl of steaming, saffron-flavored rice. Everything was absolutely delicious but for the sashimi etched from the evening's tuna, which though ruby red in color, was chewy as an old Dutch boot and tasted strongly of essence of tidal pool.

Joining us around the oilcloth was Claudia, a Polish university student, whom I'd bumped into earlier that day on the *Bukit Sigun-tang* when, walking past the Exclusive Karaoke Lounge, a grotty, cavelike snack bar off the main dining room, I looked in and a pair of haunted bule eyes had stopped me in my tracks. Tall and angular, Claudia was decked out in a full set of camouflage battle fatigues, including the floppy field hat—a present from the government soldiers in Ambon who, Allah be praised, had decided to be nice to her. She spoke her English combatively, but her youthful bravado hadn't quite stretched over the obvious fact that she was desperate for companionship.

That much became plain over dinner. Claudia had traded in her battle gear in for a clean T-shirt and shorts, revealing a pair of long shapely legs and previously hidden curves that appeared to have a mesmerizing effect on Ramon, princely bachelor of the lonely Bandas. And it was under his solicitous questioning that Claudia's story tumbled out. Inspired by the chronic political turmoil in her native Eastern Europe, she said, she'd decided to make a study for her senior thesis on separatist movements in exotic Indonesia. She'd jumped on a plane, then a ship, and in no time at all had managed to demonstrate just how easy it is to locate trouble in this inner-connected world of ours by arriving in Ambon just as the bombs began exploding and the military rang down its shoot-to-kill curfew. (Developments our friend, Captain X, had neglected to tell us about, by the way.) Claudia explained how the eager young soldiers had taken her under their collective wing, sharing their rations, and giving her a bed in their barracks.

Ramon winced, and said, "Well, you were lucky there."

"Luck had nothing to do with it," sniffed brave Claudia, taking brief offense, before going on to confess to some decidedly uneasy moments. The most frightening of all, she said, had been waking up at three A.M. in her steerage bunk on the *Bukit Siguntang* to find a platoon of cockroaches marching up her chest while a man she did not know watched, bug-eyed and smiling, from a distance of a few inches.

Above our heads the stars hung like crushed diamonds on blue-black velvet above the richer blackness of the bay, and as Claudia's cathartic words poured into the night, the rest of us sat around the table, nodding and smiling in the manner of a sympathetic if somewhat erratic adoptive family.

"Pass the banana fritters, would you please," said Uncle Ramon, eyes glittering, while I thought, What a world we inhabit! Two hundred miles to the north in Ambon, Muslims and Christians were reenacting a battle that was hitting its stride when the Muslim Umayyads swept through Spain in the eighth century and the First Crusade sent Christian soldiers marching into Jerusalem in the eleventh. But here in momentarily peaceful Bandanaira, Muslims and Christians, or their diluted cultural equivalents, sat around a table eating island treats and enjoying one another's stories.

Next it was Tanya's turn, and over the strong dark local coffee, she offered a riveting glimpse of the waxy underbelly of Suharto's old inner circle. Famously pampered, Suharto's six adult children were well-known for spending lavishly on cars, houses, vacations, and parties. (Later that same year, Tommy, Suharto's youngest son, would flamboyantly encapsulate the spoiled-brat concept when, sentenced to jail in a land scam, he went into hiding from or, according to some accounts, with the help of the police, only to be eventually arrested for having the sentencing judge, a Supreme Court justice, rubbed out in a gangland-style hit.) Some individuals in this clubby little demimonde allegedly took things a titillating step farther by arranging sex parties as a further means of exercising, among other things, political control.

Few of the naive young partygoers realized what they were getting into, of course, until they were blackmailed into supplying dirt on friends or relatives that could be used as a means of further blackmail. If the sexual recruits refused, it was suggested to them that the group, and possibly the world at large, might easily learn to get along without them. As Tanya talked, I was reminded of stories I'd read about the Nazis in Europe under the Third Reich—members of the "master race," running the place like a bunch of gangsters, showing off their mastery by prancing around in their birthday suits, wearing masks, flirting unwholesomely with the occult powers.

Then Tanya shocked me by saying that I'd met one of these sexual operatives, at the airport in Jakarta.

"You're joking," I said, but then suddenly I remembered a cowering young woman with China-doll bangs who'd been struggling with Tanya for the honor of pushing her luggage cart toward the check-in counter. When introduced to me, she bowed in such an exaggerated fashion that I'd mistaken her for Tanya's maid. Frankly, the idea that this mousy specimen could be wrapped up in some kind of elaborate sexual sorority seemed incredible.

"No joke, Pak Tracy," said Tanya. "That one, she acts so meek and mild but I know why she came to see us off."

I shook my head. I couldn't imagine.

"She wanted to find out who I was going to the Bandas with so she could report back," said Tanya.

Report back? "Oh, come on, Tanya," I said. Even in the unlikely event Suharto's former minions were behind some vast conspiracy to stir up trouble all across the big country and destabilize the national government, as Indonesians then widely believed, why would anybody be interested in the comings and goings of our little crew?

I looked over at Ramon, expecting—hoping—he'd join me in a good laugh. But he was dead serious, too. "The information could be useful," Ramon said with a resigned shrug. After all, Tanya was a prominent person in Jakarta society. Now here she was taking an American journalist from a prestigious magazine into the tempestuous Moluccas.

"Oh please," I said, laughing out loud, though not nearly as confidently as before. Tanya and Ramon traded looks that flickered somewhere between "Boy, is this guy dumb", and "Let's not scare the pants off him, shall we?"

But it was Norman who finally spoke up. "Boss, look at it this way," he said. "What if for instance, just hypothetically speaking of course, a group of provocateurs wanted to do something and blame it on somebody else?" Might they conceivably eliminate a certain bule somebody, wait for the expectable international diplomatic ruckus, then blame it on—take your pick—either Muslim fanatics or Christian thugs, depending on whatever suited their interests at the time?

I gulped on my bananas as I realized the "bule somebody" Norman was talking about was me. In the political logic of Indonesia, unfortunately, the scenario as outlined made perfect sense. That was precisely the sort of tactic the military, or renegade elements of it, the so-called Dark Command, was suspected of using all the time.

Sardonically, I thought how nice it was of my friends to wait to share this insight with me now that we were locked deep in the shank of the Moluccas. Had they told me back in Jakarta it might have spoiled all the fun.

After dinner Tanya generously offered Claudia a room at the hotel, where she would be reasonably safe. But Claudia declined, choosing instead to head off up the dark, twisting road to her lodgings at a dollar-a-night youth hostel. I didn't like the idea of a lone bule woman roaming such a volatile neighborhood at night, but Norman was philosophical. Separatist Girl, as he now called Claudia, "must by her nature remain separate," he said. He then went to make sure the hotel boys kept an eye on her. When Tanya raced off to try and reach Captain X again, I joined Ramon, who was sitting on the patio sofa facing his giant TV.

"Still no news about Ambon on CNN," said Ramon as he aimed the remote and flipped channels to MTV, where a glistening, semi-clothed pop diva wriggled on screen to a throbbing hip-hop beat. Ramon watched with the same hungry eyes he had lavished on the Gouda cheese, and then said in a confidential tone, "Do you think that Polish girl is very beautiful?"

Ah ha, I thought, so the young prince is smitten. "She's pretty," I said cautiously, not wanting to needlessly stir up any ground-scraping male rivalries here in the contentious Bandas.

"Not beautiful?"

"Well, that's in the eye of the beholder, now isn't it, Ramon?"

Ramon smiled and seemed reassured, but he had every reason to feel vulnerable. Whatever the exact nature of the handicap I was never told, but the fact was that his quick and active mind had been trapped in a balky, uncooperative body that made walking a chore and quickly sapped energy in the beastly local heat. The condition had also helped catapult him to stardom as a child movie actor. (It still strikes me as odd in the extreme that I should manage to wind up in the far Spice Islands in the company of Norman and Ramon, both bona fide Indonesian movie personalities.) In the early 1970s, Des had cast Ramon in a film he called *The Grandson,* the tale of a crippled little street urchin who is eventually plucked from sad mis-adventures by a wealthy Bandanese grandma. Indonesia audiences had eaten it up, and the proceeds from the film helped Des set him-self up in the tourist trade. It had also allowed him to send Ramon to a fancy boarding school in London, though not for long.

"They gave me the boot," Ramon chortled, and I gathered from our conversation it wasn't the only school to show him the door.

"You've been a bad boy," I teased.

Ramon chuckled naughtily. "When I went to college in San Francisco," he offered, guffawing, "the girls called me Ramone . . . *Rah-moaaan!*"

It was then I decided I liked *Ramone,* and I think he was begin-ning to like me. Anyhow, the Bandanese ice was finally broken, and our conversation took the short hop from sex to war. I asked Ramon who he felt was responsible for instigating the local bloodshed. Frowning thoughtfully, he said, "It's really blind hate here now, Tracy, but basically, you know, it's more cultural than religious."

The Spice Islands had harbored countless local clashes over land boundaries or scarce resources that were old when the spice-seeking Europeans first arrived to amplify the tensions. When the Dutch showed up in the late 1500s there were still large numbers of Hindus in the islands, as well as a burgeoning Muslim population, and the interlopers quickly set about winning souls for Christianity by supplying both sides with powder and shot.

"They essentially instigated sibling rivalry," said Ramon, "keeping the locals busy" while the Dutch funneled out the wealth. "And believe me," he added, "those fights are remembered in the villages to this day."

The funny thing about the current mess, said Ramon, was that while the historical ingredients were there, "you can't have an uprising in five minutes. The kampongs, the villages, just aren't that well organized. You need to have an emcee."

"A provocateur?"

Ramon nodded. "Provocateur" was a catchall word people used when they wanted to blame outside forces for stirring up trouble among neighbors. Conspiracy theories focused on political schemers, rogue military units, or gangsters, who sought profit from sowing discord—or all of the above.

Talk ran in circles, but there was a discernible pattern to events. A letter written on faked church stationery suggesting a "cadre of Christ" was forming up to attack Muslims would be circulated in a Muslim community, for example. Alarmed, the Muslims would then strike at the Obet in what they thought of as self-defense. Shadowy figures, not infrequently dressed in the black ninja costumes popular in Asian martial arts movies, meanwhile, were often said to be seen passing out literature, bullhorns, knives, and other essentials of "spontaneous" riot.

"The organization has to come from the outside," said Ramon with finality. But whoever had stirred the pot this time—freebooting military units, thugs from Jakarta, and almost inevitably, Ramon thought, Ambon's old-line Christian political bosses, who had been cozy with Suharto and therefore had the most to lose from a Muslim realignment of the political landscape—"they didn't plan on it going on for this long, and now it's all gotten away from them."

However fuzzy the details, Ramon's point was clear: It takes more than a village to raise a terrorist. "But there's something that's new, too, isn't there?" I asked, pointing to the TV screen, where a platoon of near-naked dancers now writhed like snakes.

Ramon nodded—"Yes, yes, of course," he said. Technology had allowed the battle in the Moluccas, in effect, to "go Hollywood." As the fighting raged and spread into the far islands, Christian and Muslim groups across the country had taken up sides and begun circulating videotapes and DVDs featuring pictures of truckloads of dead bodies and other ghastly, eye-popping atrocities allegedly carried out by the opposition. Meanwhile, the teapot struggles for limited land, resources, jobs, and education among the area's many competing ethnic groups, who also happened to be either Christian or Muslim, that had in fact put the islands on the boil—all the boring old plot lines—had lost their credence. Mayhem in the Moluccas, as anthropologist Paul Michael Taylor would note, could now be seen as nothing less than a great "cosmic battle."[1]

It was not an isolated phenomenon. Similar production techniques had by then been used to showcase many, if not all, of the nasty little communal conflicts tormenting the post–Cold War world, from Rwanda and Somalia to Kosovo and Sri Lanka; history had gone virtual and was being madly twisted in the editing process. But of course what neither Ramon nor I could have possibly guessed on this night, a full sixteen months before the attacks on New York and Washington on 9/11, was that the Bandas and New York, linked historically by the alchemy of nutmeg, would soon also be connected by the punishments of jihad—and that Osama and his henchmen would wind up with VHS copies of both sets of atrocities in their video libraries.

Those of us who aren't big fans of an implacably hostile worldwide Islamic revolution should have been paying more attention. But the fact is that the drama in the Moluccas did exceedingly poor box office in the U.S. and Europe. For most Americans living back

---

1. From testimony before the United States Commission on International Religious Freedom, *Hearings on Freedom Violations in the Moluccas, Indonesia*, February 13, 2001.

there in the world before 9/11, enjoying the longest period of economic expansion in our history, and enwrapped in our latest contribution to world culture in "reality TV," the threat of radical Islam was little more than a tiny cloud on a very far horizon. With the story far removed from familiar geopolitical borders, even the ordinarily ravenous eye of CNN (efforts of courageous local reporters to get their stories on the air notwithstanding) largely ignored it.

No, parked there on the patio in the starry night, and despite the theoretical benefits of the global information superhighway zooming at us through Ramon's big TV, we were, as the Japanese say, frogs sitting at the bottom of a well. Unable to see much of anything beyond our immediate circumstances, we abandoned politics and returned to our earlier topic.

"Do you think that Polish girl will come in the morning?" asked Ramon, hopefully.

I was sure of it, I told him. Having come all this way, I wasn't about to miss seeing Palau Ai and Palau Run, the two islands that had been of pivotal importance in the Anglo-Dutch spice wars. We were planning to leave first thing the next morning, and at dinner I'd overheard Tanya inviting Claudia to join us.

Ramon seemed pleased. On the screen, meanwhile, another diva was crouching on all fours, panting like a jungle cat as she performed a series of calisthenics guaranteeing the maxim display of cleavage while maintaining an expression of utterly false innocence. (Sometimes you really do have to wonder if we Americans think about the effect we have on the rest of the world nearly as much as we should.)

"Sweet dreams, Tracy," said Ramon, sweetly.

"Goodnight, Ramon," I said. "Thanks for the education."

As I walked up the stairs to the balcony, the soft, warm air blew in gentle puffs against my face. When I entered my room, instead of a mint on my pillow I found a dead palmetto bug as big as my thumb. As I crawled into bed, I comforted myself with the thought that royalty, rock and otherwise, had lain there in happier days.

8

ORIGINAL SIN

State-sponsored terrorism literally started with a bang in the Bandas when the Dutch arrived to impose their will in 1599. No sooner had Vice Admiral Jacob van Heemskerck anchored his ships, the *Gelderland* and the *Zeeland,* than mighty Gunung Api blew its top and rained down hot coals on the lagoon. That he'd arrived smack in the middle of an interisland war in which Bandanese canoes zipped back and forth decorated with the bloody noggins of vanquished enemies may have added to van Heemskerck's dour view, as shared with his ship's log, that the locals were so untrustworthy, "crooked and brazen" that a "man needs seven eyes if he does not want to be cheated."

But in fact it was the Dutch who had cheating on their minds—or its colonial equivalent, otherwise known as "trade." Insisting that the Bandanese grant them a permanent monopoly on the traffic in nutmeg, the world's third most valuable commodity after gold and silver, the spice chasers offered in return the most spectacularly inappropriate goods imaginable—smothering Dutch woolens, velvet, damask, and other items of little practical use in the blazing tropics. To the shrewd *orang kaya,* the island elders, these demanding, ill-tempered barbarians were essentially no different than their Portuguese and Spanish predecessors, and so they decided to deal with them in the same way, which was basically to humor them.

Big mistake. Worn down by the badgering Dutch, the orang kaya eventually agreed to put their marks on something called the Eternal Compact (that first word being the real killer), which granted Holland's Vereenigde Oost-Indische Compagnie (VOC), or Dutch East India Company, its desired monopoly. In return the islanders got unasked-for and unneeded protection from other European spice competitors; the Portuguese and Spanish had pretty much faded into the Bandanese sunset by then, and the English were comparatively popular because they offered vastly better terms of trade than the parsimonious Dutch.

While clearly not up to speed on the bossy concepts of European contract law, the Bandanese were very far from stupid. Having signed various agreements in the name of the king of the Bandas, a personage who did not technically exist at that historical moment, they not unreasonably adjudged the Dutch pact to be as phony as a counterfeit doubloon. But the legalistic Dutch had a sharply different take on the relationship. When the orang kaya refused to abide by the agreed-on terms, the local VOC reps promptly set out, according to Willard Hanna, to enforce "their stated principles by landing soldiers, burning villages, killing resisters, confiscating stocks, and demanding ever more sweeping concessions."

With other means of conflict resolution denied them, the Bandanese opted for a modified amok defense. In 1609, when the Dutch sailed in and put a thousand men ashore at Naira to start erecting castlelike Fort Nassau, against oft-stated Bandanese objectives, the inwardly smoldering orang kaya said, essentially, "Okay, fine, have it your way, but let's talk." Then, turning on that famous Bandanese charm, the islanders lured the Dutch commander, Peter Verhoef, and his forty senior officers into a shady island grove, where they slaughtered the outlanders to a man, the severed Dutch heads reemerging from the conference site on the end of Bandanese pikes.

Amsterdam, we have a problem.

The phones were still dead the next morning when we set off for our tour of the magical nutmeg isles. Down on the esplanade the boys were gunning the twin outboards on Des's speedboat, filling the succulent Banda air with gasoline fumes, when Separatist Girl arrived to join us. She was wearing a bikini of such throbbing metallic blue intensity, held together with an intriguingly intricate series of biker zippers that I thought poor Ramon's eyeballs might pop right out of his skull and into the water. And then, to my amazement, we pulled away from the dock, leaving Ramon behind.

"Ramon's not coming?" I asked Tanya, shouting over the roar of the engines.

"No," cried big sister, crisply and without explanation. I suddenly remembered the previous evening and Ramon's pointed references to "sibling rivalry" as a cause of political turmoil in the Moluccas, and I wondered if his choice of words might have a personal meaning as well. Whatever the reason for his nonparticipation, I felt sad as I watched the resident squire wave forlornly from the dock, grow tiny, and then disappear altogether. Poor *Ramone*.

The open sea beyond the lagoon was deep and wild-looking but deceptively calm, and we made our first stop, Palau Ai, in about thirty minutes. Tramping up the hill from the landing, we passed through a crumbling stone portico, heavy as the entrance to an Egyptian tomb, and into the ruins of the old VOC fort known as Benteng Revenge. The thick, vine-laced walls enclosed an area that looked to be the size of a professional baseball diamond where three men worked a crop of standing corn, their machetes whispering to the ground. The men raised their heads and fixed us with some very serious looks until they recognized Tanya and broke into broad smiles. While the princess of the islands engaged their leader in laughing chatter, I had myself a look around.

I knew from my homework that interestingly bloody things had happened here long ago. The old battlements, still robustly intact after four hundred years, for example, marked a pivotal point in the war between the English and Dutch for control of the spice trade. By 1610, only the highly annoying presence of the English on Ai and Run stood between Holland and total mastery of all the nutmeg in the world. It won't come as a big surprise, then, when I tell you that the Dutch landed a thousand men at the waterline on Ai on May 14, 1615, with the express purpose of demolishing the island's small English trading post—but it did come as a surprise to the Brits. Judging themselves to be vastly outnumbered, the frantic factors hightailed it to nearby Run, leaving the Dutch to celebrate their famous victory on the beach. But the English had learned a thing or two from the tactically nimble Bandanese by now, and later that night they dispatched a native mercenary force that managed to sneak up on the besotted Dutch and, killing or injuring a great many of them, forced a humiliating retreat.

Ultimately, though, Anglo-Bandanese trickery proved no match for Dutch military muscle. The following year the determined VOC reps returned with more men and more cannon, and this time methodically pounded Ai until the defenders quite literally shot their last wad. As author Giles Milton notes in *Nathaniel's Nutmeg,* the Dutch commander, Admiral Jan Dirkz Lam, "took no chances once he had conquered Ai. He built a sturdy fort close to the shoreline, provided it with a permanent garrison and gave it the appropriate name Fort Revenge." He also equipped it with a dungeon where the jailed English found their jailers to be less than accommodating. " 'They pissed and **** upon our heads,' " Giles quotes one captive named Bartholomew Churchman as reporting, " '. . . untill such times as we were broken out from top to toe like lepers.' "

Palau Run—that most prolific nutmeg island of them all—fell to the Dutch four years later. And that effectively and very unhappily, as far as the Bandanese were concerned, put the entire island chain under the de facto control of VOC Governor General Jan Pieterszoon Coen, a man whose essence one modern Dutch historian neatly captured by concluding, "His name reeks of blood." In any event, it was Coen who sailed into the harbor at Naira in the spring of 1621 with 13 ships and 1,600 marines, and 80 Japanese mercenaries "expert in the art of execution," and gave the Bandas their first real taste of sustained Western-style cruelty.

Coen of course felt perfectly justified in punishing the Bandanese. Vowing to repay the 1609 Verhoef massacre, he ordered his marines to round up all Bandanese belongings and toss them onto giant bonfires. As the family heirlooms sizzled and popped, the Dutch torched Bandanese houses and canoes. And when a few of his squeamish charges refused to take part in the pillage and plunder, Coen threatened to have them hanged for treason. The few Bandanese natives not butchered outright were exiled to less lucrative islands, where their troublemaking wouldn't interfere with Dutch profit-taking. Meanwhile Coen had the forty-four disputatious orang kaya tossed into a bamboo enclosure, where a half-dozen of his Japanese swordsmen went to work, briskly beheading and quartering them.

That particular spectacle so sickened a young Dutch Navy officer named Nicolas van Waert that he confessed to his diary, "Thus did it happen: *God knows who is right.* All of us, as professing Christians, were filled with dismay . . . *and we took no pleasure in such dealings.*"

Within a matter of weeks, Coen's ethnic-cleansing campaign had resulted in a breathtaking ninety-six percent drop in the local population, to a mere six hundred people. Meanwhile Coen redrew the map, dividing the Bandas into sixty-eight *perken,* or plantations, and bade his newly appointed Dutch masters, the perkeniers, to import slaves from elsewhere in the Moluccas to offset the disappearance of the local labor pool. Finally, in parting, Coen ordered his men to raze the nutmeg groves on Ai and Run, lest the English get any funny ideas about returning to reclaim their former prizes.

Having made the islands safe for commerce and Christianity, Coen, though mildly reprimanded for his bloody excesses by King Heeren VII of Holland, was promptly paid a handsome royal bounty in gold, and in short order the Dutch spice merchants were boasting of the Bandas as the "brightest star of the V.O.C. constellation."

• • •

In *The Pillars of Hercules,* Paul Theroux accurately observes that expectant, "abnormal silence . . . is more typical of life in a war zone than noise, for war is nothing happening for weeks and then everything happening horribly in seconds." On Ai, with its gently sloping hillsides, and birds trilling in sweet, flowering jungle groves, it seemed as if nothing remotely dangerous could have happened for a very long while. But Tanya assured me my eyes and ears again deceived. To make her point, she marched me along one of the island's lush trails, the overhanging grass still cool and wet from a morning downpour, until we came at last to a small cottage set in a clearing among the Java almonds.

A tall gray-haired man stood on the porch and stared at us without smiling, but flapped a big bony hand in welcome when he caught sight of Tanya. "That's the local preacher," she whispered to me as we walked up the little path. "They burned down his church."

Plastic patio chairs were produced and we sat down. Rangy and rawboned, the preacher wore a soiled pinstripe shirt and heavy twill trousers hoisted to his midsection by a pair of old-fashioned braces. Maybe it was the man's backwoods-style dwelling, with the little plume of smoke curling from the chimney, or his dignified melancholy, but he had very much the demeanor of an Abe Lincoln in his depressions, I thought—a man who had seen too much in too short a time and carried the world's weight on his shoulders.

I said, "I'm sorry about your church." The preacher looked down at his hands and smiled sadly but said nothing. "Who do you think was behind it?"

"I don't know," he said, still staring at his big knuckles.

It is times like this that remind me, too late, that I'm not really cut out for the reporter's pushy craft. Still, here I was, having traveled ten thousand miles through jihadis and the *Bukit Siguntang*'s rich insect life, and so I pushed: "I was told it was Muslims from Ambon."

"I don't know who it was," the man repeated quietly. "They just burned my church. That was all—there was no further violence."

"If somebody burns down my church," I pressed, but obliquely in the Asian manner, "I guess I'd have to suppose they're angry about something."

The old preacher nodded sadly. "Well, it's Ambon, isn't it?" he said at length. Everything was topsy-turvy now. Half his flock had fled to safer islands down the line. He took his responsibilities as a village leader seriously, and so he and his family had stayed on. Someday, he hoped things would go back to what they'd been before—but of course everything about him except his words confirmed that nothing would ever be the same.

When I rose to go, and I shook the man's hand, he said in an apologetic, disbelieving tone, "Muslims and Christians have always gotten along so well here."

I smiled and nodded and thanked him for his time, and our little team walked back through the dewy grass to the main trail. But I must say that I carried that sad old preacher with me for a long time afterward—maybe because his forbearance seemed to stand for so many people I'd met who steadfastly refused to believe the hate-filled propaganda on either side, Muslim or Christian, until escalating violence inevitably made common sense an unaffordable luxury.

Over the months, I'd talked to dozens of refugees from various parts of the Moluccas. That was only a minuscule sampling of the half-million people the U.N. said had been rooted out of their homes, but still, in all, I never ceased to be amazed at how their stories of individual tragedy were at once horribly unique and remarkably the same. One night under a naked electric bulb in a steamy old rattan factory, a grizzled former Army sergeant described for me how Muslim hoodlums had ransacked and burned his home, and then expressed his anxiety about the safety of Muslim neighbors he'd been forced to leave behind. A lemur-eyed civil servant told how he'd fled his island because he feared his kindly Muslim landlord might come to grief for renting a room to a Christian.

I was moved to awe by such good and decent people—how could you not be? Cut loose from the anchor of home and community, they nonetheless clung to a generosity of spirit and a reverence for the truth that defied understanding. A mere bule giant, I tell you

I felt very small in comparison, in part because I suspect that, were the situations reversed, I wouldn't acquit myself nearly so well. Norman, translating our conversations, was made sick to his stomach on at least one occasion because, his jovial Defender of Java shtick aside, he too was a good and decent son of Indonesia, deeply troubled by his country's misery.

Back in the boat, we made a beeline for Run, which appeared on the horizon like the hump of a mythical creature, its spine green with the tall kanari trees signaling nutmeg groves inside. We were breasting a series of big waves when Norman shouted, "Hey," and pointed over the side. We all looked as first one glistening tube broke the surface, then another and another. Just then the sun disappeared behind a cloud, the sea grew opaque, and I suddenly saw we were surrounded by a school of a hundred or more bottlenose dolphins.

"They finally checked their e-mail," shouted Tanya, laughing, as the rollicking creatures enclosed the boat and escorted us all the way to Run. Ah, this is more like it, I thought excitedly. Paradise at last!

"All roads are long that lead towards one's heart's desire," wrote Conrad in my personal favorite, *The Shadow-Line.* But some roads are just a hard slog to disappointment, and despite the happy dolphin buildup, Run was supremely depressing. Contrary to Tanya's promise, the village children did not line the jetty and sing us ashore according to an old island custom. Instead a dozen doll-eyed boys and girls gathered at the landing to stare at us unsmiling, as if they'd just been memorizing excerpts from *Lord of the Flies.* Tanya had also promised a glimpse of the old curing sheds that still stood near the island's summit, but when the trail vanished into the sheer jungle, we gave up and turned back.

As on Naira, satellite dishes sprouted from village roofs. A doctor visited periodically on Des's orders. There was a small schoolhouse presided over by a teacher from Java. But frankly, Run seemed to be living under some kind of historical curse. The nutmeg groves had been razed and replanted twice since the gory days of Jan Coen. In the 1990s, world market prices even improved a little. (Des attributed this to growing world demand for Coca-Cola, which he and others surmised, used nutmeg as its secret ingredient.) But it was too late for Run. Nutmeg trees produce for sixty years, but geriatric trees produce weak, spindly offspring, and the island's forests, not properly rejuvenated, were dying. Worse, the money Suharto had promised Des to revive the traditional industry had vanished with Suharto's mandate, and Run was like the rest of the world in one respect—no loot, no luck.

When it was time for us to leave, the kids lined up and watched as Claudia and I heaved our outlandish bule bodies over the sideboard into Des's motorboat, their circular eyes remote and arms hanging at their sides.

"What gives?" I said to Tanya. "The kids haven't sung a peep."

"Yeah, I know," she confessed. "I forgot the sweets." The singing, it appeared, was a strictly contractual deal—no candy, no musical prayers for a safe journey over the bounding seas. Small of me, I know, but our wonderful trip to the nutmeg islands was over, and frankly I was glad to be going.

Smugness is a dangerous luxury for the foreign sojourner, and the gods of the Bandas quickly served up a little reminder of who was really in charge around there. It happened when we stopped for a picnic lunch at nearby Nailaka Island, a tiny uninhabited spit of sand that extends from the northeast end of Run like the big curved claw of a fiddler crab. As we drew close in, Norman leaped from the boat, video camera whirring. He was determined to capture the Manhattan Viking's arrival at the end of the earth for a film skit he planned to call "A Long Way from Long Island."

"Take one," shouted Norman as I put my leg over the side and immediately plunged to my chest on the near-vertical berm. Several moments of thrashing, cartoonlike panic ensued in which my feet, refusing to stay planted on the treacherous dissolving ledge, headed for the open ocean under the force of a powerful undertow. Had Norman not helped pull his floundering bule boss to safety there would have been little to stop me until I washed ashore in Australia, six hundred miles due south.

Properly chastened, I hotfooted it over blistering white sands with the others until we found a shady spot under a gnarled tree (not nutmeg—none had ever grown here), where the asbestos-footed boatmen laid out our lunch on a pockmarked blanket of lava. As we sat around on the bumpy rocks in our bathing suits, squinting into the powerful sunshine, towels wrapped around our heads like a bunch of desert vagabonds, I felt safe and happy for the first time since we'd left Makassar, in part I suppose because from this rare vantage point the world looked so spectacularly empty. All around us was an impossible immensity of blue, blue water, which was joined at the horizon to a soaring vault of sky only a shade and a half less blue. And in the distance, minuscule now but nonetheless imposing, the bright green cone of Gunung Api rose in a blazing field of hypnotic light.

I knew from looking at my watch that back in Manhattan it would be getting on toward midnight now, the dynamo of the great city having slowed to a dull roar as the nonstop traffic thinned out under my window on First Avenue just north of the United Nations building. How strange it was, I thought, that the vast majority of Manhattanites, having wound up one day and gathering energy for a new one, would be blithely unaware of the long-ago swap that had secured the unimaginable future that was now their exciting, tumultuous present. Back here at the other end of the earth, meanwhile, there wasn't so much as a fishing boat or a skiff to mar the panorama.

Returning to Bandanaira was like going back to the big city after a restful country vacation, meaning it was fraught with the tensions of unfinished business. Tanya tried the phones again but still without luck. And so we ate our dinner on the veranda, but this time without exuberance. The *Bukit Siguntang* was scheduled to return the next day from its apogee at Dobo on the outer edge of the Moluccas. It had hardly escaped our attention, however, that if the Navy had succeeded by now in putting its embargo in place, we'd be waiting for a ship that might never arrive. Unspoken anxiety hung over our large slabs of banana cake, and then Tanya blurted out, "I'm going to get through to Captain X if it kills me!"

She repeated her earlier argument that flying into Ambon

would be much safer than taking a ship packed at minimum with desperate refugees and freelance criminals. After arriving at the airport, all we'd have to do was amble across the tarmac to the civilian terminal, and fly out on a commercial jet. If the planes were grounded, we'd simply stay in Ambon under the protection of the captain until the smoke cleared—let *him* worry about our safety.

Under virtually any circumstances I can think of, I'd have regarded the prospect of the armed services swooping in to rescue us as the stuff of boyhood fantasy, and I would have been gung-ho eager. But our incarceration in paradise had given me time to think, and for reasons that could only be described as Normanesque, I was developing bad vibes about flying off the island. Mind you, I was by no means enamored of the *Bukit Siguntang,* with its concealed knives and aggressive cockroaches, and its history of mysterious disappearances. (I'd learned by now that even the jihadi-free *Bukit Siguntang* and its sister ship, the *M. V. Rinjani,* had a habit of swallowing its Christian passengers; only recently an Ambonese woman, returning from her Ph.D. studies in Canada to visit her family, had been plucked at night from steerage by a gang of freelance Muslim vigilantes and never seen again.)

On mental review, however, I had to admit to myself that Captain X didn't exactly come up aces in the reliability department. First, the embargo he'd predicted with an insider's timing had failed to materialize when he said it would. Next, Claudia, along with her reports of the dangerous fireworks in Ambon, had brought us the news of that military curfew about which Captain X had shared nary a peep. No, better to stick with the ship, I thought, which at least tried to keep to a schedule and was therefore marginally predictable. If the ship didn't show up, I supposed we'd just have to wait until we got as sick of eating our weight in tuna and bananas as Ramon.

I was working out how to say all that diplomatically when Ramon saved me the trouble. *"Taan-yaaah,"* he cried out, "don't be a fool. The ship is ten times safer. What if you get stuck in Ambon? You could all get killed!"

Tanya gave her foot a little stamp. "I'm not going back on that ship!"

"But Tanya," I said smoothly, "Des said from the beginning that the ship was the safest bet."

"Tell that to the fucking cockroaches," she snapped, tossing her head.

Startled by the flash of anger directed at me, which was so out of character for Tanya, and eager to head off a full-blown Bandanese standoff, I decided to play the peacemaking uncle. "Okay, Tanya, I tell you what," I said. "You get Captain X on the line and tell him I'll pay to have his boys pick us up and get us as far as Ambon. If he can guarantee our safety, and you can arrange it, we'll fly Navy."

"Right on," said Tanya, pausing to fix Ramon with a superior look. Then without further delay she hurried off across the cool, flat stones to hit the phones.

Feeling absurdly proud of myself, I marched upstairs to my room, buffeted by the spicy, lazy breeze, and absolutely secure in the knowledge that Tanya would never in a million years succeed in getting her dear Captain X on the line.

9

ESCAPE

The next morning Norman, Ramon, and I were gathered around the table by the banyan tree, dawdling over our banana pancakes, when Tanya came striding across the courtyard. Her hair still wet from her morning mandi, and combed straight back off her forehead, she had the ebullient, don't-screw-with-me look of a Wall Street power babe who had just closed a multimillion-dollar deal. We all sat up a little straighter in our chairs.

"The plane will be here at noon, boys," she announced triumphantly. Norman, Ramon, and I exchanged astonished glances as Tanya explained that she'd been forced to stay up half the night, but damned if she hadn't finally managed to get a call through to the elusive Captain X, who said he would be only too delighted to fly us out to Ambon—for a thousand dollars cash one way, the same deal as before.

"That okay by you, Pak Tracy?" inquired Tanya. From the way she said it, it was pretty clear she wasn't going to take no for an answer without a considerable to-do. And all at once I was vacillating again. Despite my reservations about flying, the concrete offer of military escort to Ambon really was, on second thought, something to hang your hat on. I glanced over at Norman and Ramon, who looked at me dolefully—they knew what was coming. Then in the finest traditions of local politics, I abruptly switched sides. "Cash or plastic?" I asked Tanya.

"Yahoo," she whooped, clicking her feet on the flagstones in a little victory dance. And suddenly I was feeling a little cocky myself as I realized, contrary to popular wisdom, maybe you could buy your way out of trouble after all. I mean, with the military of a great nation behind you, what could possibly go wrong? (I was going stupid again; wishful thinking had allowed me to conveniently disremember what I already knew of the sad state of repair of TNI's facilities and equipment.)

"Hello, Navy flyboys, goodbye S.S. Cockroach!" said Tanya, tilting her head back and unleashing her full, infectious roller-coaster laugh. As it swooshed and dipped we all joined in—all except for Ramon, that is, who looked as if he might have swallowed one too many slices of his beloved Gouda cheese. Defiantly but at low volume, he said, "It's a mistake."

Tanya ignored him as she plunged into final preparations for what Norman promptly dubbed Operation Banda Escape. First, seeing as how Banda's airstrip had been closed for well over a year, she sent word to the home of the local man who filled in as director of aviation, instructing him to get the field ready to receive an incoming plane. Just to be on the safe side, she then dispatched one of the hotel boys to go shoo away any livestock that might be grazing on or near the runway.

At eleven o'clock sharp, as the boys piled our luggage into Des's SUV, the kitchen ladies lined up in the narrow alley behind the hotel to wave goodbye, and there were many warm smiles and friendly gestures involving the touching of hearts with the hands. Claudia was there, too, of course. I'd invited her to fly with us to Ambon and, seeing as how she was traveling on a student budget, I offered to pay the forty bucks for her connecting flight to Makassar as I was feeling guilty about abandoning her to dangerous steerage aboard the *Bukit Siguntang,* this time all the way back to Jakarta. True to her separatist tendencies, however, she said she was sticking with the ship. Intrepid or dumb, I couldn't decide which—but I couldn't help admiring her youth and her guts.

"Looks like a clean getaway, Boss," said Norman as we drove through the little town and wound up the hill toward the airport. Yes, we were at last on the move, and forward motion, right or wrong, rarely fails to make my spirits soar. Plus, it was a perfect day— the sun blazing away up there in a sky of cloudless blue. It really is amazing, I stopped to think, how much more fun adventure is when you're reasonably sure you're not going to have to pay for it with your life, and suddenly our little escapade on Banda seemed the very height of adventure. Colorful tropical island, hemmed in by fighting, real live combat pilots flying in to the rescue—what could possibly beat that?!

So what if the Ambon airport was shut down again? I thought confidently. We'd simply camp out at the military base under the authoritative wing of Captain X until we could fly out, just like Tanya said. Who knows, it might even be an interesting experience. Feeling downright giddy, I intoned, "And so we bid a fond farewell to the beautiful Banda Islands," mimicking one of the corny TV travelogs that had suckered me into dreaming of far places like this one when I was a boy. Everybody laughed as we hit the crest of the hill and below and behind us the turquoise harbor slipped from view.

It was at that very moment the first raindrop splattered against the windshield. It was big and fat and landed with the sound of a grape being squashed underfoot.

"Uh-oh," said Tanya under her breath. But it didn't take an island girl to interpret this meteorological omen. Even an ignorant bule like me knew what a big fat raindrop meant in this neck of the woods. In the five minutes it took us to get to the airport the skies had opened and the rain was coming down in buckets. We pulled into the airport's parking lot like an amphibious landing craft splashing ashore and then quickly ducked inside the tiny stucco terminal.

The airport man came hustling into the waiting area, which had no electric lights and smelled of wet hay, and greeted Tanya with great formality. In his ill-fitting uniform shirt, which he was still tucking in, he looked like an underemployed washing machine repairman suddenly on an emergency call. Excitedly, he reported having established radio contact with the pilots or maybe he'd just heard voices swimming through static; it wasn't clear to me which. Anyhow, the idea was that Tanya's Navy flyboys were still on course.

Under the circumstances, that did not strike me as necessarily cheery news. One good look at the lay of the land thereabouts and you could tell that flying into or out of "Banda International," as Tanya affectionately referred to it, would be no mean feat even with ideal weather conditions. Set in a sort of tropical salad bowl between rocky peaks, which channeled air currents through a narrow, whistling gap, the airstrip was a natural wind tunnel of unpredictable ferocity. At that particular moment, as I stood there looking up at a sky seething with masses of angry roiling clouds, it was like watching a gumbo simmer through the bottom of a glass stewpot.

True to her nature, Tanya chose to interpret events with an optimistic spin. "See, no cows," she said as great spouts of water continued to gush from the eaves of the airport building. "If the rain stops for just ten minutes, we'll be okay. The pilot can . . ."

Tanya was interrupted in midsentence by a deafening thunderclap as the heavens opened wider and the rain fell harder than before, bouncing off the surrounding asphalt like BB shot. "This will blow over soon, yah," she said, shouting to be heard over the racket but suddenly not sounding all that sure.

Consistent with my gloomier gestalt, I was actually feeling much relieved. I certainly had no intention of going up in that sort of violent soup, and I knew no pilot in his right mind would ever try to land in it, either. So we'd be taking our leave of paradise by ship, after all, I thought. I looked down at my watch. Provided the *Bukit Siguntang* had not been burned to the waterline and scuttled somewhere in the far islands, it should be pulling into the harbor right about now.

"Excellent decision, Boss," said Norman when I shared the news with him. "But if we stand around here too long waiting to see what happens to Tanya's friends," he added, "we won't make the ship, either." In that case, Norman reasoned, we would be marooned on Banda for at least another week and, depending on events, possibly forever.

"Good point," I said. "Let's get the hell out of here, pronto."

I turned, and was preparing to return to the car when I heard a sound that yanked my head skyward. It was a low, very faint droning noise at first, like a honeybee drowning in a dish of olive oil. By tilting my head to the side and going snake eyes, I could just make out a tiny black speck agitating the horizon. That angry bee was our plane.

"Oh my God," said Tanya, "I think he's going to try to land!"

The plane did indeed draw closer, bobbing and rocking through the roiling, rain-lashed skies. It circled the field twice, as if the pilot was having trouble finding the runway, and then suddenly started growing bigger and bigger.

Tanya was now in a complete tizzy, her unshakable confidence in Captain X and his men suddenly altogether too shakable. "Oh, if they crash," she cried, "it's all my fault!"

"Tan-*yah*," cried Norman. "Don't say *that*!"

He then turned to me and whispered, "They're never going to make it, Boss," while we stood watching with morbid fascination as the gusting wind batted the little plane around like a cheap toy.

Then all at once I heard Tanya let out a startled yelp. A little incongruously, I guess, I swiveled my head, expecting to see the Jihad coming through the windows, with Jaffar Umar Thalib himself in the lead, scimitar flailing. Instead Tanya was pointing, open-mouthed, at a handsome souvenir calendar that lay on a large table in the middle of the room. It was a promotional item put out by the Pelni shipping line and flipped to which month I forget—but the one featuring a large rotogravure photograph from the bridge of the *M. V. Bukit Siguntang,* with none other than Captain Farad Alam Harahap staring sternly out to sea.

"Oh my God," cried Tanya, rolling her eyes heavenward. "It's Harahap! It's a sign from Allah! We should have gone with him on the ship, after all!"

In the very next instant, the airport man appeared at the door. "Come quickly," he said, waving us on. "The plane is about to land."

Tanya, Norman, and I rushed to the front of the building and took our places under a little canopy on the verge of the runway. As we did, the plane, a trim Nomad eight-seater with a white fuselage, swooped in low over the treetops, its wings waggling wildly, and shot past our noses at a speed that seemed altogether too fast. Its wheels had not so much as tapped the ground before it barreled out of sight behind a hillock blocking our view of the lower half of the runway.

Tanya raised cupped palms and bowed her head, the universal Muslim gesture symbolizing the individual's submission to Allah's will. *Inshallah.* She followed this up by hurriedly making the sign of the cross with a zigzagging thumb and forefinger. "Covering all bases," she said, lifting her eyebrows at me in a theatrical aside. "My mother was a Christian, from Manado, yah?"

In the next instant, we heard a series of muffled shouts from the lower runway, and then a teenage boy, gasping for breath, his eyes round with fright, came tearing around the corner. "The plane's crashed!" he cried. "The plane's crashed!"

"Oh my God! I knew it!" shrieked Tanya as I ran the short distance out onto the tarmac. At the far end of the runway, where it fell away to the ocean cliffs and the rain-dark sea, was our plane. Nose down, it resembled a large broken grasshopper. The crew—pilot, copilot, and navigator—were outside the wreckage, milling around in dizzy circles, holding their hands to their heads.

Quick-thinking Norman had jumped into the airport manager's car and raced to assist the staggering crew, but soon returned to the terminal. His heroic impulse had hit a slight snag when one of the pilots fingered his pistol and threatened to shoot if he came any nearer. But Norman was forgiving when he learned that both the pilot and copilot were fellow Javanese. "Defenders of Java under stress, Boss," he said sympathetically, in a sort of what's-an-occasional-shooting-among-kinsmen tone.

Luckily no one was seriously hurt. The plane was a different story, however. Just as its wheels had made contact, a stiff crosswind jerked it off the runway and into the grass, which was easily six feet high. The grass had then wrapped itself around the axles, yo-yo-ing the machine to an abrupt stop, smashing its landing gear, and bashing in its nose. Norman doubted the crumpled mess would ever leave the island.

In due time the pilots came hobbling into view, bruised, bloodied, and mightily chagrined. Ignoring all inquiries about their condition, they marched straight up to Tanya and, steepling their fingers, dipped their heads in a penitent bow before the princess of the islands.

"We Javanese know how to respect authority, Boss," said Norman admiringly.

Graciously, Tanya accepted their apologies and then turned to me and said under her breath, "There go their promotions, yah?"

Word travels fast on a small island, and by the time we got back to the hotel Ramon was in a state. "Thank God, you're okay," he said, and being essentially a decent, gentle soul, he added, "It's karma," instead of what I would have said, which is, "I told you so."

Then, as an afterthought, I looked out across the courtyard to the steamer dock, and my heart stopped. The ship wasn't there! But my worries were premature. Before long, and with great relief, believe me, I could make out the trustworthy hull of the *Bukit Siguntang* as it threaded its way through the narrow opening athwart Crab Island and came slowly gliding across the lagoon. Dwarfed by Gunung Api in the background, it looked like an oversized model boat in a very exotic bathtub but a wildly majestic sight to my eyes nonetheless.

Tanya went upstairs to console the pilots, who were nursing their wounded egos on the second-floor balcony. But when I moved to follow, Norman stopped me with an upraised hand.

"Better wait here, Boss," he said. "Javanese at a delicate moment, you understand . . . not a pretty sight."

"Have it your way," I said without heat—I'd had enough high

drama for one day. And so I wandered out onto the veranda and took a seat near my favorite banyan tree, where a glass of steaming kopi appeared at my elbow as if by magic. As I sat there sipping, looking out on the harbor, I suddenly realized something was missing—it was as if my fear, that indissoluble heaviness that had wedged itself under my rib cage like a chunk of granite since embarking on Operation Banda, had in the blinking of an eye completely disappeared.

Maybe it was simple relief over escaping the false salvation of the Navy rescue, or my anticipation of the calming, forward motion of the *Bukit Siguntang*. Whatever the reason, and without my conscious permission, my psyche had apparently decreed our ordeal officially over. And as the poet says, when fear subsides we appreciate beauty. The rain had cleared off now and it was once again a perfect day of blue, untroubled skies. Unlikely ever to sit at this table again, unless drugged and kidnapped, I thought, I fixed the main points in my mind—the picturesque little bay, the towering green volcano, and the nutmeg forest shrouding the tip of Banda Besar, the source of original turmoil in the islands.

This being Indonesia, of course, the splendor of the moment was inextricably mingled with chaos. Over at the landing, the ship's narrow gangway was already in a human knot, as embarking passengers fought their way up while disembarking passengers fought their way down. From somewhere below, an electronic boom box blared out the earthy, Arabesque rhythms of the *dang dut,* Indonesia's riotously popular Arabesque pop music, redolent of smoky city nightclubs with zaftig belly dancers wiggling bare midriffs. Meanwhile from the upper deck the ship's loudspeakers rang with the trembling, pulsating notes of the muezzin calling the Faithful to the midday prayer.

It was a lovely, confusing sort of a jumble, and I was sitting there, lost in reverie, when Norman strode across the courtyard, all bustling efficiency. "Not going troppo on me, are you, Boss?" he said.

I stared at him blankly. "How's that?"

"It's time to pay off the flyboys," he said, his right knee pumping impatiently.

"How silly of me," I said. "In all the excitement I guess I over-looked the fact that I'd have to pay for the flight whether we actually flew or not."

Well, I thought, at least I'm not being asked to spring for a new airplane. I reached into my pocket for my passport folder and pulled out ten damp but perfectly steam-ironed one-hundred-dollar bills. "I know your Javanese pilot is in a delicate state," I said, handing over the cash, "but see if you can't get him to sign a receipt without get-ting shot."

"His condition isn't that delicate," said Norman, briskly count-ing off five bills and handing the rest back to me. "Our deal was for a thousand bucks out and back," he said, with a shrewd wink. "So it's half-pay for halfway, Boss."

The Navy didn't put up a fight. At least I heard no gunshots ring out from the balcony, and when Norman returned, he was fanning himself with a sheet of wilting, oatmeal-colored paper. The pilot had scrawled his signature under Norman's neat block printing: "For charter flight from Ambon to Banda." Moreover, Norman had drawn a line through the figure of "U.S. $1,000.00," written in five hundred, and added the further helpful notation: "One way only. Plane crashed."

It was time to go. I stuffed the receipt into my pocket, shook hands with Ramon, and said goodbye. You appreciate intelligent friends in a crisis situation and I was going to miss his company. To prepare for a preemptive strike against the *Bukit Siguntang*'s insect armies, I walked across the alley to a dusty little shop, where I pur-chased the last two economy-size cans of a powerful antiroach spray. Produced by a big international pharmaceutical concern, the chem-ical was said to have been banned for use in the United States but was apparently still okay for destroying roaches in places like Indonesia, where it was aggressively marketed and widely admired.

We set off for the pier in the midday heat. With Tanya leading the way, we passed through the cyclone fencing, clambered up the gang-way, and once again entered the humid belly of our great sea-mother, where we were immediately and warmly embraced by Pontoh. He then harangued his two long-abused junior pursers until they somehow finagled a pair of cabins, one for Tanya and Separatist Girl (who for the sake of group solidarity had consented to bend her principles and upgrade from steerage), one for Norman and me, all on an overbooked ship with no beds and very little free deck space, let alone any staterooms, to spare. *Inshallah.*

Two weeks later I was back in Manhattan, where my wife, Toshiko, and I immediately sank our puny cut of Nasdaq loot into renovating our dilapidated East Side apartment, and I was plunged headlong into the lesser jihad of defending my pocketbook against architects, electricians, plumbers, and cabinetmakers. Safely back home in America, I sorely missed my friendships with Norman and the remarkable Alwis. But I was relieved and grateful (quite mistakenly, as it turned out) that I'd put the Laskar Jihad and the roiling mess of Indonesia behind me for good.

A few weeks later I read that Indonesia's embattled president, Abdurrahman Wahid, after prolonged stewing and inaction, had finally declared an official state of civil emergency in the Moluccas. To the surprise of many, perhaps including his own, the military actually attempted to carry out their orders this time, having already allowed thousands of jihadis from Jaffar's group and others to slip into the islands and raise holy hell. A few months later the militants aggressively widened their jihad, feinting east to Irian Jaya, and ultimately zeroing in, most disastrously, on Poso, a Christian enclave in Central Sulawesi, sparking yet another undeclared war that would wind up costing thousands of additional lives.

The following year Jaffar Umar Thalib would supervise a kangaroo Islamic court in the Moluccas that sentenced an alleged adulterer to death by stoning. Though briefly detained by police, Jaffar would never be prosecuted for the crime. Instead, he became the darling of mainstream Islamist politicians in Jakarta who found his swashbuckling cachet with conservative Islamic voters helpful to their own ambitions. "This is a country of equal opportunity impunity," said Douglas Ramage of the Asia Foundation in Jakarta, as he limned the bizarre state of the nation for the *Far Eastern Economic Review.* "Nobody gets punished for anything."

Meanwhile things went quickly downhill for President Wahid. In

June 2001, Indonesia's first democratically elected president in over four decades was impeached on charges of gross incompetence, and was succeeded by a democratic challenger, Megawati Sukarnoputri, who also happened to be the daughter of the self-styled former god-king, Sukarno. Islamic fundamentalists were unimpressed. Though a Muslim, Megawati was inescapably a woman, and therefore in the eyes of her militant co-religionists unfit to lead a Muslim country. As on the bridge of the *Bukit Siguntang,* it was not entirely clear who, if anyone, was in control.

In all the chaos, one particularly portentous event went virtually unnoticed, however. Two months after our hairy ride through the Moluccas, a man named Omar al-Faruq, later arrested by the CIA as Al Qaeda's senior operative in Indonesia, took Ayman al-Zawahiri, Osama bin Laden's top lieutenant, on a tour of the embattled Moluccas, allegedly scouting a site for a terror camp of the sort the *New York Times* would eventually call "an international training center like Afghanistan under the Taliban." It remains unclear whether that camp or others ever got much beyond the rumor stage, but the larger point is really this: Terrorism loves what the diplomats call a nuisance conflict. And while infighting among the militant groups involved in the eastern campaign would eventually splinter the effort, opening the way for the signing of a peace accord, the Moluccas had given terrorism in Indonesia a frightening new impetus. In fact, the struggle there had become to the development of terrorism in Southeast Asia what the fighting against the Soviet occupation of Afghanistan had been to Al Qaeda a decade earlier— the great catalytic event for a new generation of holy warriors, blooded in fighting, inculcated with a romantic, overarching vision of the world Islamic revolution, and bonded to large numbers of like-minded comrades from across the region. Emboldened jihadis would soon bring bloody chaos to Bali and then into the heart of downtown Jakarta, and in so doing toss up a whole new cast of characters for the terrorism detectives in the U.S. and Asia to consider. While far from panoramic, violent Islam was now most assuredly a growth business in Indonesia, and it had attracted the attention of investors and adventurers the world over.

• • •

Luckily, meanwhile, the spirit of the old-time Moluccas was still very much alive in the form of Des Alwi, enterprising sultan of the Bandas. When I met him over breakfast at one of Jakarta's five-star hotels during a later visit, he had just published his memoirs in Bahasa Indonesia. Looking remarkably hale and hearty at seventy-five, he was coming from a local TV studio, sleek in a double-breasted suit with his hair slicked back and bushy eyebrows neatly combed.

"You see, Tracy, it's like this," he said with a mischievous wink, "I'm pushing my new book." Then, autographing a copy he'd brought for me, he said, "I feel like Hemingway!"

"Yes, the old man and the fish," cracked an old Alwi family friend, a senior adviser to President Megawati, who had joined us at the table, and soon the two men were horsing around like a couple of island boys.

"Oh, by the way, Captain X is now Admiral X—he got another star," said Tanya, who was of course on hand, looking radiant and happy and pushing new promotional schemes of her own.

"What about the two pilots?" I asked.

Tanya shrugged. "Poor guys," she crooned, emitting a rocketing laugh. "Nobody's ever heard from them again, yah?!"

Then, in typical tropical fashion, the mood shifted dramatically. Des glowered, predicting dourly that although peace had been declared in the Moluccas, and a treaty signed, nothing would ever be the same again, especially in the formerly sweet and lovely Ambon. Too much damage had been done to the local psyche to be fixed by words on paper. It would take generations to undo the hurt; meanwhile the physical city had been completely wrecked.

Ever the wheeler-dealer, though, Des said he was working on a scheme to move the regional capital to the nearby big island of Ceram. "And good news, Tracy," said the sultan, his mood lightening again, "the last of the Muslim refugees have left Banda."

The Christians were starting to return, too. Even a few intrepid tourists were filtering back, like the young Dutch couple who had unwittingly tested out the shark pool. "Late one night," said Des, tapping me on the arm, "they suddenly decided to go for a dip in the nude, you see."

Only the next morning did the swimmers discover they'd been paddling romantically among the great predators of the sea. "Can you imagine, Tracy!?" said Des, his shoulders heaving in mirth. "What if they got in there, you know, and the shark grabbed the wrong thing? Oh my God!"

Des warbled with laughter, a sound not unlike the cooing of the endangered Banda pigeon, and then he suddenly grew angry again. "That whole damn thing about the Muslims attacking the bus driver was all trumped up," he blurted out, referring to the attempted robbery in Ambon still widely believed to have triggered the blowup in 1999. "The Army was behind every damn thing!"

"How do you know that, Des?" I said.

Des stared at me in disbelief. "It was the Army that burned my hotel in Ambon, Tracy!" he cried. "Yah! But first they stole all the air conditioners and television sets from the rooms and took them to Army headquarters several miles away."

Ambon was a very small place, with a limited cast of characters, and Des knew them all—"I sent my man in there to, you know, investigate." After he was satisfied he'd distilled truth from conflicting accounts, the sultan personally marched up and demanded to see the storeroom.

"They had all my stuff right there! They made no attempt to hide it!" said Des, adding that somebody had even doctored his furniture to make it look as if it had survived a fire.

"What did they say when you confronted them?" I asked.

"They said they were protecting it!" Des snorted, emitting a high-pitched shriek of incredulity. "Terrible!"

By now the Bush administration was in office in Washington, pressing Jakarta to act more aggressively in its new Global War on Terror, and officials were exasperated with what they saw as Indonesian foot-dragging. To aid in that fight, the Pentagon was angling to reestablish aid to the Indonesian military, which Congress had cut off during the Clinton years over TNI's long ledger of human-rights violations in East Timor and other places. And this to Des was precisely what the Americans so miserably failed to understand about Indonesia. When God-fearing Indonesians looked under their beds at night, it wasn't Al Qaeda or Osama they saw hiding there to haunt their dreams, but their very own military, which the United States of America had helped fund and train during the bulk of the Suharto years.

Historically, said Des, "it was always so easy to blame the Muslims in the Moluccas—they were poor, they were stupid, they were dangerous. But nobody ever really tried to solve the basic social and economic problems." Meanwhile elements in the military had played all sides against the middle until savvy militants like Jaffar had figured out how to use them to capitalize on the chaos for their own revolutionary goals.

"Well, now you see what happens," said Des grumpily. "The radicals have stepped in and used the Molucca tragedy as an excuse to publicize their cause, which includes this global jihad business."

Des clucked his tongue loudly, indicating there would be further hell to pay. He then laughed, lowered his head confidentially, and said, "Tracy, I've got three planes now, ready to go, to move tourists from Ambon to Banda."

"But is it really safe now, for tourists, I mean?" I was remembering, perhaps unfairly, how Des's previous advice on this score, while in hindsight technically correct, had nevertheless led to Norman, Tanya, and me being dropped into the lap of the roistering Laskar Jihad.

"Oh, it's completely safe now, Tracy," he replied indignantly. Des then leaned over the table and added with his impish grin, "Well, maybe not totally safe, you know. That's why the airplanes will sleep on Banda."

PART TWO

10

BATTLE OF WILLS

October 13, 2002, 10 A.M.

Toshiko and I were sitting down to a late breakfast in our Manhattan apartment when I flipped on CNN to catch the headlines and saw Bali, half the planet away, dancing in flames. In the pictures it was the wee hours of Sunday morning in the Far East, and as terrified faces rushed past the camera, the giant fires leaped wildly over thatched roofs and jagged palms. A disembodied announcer's voice said that two popular tourist spots on the fashionable bule playground at Kuta Beach, the Sari Club and Paddy's Irish Bar, had been bombed. Hundreds of patrons, mainly foreign tourists, were dead or grievously injured.

Watching the looped images played over and over again for chilling effect, my first coherent thought was not of terrorism, which this obviously was, but of Norman. He'd recently moved to Bali to start a new business, a fancy boutique bookstore, and I fired off an e-mail to see if he was okay.

"I'm okay, Boss," came the reply, "but my dreams are shattered in pieces overnight." Nobody would be buying books or anything else in Bali now, at least for the time being. Meanwhile, Norman reported, friends living near the blast site had found their backyards littered with severed arms and legs.

And so it was that we—all of us—had stepped, darkly, into a new phase in the war against terrorism. Heretofore, the criminals had targeted mainly "power" sites—the World Trade Center, the Pentagon, U.S. embassies in Africa and the Middle East; in recent months, however, Western intelligence officials had been picking up muffled signals suggesting that Al Qaeda and its local henchlings might be zeroing in on "soft" targets in Southeast Asia—the resort hotels, restaurants, bars, and discos where "white meat," the chilling terror code for Americans, went to see and be seen.

Now, in Bali, the self-styled soldiers of Allah had literally scored a billion-dollar hit. In striking one of the world's truly mythic getaways, the largest terrorist attack since 9/11, they not only burst the bule bubble of tropical splendor, but had slammed a $5.4 billion-a-year tourist industry important to Indonesia's cash-strapped economy. Overnight, tourists became rare as snowflakes in Bali. Hotel occupancy hemorrhaged. "Flirt with the bule and their sinful, hedonistic ways," the bombers were in effect telling Indonesia's political and business elite, "and behold the fire that will ruin you."

For the "white meat," the message seemed even plainer: "You are safe nowhere, not even in your green and luscious dreams."

By this time of course my own daydreams had come to focus almost exclusively on returning to Indonesia as fast as I possibly could. Amnesia sets in quickly for the addicted hack, and the mind-numbing fear that gripped me during our quixotic tour of the Banda Islands had long since retreated to the back burners of consciousness, pushed there in no small measure by the life-changing events of 9/11 and the desire to get a better look at who or what we were up against.

In addition, America now faced a vexing new dilemma. Our retaliatory strike against Taliban and Al Qaeda strongholds in Afghanistan had succeeded in smoking the "evildoers" out of their holes, just as President Bush had promised. On the run, however, many of our enemies, archvillain Osama included, had simply found newer, deeper holes to hide in. By pitching the Global War on Terror onto a gauzy, geographically diffuse plain in Central and Southeast Asia, the Bush team had effectively expanded the circumference of our ignorance, and tracking down terrorists in suspected haunts like Indonesia was proving as difficult as chasing wisps of smoke through the jungle. (And ultimately, in my opinion, it was understandable frustration with this porous new battlefield that helped stoked the Bush administration's ill-conceived desire to "focus" our efforts on Iraq.)

Yet horrible though it was, the darkness in Bali did produce a ray of light. In carrying out such a daring plan, the terror ghosts had tipped their hand, leaving behind them a trail of solid evidence. The serial number on an engine block plucked from the rubble quickly led to a ghastly grinning garage mechanic named Amrozi and behind him to the small, well-hidden terrorist organization with big ideas called Jemaah Islamiyah. Based in Indonesia, with cell groups embedded in neighboring Singapore, Malaysia, the Philippines, and southern Thailand, JI's master plan ostensibly called for sweeping pretty much all of Southeast Asia into an Islamic superstate they called *Daulah Islamiyah,* or the New Caliphate, in keeping with a vision shared by Islamic revolutionaries the world over. (On the radicals' calendar, the last Caliphate had ended with the crumbling of the Turkocentric Ottoman Empire in 1924; the new one would extend and enhance the old model, running from Morocco to Manila, as the saying went, and put as many of the world's 1.2 billion Muslims as possible under the rule of Islamic law. Come the revolution, JI's Asia would be the Caliphate's important eastern suburb.)

Asia's extremists were thinking big, and like many people who fancy themselves Asia hands, I'd been guilty of thinking small. Radical Islam had never been a panoramic problem in the multicultural societies of Southeast Asia, and in spite of my brush with Jaffar's troopers in the Moluccas, I'd come to view resurgent Islam in "my" part of the world mainly as a rising but modest danger to the stability of two or three shaky governments. And so I was duly flabbergasted when Jemaah Islamiyah popped onto the world's antiterror radar screens in December 2001 with plans to ring in the approaching New Year with a terror extravaganza designed to rock the region to its core.

The target was orderly, ultramodern Singapore, and as uncovered by the city-state's sharp-eyed Internal Security forces, JI's plans included blowing up the U.S., Israeli, British, and Australian embassies, as well as a subway complex frequented by local U.S. military personnel. There was a wild auxiliary scheme to spark a diversionary war between multicultural but predominantly Chinese Singapore and its peaceable but predominantly Muslim neighbor, Malaysia. The most flamboyant entry, though, was a variation on 9/11 in which terrorist-pilots would crash a hijacked passenger jet into the control tower at Changgi International Airport. When the Singapore cops foiled the attack, the theory ran, Jemaah Islamiyah, working on direct orders from Al Qaeda, had simply moved to a less ambitious Plan B, and ripped open Bali's soft tourist underbelly.

All of this, as I say, puzzled me no end. I mean, you don't just slap together plans of that magnitude overnight—they require time, thought, money, reconnaissance, and lots and lots of logistical support. And yet in all my previous travels in Indonesia, nobody, neither diplomat, pundit, nor spy, had ever so much as uttered the words "Jemaah Islamiyah" in my presence, let alone mentioned the group as a force to be reckoned with. How could a band of such murderous but apparently well-organized thugs have sunk their claws so deeply into the Asian landscape and drawn so little attention?

An oversight of that magnitude demanded some fast answers. Accordingly, reporters for CNN and other key players in the international media pieced together a neat and compelling picture based on what was considered the most newsworthy information then available. JI was not only Al Qaeda's special Asian clone, it was suggested, but Osama had an Asian doppelganger, too—a lean, ascetic, Koran-thumping fundamentalist preacher named Abu Bakar Bashir. And if ever there was a made-for-media villain it was this character. With his scraggy fringe of graying beard and eyes magnified by bottle-thick glasses, he projected an image of mystery and menace, handily reinforced by the fact that he headed an equally mysterious Islamic boarding school in Ngruki, a tiny village deep in the Islamic heartland three hundred miles southwest of Jakarta. The further news that many of the suspects under indictment for the Bali bombings, as well as individuals arrested in the botched terror raid on Singapore, had studied at Ngruki or were otherwise linked with Bashir only seemed to cinch his role as the leader of Indonesia's branch office of Terror, Incorporated.[1]

The media's case against JI, abetted by officials in Washington and the region, seemed to neatly jibe with history, too. In 1985, accused of treason and on the lam from Suharto's security goons, Bashir had fled to neighboring Malaysia, where it is now generally believed he set about stitching together his pan-Asian terror network. That he reportedly accomplished with the help of a select group of former pupils who had recently fought to oust the Soviet Army from its then-occupation of Afghanistan, and where they'd also conveniently cemented ties with future Al Qaeda leaders. After the Suharto regime collapsed in 1998, Bashir returned to Ngruki and took advantage of Indonesia's new political freedoms to once again spread his radical creed. And now Indonesian police were convinced that the great gray wizard not only talked like a terrorist but walked like one, too. Very soon they had implicated him in a nationwide series of church bombings on Christmas Eve 2000, as well as a plot to assassinate President Megawati. And so the Western media seemed to have it just right—Indonesia's axis of evil had been identified, and with it the wolfish grandpa who took his orders straight from Osama's board of directors.

Like most people, I sincerely hoped that the case against Bashir and the JI was every bit the slam dunk the government-media consensus publicly said it was. Yet you had to wonder if the dots hadn't been connected a little too neatly to encompass messy reality. If my

---

1. Bashir's heated denials of JI's very existence only added to his suspect image: "Jemaah Islamiyah," he told CNN interviewer Maria Ressa, "I am sure is a manipulation, a fiction that was created to arrest people." According to Bashir there was no such thing as Al Qaeda, either. Americans and the Jews were the real terrorists, using their lies to besmirch and attack Islam.

years in Asia had taught me anything, it was how lines you swear run arrow-straight from points A to B can suddenly go all squiggly on you before they vanish into the jungle entirely. More to the point, nearly everyone you talked to privately confessed there was still a whole lot of guesswork involved in drawing anything approaching a definitive picture. (As one former CIA official commented, "Frankly, we don't know what's out there.") And even if Abu Bakar Bashir had given the orders that flipped the terror switches in Bali, did it really tell you everything you needed to know about how radical Islam functioned in its new incarnation in Southeast Asia? (To underscore the dangers in imposing the wrong template on reality, let me just offer five further words: "Iraq" and "Weapons of Mass Destruction.")

You see where this is heading: I was raring to get back into the field, and inventing all manner of excuses as to why my unasked-for presence was absolutely essential in helping George Bush and the GWOT irregulars crack the puzzle of Asian terrorism. But as I said earlier, I was thinking of Norman, too. In the odd way that life throws people into one another's paths, and perhaps because, according to my rough calculations, he'd saved my life on at least one occasion, and possibly two, I now thought of Norman with great affection, as a talented son or maybe a clever, courageous younger brother. In any event, I was absurdly proud of his intelligence and accomplishments (as if I had anything remotely to do with them) and interested in his future. And lately Norman's future had taken something of an unexpected turn.

His dream of opening that upscale bookstore near Bali's Kuta strip, where sophisticated bule tourists and affluent Indonesians would mull the world's great literature in English or Bahasa Indonesia while sipping lattes or organic fruit punch, for example, had been inspired by an astonishing piece of news he'd received in an e-mail from Europe. In it, a former bule girlfriend living in Amsterdam informed Norman that in addition to a brief, romantic kindling of Dutch-Indonesian relations, they now had something else in common—a beautiful baby daughter whom we'll call Annie.

The discovery had instantly transformed Norman's life. Putting his carefree bachelor days behind him, he gathered his new instant family to him in Jakarta, and embarked on a career as a doting father. When he adjudged the frenetic capital too raw an environment for his darling little Annie, he moved everybody to leafy Bali, where she could frolic in safety among the frangipani and the broad-leafed banana trees, while Papa Norman, thanks to a wealthy investor friend in Jakarta, became a purveyor of fine books and coffees.

There was only one small flaw in Norman's plan. Annie's mother, an intelligent, ambitious young woman, had taken a more or less instant dislike to Bali, and grew quickly bored with the island's breezy, lackadaisical ways. After a few months, she decamped for Europe, taking baby Annie with her. Mother Holland would provide until such time as Norman proved his husbandly mettle by making a go of his book operation.

The challenge appealed to Norman's innate nobility. With the dark, cheery aplomb of a Javanese superhero, he worked night and day on his business plan, leased a promising corner lot in downtown Kuta, and pored over blueprints with his architect. And then, in that one fiery Saturday night of terror, Bali's tourist industry was dead and gone, and so were Norman's hopes of combining commercial success with domestic tranquillity. Nobody in his right mind would invest in Bali now, which is what Norman's backer apologetically told him when he backed out of the deal.

"I'm okay, Boss, but . . ."

You didn't have to be telepathic to tell that Norman was sailing some heavy psychic seas. And so, a little cryptically, I told him to hang on—I might have something to take his mind off his troubles. My agent, Philip Spitzer, had been working on a book deal that would pay my way back to Indonesia, and throw a few bucks Norman's way into the bargain. And since my faith in Philip, a man as gentlemanly as he is persistent, is as boundless as my faith in Norman, I got to work brushing up on current events.

It was then I began to wonder if returning to Indonesia had been such a hot idea, after all. What I was reading in the various news services, for instance, made this country I loved and thought I knew a little something about sound as relentlessly dangerous and unlovable as the battlefields of Afghanistan. If the reports had it right, the

Bali bombings had flung Jakarta into the grip of a powerful hysteria. Its international schools, American, Australian, and British, had emptied until security features like new "blast walls" could be installed. Other accounts raised the possibility of snipers working the city's rooftops, zeroing in on "white meat" as people walked the streets or drove to work. "I've been in six countries," one American executive told the *New York Times,* "and never had a post where the schools were targeted."

I've worked around the news media long enough to know that even the savviest reporters can get swept up in the heat of the story (it's even happened to me a few thousand times), and so I've always prided myself on maintaining a healthy degree of professional skepticism about what I read in the papers or see on TV. But frankly I'm not so sure anymore. Let me put to you this way: Who among us can resist today's electronically driven media, where corporate interests increasingly oblige otherwise skilled and sensible reporters to dance to their tune, and in so doing ensure dark and superficial themes be driven home with a mindless, irritating repetition once reserved for TV commercials selling aspirin or laundry soap?

Not me. Adding to the media conditioning was the fact that not two blocks from my apartment in Manhattan, diplomats of many nations were gathering at the United Nations to debate the best way to handle the dangers of Iraq, with Bush administration officials demanding that Saddam Hussein choke up his alleged stockpiles of WMDs or face the mother of all shellackings, while our allegedly wimpy European allies argued such an adventure would, among other things, set the Islamic world afire.

Contemplating a fast-approaching visit to Indonesia, a country about which I could see I apparently knew very little at all, and now supposedly crazy with anti-American rage, I was suddenly feeling a little weak in the knees myself. But at least my friends were supportive. When they heard I was headed for the place they recognized from the news as Terror Central, they expressed their concern in sentences invariably using the word "nailed"—as in, "Don't you ever worry about getting 'nailed' over there in Indonesia?" or, "Indonesia? Jesus, I sure hope you don't get nailed."

One night at a dinner party, an expert on Asia, a man wise in the ways of Indonesia and given to solid, bankable judgments, surprised me by saying, "You wouldn't catch me going there now."

Why not? "Too easy to get nailed." [2]

Time was running down as fast as my enthusiasm when I got in touch with Norman and gave him the details. He was back living in Jakarta now, alone and restless, and despite having just landed a good-paying job, he had jumped at the chance to hit the reporting trail with me, and had tendered his resignation. Norman openly scoffed at America's dark view of Indonesia as a typically hysterical American overreaction unmatched by real events. (Memory may err here, but if I'm not mistaken, he may actually have used the term "drama queen.")

"Come on, Boss," he pronounced confidently. "If we survived our trip on the *Bukit Siguntang,* we can survive anything."

By Jove, I thought, Norman is right—I'm taking this whole thing too seriously, listening to people who don't know a damn thing when Norman is right there on the spot. My hopes quickly revived. As the days and weeks rolled by, and Norman got busy arranging our itinerary, however, I began to detect a subtle and troubling shift in his psychology. Below the cheery surface bravado, a less confident tone was creeping into his e-mails.

"I am not as fearless as before," he ventured in one particularly

---

2. I was in good company, as it turned out. In Jakarta, the American ambassador, Ralph "Skip" Boyce, would tell me a good story about meeting his newly arrived counterpart from Afghanistan. The Afghani envoy told Boyce that when his friends in Kabul heard the news that he'd been posted to Indonesia, they reacted in horror. "Oh, my God," they'd said. "You're not going to Indonesia?! That's the center of Al Qaeda!"

"How weird is that?" said Boyce, with an astonished chuckle. Even the citizens of war-ravaged Afghanistan, Al Qaeda's former GHQ, were convinced that anyone venturing into Indonesia was automatically a candidate for getting nailed. The very real threats of terrorism aside, Boyce attributed this distortion to what he called the "CNN effect"—the steady run of narrowly focused news stories out of Indonesia in the international media, which often portrayed the country "in negative and violence-prone fashion, which belies the day-to-day realities." Familiar as I was with the not infrequently grim features of that daily routine, it would be hard for me, on balance, to disagree with him.

introspective installment, "and haven't utilized my gut instincts for a while. But since one by-product of this project is to inspire the world with our triumph of will, count me in."

Triumph of will?

On the theory that we couldn't piece together a satisfying picture of Indonesia's Islamic landscape by talking only to friendly Muslims, I tried to sound out Norman on a list of names of known fundamentalists I'd gathered by canvassing the experts in New York and Washington, asking if there was anyone we should avoid for safety reasons.

Norman responded skittishly. He said he really couldn't say—all those Arab-sounding names were Greek to him. He signed that particular e-mail, "Noorman bin Intimidata." When I opened my mailbox a few days later and got a message referring to our quest as "Operation Enduring Tracy," I reached for the phone.

It was one o'clock in the morning in Jakarta and, ominously, Norman was still up and pacing the floor. "Boss!" he said, his voice sounding startled and weary.

"Norman, what the hell is going on with you?!"

"What do you mean?"

"Your e-mails, man! Frankly, it sounds to me like you're freaking out."

"Mild freak-out, Boss."

"Okay, let me see if I understand you," I said, uncorking my mystical powers of bule deduction. "Am I correct in assuming that you are torn by this whole business of my trip?"

"Correct, Boss."

"On the one hand, you're afraid I won't come, in which case you'll be unemployed and broke. On the other, you're afraid I *will* come, in which case you may be dead?"

"Nice detective work, Boss. You've put your finger on it as usual," he said, chuckling mirthlessly.

My deductions were hardly Holmesian. Like many millions of Indonesians, Muslim or not, Norman hadn't ever really troubled himself to examine the serried ranks of militant Islam too closely, and for good reason. The Islamists were a famously prickly bunch, and appearing to be even mildly critical of them could be dangerous. Many people had simply hoped their fanatical sound and fury would be sluiced away in a new high tide of democratic reform. But nearly five years after the fall of Suharto, with the Megawati government mired in corruption, infighting, and seemingly incapable of resuscitating a flagging economy, Islamic anger was more a factor in the life and politics of the nation than ever. After Bali, Norman, like Indonesia as a whole, was suddenly forced to engage the issue, and he found himself with little to go on but his own understandable fears. (The Bush team and the cognoscenti in Washington called this denial; I called it common sense.)

Speaking into the phone with quiet urgency, Norman said there was no use pretending—he didn't know beans about Indonesia's Islamic landscape, or which groups could be safely approached or which might be a problem.

"Boss," he said at length, "I think we need to hire a guide."

I wasn't sure I'd heard him correctly. "You're telling me the guide needs to hire a guide?"

"Precisely, Boss. We need somebody, call him our Islamic bureau chief, who can steer us through the territory. Somebody who can pass the Javanese eye exam."

Like many Javanese, Norman put great store in the all-important opportunity, in a mixed and unsettled environment, to look someone in the eye and decide whether they're telling you the truth or not, and whether a lie might result in your untimely demise. It was a very low-tech solution for someone as digitally mastered as Norman, but under the circumstances it was sound methodology all the same.

"Well, that shouldn't be too hard," I said, my hopes suddenly diving for the cellar once again. "Just go out and find somebody who knows the Islamic landscape like the back of his hand, who you can look comfortably in the eye, and then completely trust him with our lives."

"Okay, Boss," said Norman.

And so that was pretty much where we stood. Without a shred of self-confidence on the part of either member of our dynamic duo, Norman went out to beat the bushes in Jakarta, looking for a guide who could keep us from getting nailed, and I got ready to head for Kennedy Airport.

11

HIDDEN FORCE

Norman had changed. He was waiting for me as usual when the big glass doors parted at the Jakarta airport and I stepped into the steamy swarm of bodies beyond the steel barricades. It had been over two years since I'd last seen him, and I dare say he'd put on a pound or two around the middle (who hadn't), but that wasn't it. It was his smile. It flashed with the old hundred-and-fifty watt luminosity, but faded a little too quickly into something aloof, moody, and very un-Normanlike.

"Don't look so happy to see me," I said once I'd crammed my legs into our tiny taxi and we were roaring toward downtown Jakarta, my knees involuntarily thrusting like pistons within inches of my chin. In the distance the city rose under brooding gunmetal skies in a cluster of skyscrapers like a sci-fi Oz or, as Norman preferred, Bladerunner City.

"I don't know what it is, Boss," Norman said apologetically. "I've been snapping at people at the office, people on the street, everybody. It is just so frustrating living in this country now."

"Don't overlook the possibility of male menopause," I said. I wasn't trying to make fun of Norman's angst. On the other hand, I'd just spent twenty-three hours on an airplane, and I was hoping a little tactical flipness might pull the old Norman out of his cranky new shell. It didn't work. As we rolled through the outskirts of the great city, and its scrublands, factories, and ubiquitous billboards zipped by, Norman stared uneasily out the window, and said with a bitter edge to his voice, "This country doesn't provide opportunities for my ambition."

"Depends on the ambition, I guess," I said, bouncing my eyebrows, hoping some truly juvenile humor might do the trick. Norman responded with a brief, reflexive brow flick, flashed a subliminal grin, and then frowned more intensely than before.

"Well, okay, then there's the whole personal mess, too."

Norman said he'd quarreled by phone with Annie's mother, who was still in Europe with their daughter, and she was now refusing to take his calls. "She doesn't want to live in Indonesia, Boss," Norman said disconsolately. "It frightens her."

Watching the spires of Bladerunner City pull closer, I said, "And you blame her?" I was trying my best to keep the conversation light, airborne, but Norman kept dragging it down to earth. "Seriously, Boss," he said, "tell me what you think."

"Look here, Norman," I said, adopting a stern tone, "Let's not get too existential about things. We've got a tough job ahead of us. So let all good Defenders of Java focus on their duties. Now tell me about Reza. Is he really an anarchist?"

Norman had recently hired our guide's guide, a man named Faisal Reza, and then proceeded to torture me by e-mail and phone as he continually referred to Reza as "the Anarchist."

"No, I think Antonia just likes to say she's married to an anarchist because it sounds more romantic." It was truly a small world. Antonia, a voluble and gracious Italian news correspondent and linguist, an old friend of Norman's, whom I also knew and liked, had turned out to be the wife of our new Islamic bureau chief.

The fact of the matter was that Reza was the leader of a small Islamic political organization, the People's Democratic Party. One of several hundred political action groups to have emerged from the woodwork after Suharto, the PRD distinguished itself by being both Islamic and significantly to the left of Ralph Nader in its positions on most social issues. That put Reza on the exact opposite end of the political dial from jihadists like Bashir and Jaffar Umar Thalib. Still, in Norman's view, Reza knew all the key players, right, left and center, and in theory at least could lead us to the right people.

"You trust him, then?" I said.

"I looked into his eyes, Boss, and didn't see anything funny," said Norman without conviction.

"Did you ask him about the fatwa?" One of the people I wanted to talk to, a leading Muslim liberal named Ulil, had recently been socked with a death order by a fanatical fundamentalist group. Norman had been nervous about setting up an interview on the theory, basically, that the fatwa might be contagious.

"Yeah, I asked Reza," Norman said glumly. "He said he *thought* it would be okay, and then he just kind of went silent."

Well, that's just dandy, I thought—all we need is an equivocal Islamic bureau chief who *thinks* everything is okay. "I want to meet Reza as soon as we get to the hotel," I said.

"Small complication there, Boss," Norman said. Antonia had apparently chosen this historic moment in the life of the nation and our project to begin labor with their second child, and Reza was on standby duty at home.

I briefly contemplated the concept of a housebound anarchist adviser, and concluded that things were getting off to a typical start for Indonesia, meaning at once unsettling and screwball. "Let me compliment you on your choice of bureau chiefs, Norman," I said. "And such great timing, too."

"You can't control when the babies come, Boss," said Norman, chuckling ruefully. "Anyway, Reza gets liberated tonight. We'll have dinner, and you can administer the Javanese eye exam for yourself."

Every traveler needs a map, or at least a mental picture of how to proceed, and the fact that I still didn't have a clue about how to thread my way through the Islamic landscape worried me greatly. I wasn't about to flop aimlessly around till evening, and so as soon as I checked into my hotel, I picked up the phone and called Sidney Jones. Sidney headed up the Jakarta office of the International Crisis Group, the Brussels-based think-tank I've mentioned before, and I was delighted when she suggested we meet for lunch at a Thai restaurant down the street.

The café rooms were inviting, dark, and cool, with an appropriate whisper of intrigue in their potted palms and slowly revolving ceiling fans. Though badly submerged in jet-lag limbo, I was suddenly glad to be back in Asia when Sidney waved to Norman and me from a table near the entrance, and we moved to a back room where it would be easier to talk. We were settling in, flipping through our menus and munching on deep-fried shrimp crackers, when she cautioned, "Don't get hung up on just looking for Al Qaeda. You'll miss the bigger picture."

I was all ears. With her short blond bangs and glasses, Sidney looked like everybody's favorite fifth-grade teacher, the one all the boys fall madly in love with. In reality, she was a leading authority on Islamic fundamentalism and terror groups in Southeast Asia, and went about her job like the finest of detectives. Intelligence officials in the region generally acknowledged that Sidney routinely bested them at their own game. Resident news correspondents followed her meticulous reports on Jemaah Islamiyah like installment clues on the whereabouts of the Holy Grail, and occasionally gave her credit. Headed into unknown territory, I had devoured her work with the enthusiasm of a man clutching at a lifeline while being dragged behind an ocean liner.

"So where *do* you look?" I asked.

"There are a lot of ties between groups in South and Central Asia and Indonesia now that have nothing to do with Al Qaeda . . . or violence. But they still represent a growing fundamentalist Islam here."

"So?"

So it was important not to overplay Al Qaeda or Jemaah Islamiyah, she said. JI was important, organized, and dangerous. Al

Qaeda everybody thought they knew. But what Sidney's work suggested was that our Western template for interpreting international terrorism was badly in need of an overhaul.

Many of us in the West still pictured Al Qaeda as a case study from Harvard Business School—a transnational organization with a CEO figure at the top (bin Laden) presiding over a series of disciplined "profit centers" (JI being one), all moving in sync to orders from the head office. What Sidney's more refined—and decidedly more disturbing—model suggested was a world populated with multiple terror groups, each focusing on their own local goals and cooperating with others, including Al Qaeda, on tactics and strategy when it suited their purposes. (Others have since arrived at this view, but the fact is Sidney was among the first to get there.)

And that was only part of a bigger picture. If you wanted to understand where Islamic fundamentalism might be taking the world, you had to consider a general ferment that was grabbing hold all across Asia. On one level, it pitted millions of the area's traditionally tolerant Muslim moderates against growing numbers of generally peaceable but newly empowered Muslim conservatives. Mainly, it was a stark ideological split (and in broad Manichean terms, not wholly different from the deep divisions in the American body politic between those who support abortion, gay marriage, and gun control, and those who don't). Moderate Muslims favored democracy, equal rights for women and non-Muslims, and accommodation with the West. The Muslim "neo-cons," meanwhile, were aggressively pressing to convert Western-style legal systems to the tender mercies of Islamic law.

"There are a lot of factors at work," said Sidney. You had to consider that radicalization, to the extent it had taken place, was stronger among middle-class college kids than even the poor farm boys Norman and I had encountered on the *Bukit Siguntang*; how large amounts of money had coming sloshing in from wealthy Saudis eager to finance the spread of their fundamentalist Wahabi teachings; and how that in turn had affected the views of local preachers, "and the translation into Indonesian of more and more radical texts."

Sidney paused and smiled, as if at an obvious point. "And I don't think you can look at radical Islam in Indonesia without looking at manipulation by the [government] security forces."

Possibly delirious from jet lag, I began to picture Islamic extremism as a rich and complex jigsaw puzzle—or maybe a Jackson Pollock canvas, alive with crazy circles, sometimes interlocking, often not, but all seeming to move with a great erratic energy.

"In other words it's not complicated at all," I said.

Sidney laughed. But like a good teacher she kept quietly driving home her main point. The radicals were small in number relative to the size of the Islamic community as a whole, but in a country as big as Indonesia that meant there were still a lot of them out there, operating beyond the pale of the law, where they could do a lot of damage.

How great was the danger that the balance might tip, from the old-time moderate Islam Indonesia was famous for, in favor of its newer, angrier form?

"I don't know about the long term," said Sidney. Everything was now in play. "There is a growing conservatism here generally. But I don't think it's possible to say Indonesia is moving away from a capitalist economy. And that people become more overtly devout doesn't necessarily mean there's a danger of Islamic law being applied across the country."

On the other hand, she said, "You have pockets of very, very strong Islamic views where there is perceptible radicalism." Small numbers could get bigger given the right conditions—the sudden further plunge of an already weak economy, for example, or too much American pressure to go after bad guys who weren't seen locally as bad guys.

"Do people still think the Bali bombings were a CIA plot?" I asked.

Sidney smiled. Yes, wild stories had circulated. (One that intrigued Norman argued that the Kuta nightclubs had been demolished with a miniature, radiation-free nuclear device far beyond the technical capabilities of local bomb makers.) Thankfully, though, the atmosphere of tabloid titillation had died away now, Sidney said. The national police had appointed a genuinely respected and capable lead investigator, General I Made Pastika, a Balinese, who quickly set to work rounding up credible suspects and was methodically building his case. Trials were still a few months off, but already, said Sidney, "Many people think that those who were arrested for Bali are guilty."

And what of the existence of Jemaah Islamiyah?

"There's less acceptance for that," said Sidney, with a quick laugh, "and almost no acceptance of the idea that those arrested had any ties to international terrorism."

"So the Bush administration is right—Indonesia is in denial?"

Sidney shook her head. Indonesians weren't being pigheaded when they balked, for example, at evidence implicating Abu Bakar Bashir and the JI in the Bali bombings. "There's really been no evidence produced except from al-Faruq and a couple of other people, all of whom are in detention." Omar al-Faruq, you will remember, was Al Qaeda's alleged senior operative in Indonesia, whom the CIA was now sweating for information at an "undisclosed location" believed to be Bagram Air Base in Afghanistan.

Thanks to Suharto-era abuses, said Sidney, "The Indonesians have had enough experience with forced confessions" to be highly and properly suspicious of news from the jailhouse.

So what was the best way for Americans to view JI and Bashir, I wondered.

Bashir's blanket denials about the very existence of Jemaah Islamiyah notwithstanding, Sidney said, she'd been able to marshal evidence that not only did JI exist in fact, but that it was a well-organized subterranean organization with a clear military-style structure of divisions and subdivisions, and had been involved in various acts of political violence across Indonesia and throughout Southeast Asia. Yet there was very little evidence that JI was functioning in any way as a direct Al Qaeda subsidiary.[1]

---

1. A subsequent ICG report in August 2003 would conclude that while both Al Qaeda and Jemaah Islamiyah share the same radical jihadist philosophy, JI leaders sought to model themselves after Osama bin Laden, and "have almost certainly received direct financial support from al-Qaeda . . . [v]irtually all of [JI's] decision-making and much of its fund-raising has been conducted locally, and its focus, for all the claims about it wanting to establish a South East Asian caliphate, continues to be on establishing an Islamic state in Indonesia."

As we mopped up our spicy curries, Sidney said it wasn't at all clear to her that Bashir had even had a hand in planning the Bali attacks. Leads from her sources suggested that the emir had actually argued against the bombings on tactical grounds—not wanting to give his movement a black eye by killing fellow Muslims who would inevitably be among the victims. Hence Indonesian prosecutors had chosen to build their case on other fronts: Bashir's alleged involvement in the Christmas Eve bombings, as well as the alleged plot to assassinate Megawati and overthrow the government.

"We'll have to see what happens," said Sidney. Meanwhile, she added, "It might be interesting for you to try and visit Bashir's *pesantren*"—his boarding school—"in Ngruki. It's harder to drop in these days but you can try."

Her suggestion snapped me back into the here and now, and reminded me the purpose of my mission was far from theoretical. Still nervous about what lay ahead, but inspired by Sidney's infectious enthusiasm for her work in the face of threats and criticism, I said, "Okay, we'll give it try."

As we rose and walked out into the intense sunshine, I was feeling suddenly elated. Through my jet lag, over the steaming curries, and thanks to Sidney's advice, I could now "see" the journey unfolding before me. After spending a few days getting oriented in Jakarta, I'd travel to Bali to inspect the imprint left by the terror bombings, and then move on to the Islamic heartland in Central Java, now home to both Bashir's radical vision and the moderate traditions of Javanese Islam. If the real front line in the battle for the soul of Islam ran through the hearts and minds of millions of ordinary Indonesians, we'd be able to see its contours there.

While I was busy being inspired, however, Norman had slid even deeper into his funk. "Okay, out with it," I ordered when we'd paused over Mocha Frappuccinos at Jakarta's newest Starbucks outlet on our way back to the hotel.

Norman laughed dryly. Though awestruck by Sidney's masterly tour of the horizon, he said she had, in his humble opinion, failed to mention the one element that had been causing him to pace the midnight floor.

"And what element is that, pray tell?"

Well, said Norman, in his experience it wasn't only rich Arabs who were funding radical causes and getting Muslims all fired up locally. Members of Indonesia's wealthy business elite also played a role, manipulating the country's many grievances, if not for fun then surely for profit. Not infrequently they were said to funnel money to militant groups, for example, to stage violent protests aimed at persuading a competitor they really didn't want to build that factory in a particular neighborhood, after all.[2]

"When there's big money at stake," said Norman, "the big guys aren't about to let friendships or anything else get in the way if they're threatened. It's *The Godfather,* parts four through seven."

I could see where this was going. "And so you're concerned we'll stick our noses in the wrong places," I said, "and get nailed by this *hidden force?*"

"Exactly, Boss—the hidden force." From the way his eyes gleamed darkly, I could tell he liked the cloak-and-dagger sound of it.

Inspired by Norman's handy reminder of what we were up against, I pictured hope as frightened deer once again bounding for a sunless thicket. "Okay," I said, as if it were really possible in such a place as Indonesia, "let's just try and avoid the hidden force, then, shall we?"

That evening we drove across town to Norman's natural habitat, the trendy Kebayoran Baru district of Jakarta, where the coffeehouses and ferny, retro-chic bistros always remind me of California minus the blond hair. Climbing a clanging metal staircase, we entered an Italian-style café, which occupied a large glass box suspended over a

---

2. Norman was not alone in his concerns. As my friend John McBeth ably noted in the *Far Eastern Economic Review,* "In the eyes of its critics, [the dominant] Javanese culture is characterized by a feudalistic deference to leaders, creating a sense of fatalism among ordinary people, who feel they have little control over their own destiny. That leaves them open to manipulation by the wealthy political elite." And like elites anywhere in the world, business, political, or both, members of Indonesia's elite rarely failed to manipulate.

posh and very well-stocked English-language bookstore. As we stood near the doorway, a wiry young man, who looked to me to be all of about sixteen, waved casually to Norman from one of the tables.

"Hey, there's Reza," Norman said, waving back and smiling.

I was flabbergasted. This mere slip of a lad was our Islamic bureau chief? This was the basket into which Norman had, so to speak, dumped our collective eggs for safekeeping? With his shy grin, bushy black hair, and thick plastic-framed glasses riding atilt his nose, Reza looked like a high school techno-whiz temporarily locked out of the computer lab. But when he shook my hand in a firm grip and looked me squarely in the eye, I realized this fellow was no kid. Above the rows of dazzlingly white teeth and behind the bashful, smiling eyes was the wry, confident, cagey look of a veteran human campaigner.

I guess my mouth was still agape, though, because Norman, detecting possibly dangerous confusion on the part of the bule, rushed in to fill the gap with some surprising biographical detail. Reza, he blurted out without ceremony, had been kidnapped, jailed, and tortured by Suharto's fearsome Kopassus branch during the waning days of the old man's reign.

"Yah, is true," said Reza, smiling sheepishly, as if somehow embarrassed by the revelation. But when our spaghetti was served, Reza quickly got down to business. Twisting his noodles on his fork, he peered into my eyes and asked, "What is your motive?"

I blanched. Suddenly being on the receiving end of the Javanese eye exam unsettled me no end. What the hell does he mean by that? I thought. I met this guy five minutes ago, and he's questioning my motive? Does he think I'm CIA? Or just another ignorant bule out to paint Muslims in a bad light?

"Settle down, Boss," said Norman, who was reassuringly back to his old habit of reading my mind. "He just wants to know what you want to find out."

"Oh, heh, heh, well . . ." I said, flushing with embarrassment. I then explained in so many words that what I really wanted to understand was where Muslim anger came from and where it was taking Indonesia, and quite possibly the rest of the world as well.

Reza nodded approvingly. "Is okay," he said. If it was angry Muslims I wanted, he was ready to oblige. He had in fact already been trying to line up an interview with Abu Bakar Bashir. Even though police had arrested the emir a few days after the Bali bombings, and he remained in a Jakarta jail cell, Bashir often spoke with supporters by cell phone and entertained a steady stream of visitors.

"You've contacted Bashir?" I said, gulping on my tomato sauce.

Reza looked at me quizzically, as if to say, "You just told me that's why you came to Indonesia, didn't you?"

"You want see Bashir, right?"

"Well, sure, I mean . . ."

"Okay, we try," Reza said with finality. If the kingpin wasn't available, there were others associated with Jemaah Islamiyah who could give us a glimpse inside the mind-set of the group they claimed did not exist. And of course no trip would be complete without a visit to Bashir's Islamic boarding school near Solo, just as Sidney had recommended.

"Of course not," I said.

"Now, for Jaffar Umar Thalib . . ."

The sudden mention of our old shipmate from Spice Islands days sent an involuntary shiver through my pasta fork as I pictured before me the scowling face and thundering hairy calves of the stocky cleric on the good ship *Bukit Siguntang.* "You have contacts with Jaffar, too?"

"Of course I know Jaffar," Reza said, blinking, as he pushed his glasses back on his nose.

"But I thought he was out of business," I said. I'd read where the redoubtable Laskar Jihad commander had eventually, if belatedly in the view of many, been put on trial for inciting a murderous riot in Ambon. Then, less than a week after the Bali bombings, Jaffar had made the surprise announcement that he was forthwith disbanding the Jihad. (When I tried to confirm this by accessing the official Web site, laskarjihad.org.id, where I'd occasionally gone to check up on features like "Jihad Troopers at a Glance," I got instead a pop-up ad featuring a zaftig young bule woman in a tight-fitting T-shirt and work belt advertising a newfangled power tool.) Having proven himself pretty much a disappointment in the running for the title of "Osama of the East," and now supplanted by Abu Bakar Bashir, the international media had for all intents and purposes dropped Jaffar.

"Yes, Jaffar got big problem," said Reza, but in his opinion the condition was only temporary. The verdict in Jaffar's trial, expected any day now, was widely anticipated to be an acquittal on all counts (which is exactly how it turned out). Meanwhile, with war looming in Iraq, the government had put militant Islamic groups on notice—violent behavior or public shenanigans of any kind would be harshly dealt with. It was no secret that the United States, Australia, Singapore, Malaysia, the Philippines, and other interested parties in the region had been quietly seething since 9/11 over Indonesia's failure to arrest terrorist suspects wanted under international writs or to so much as acknowledge the existence of Jemaah Islamiyah. After Bali, and all the bule deaths on Indonesian soil, however, the government in Jakarta had no choice but to at least appear to clamp down on its more notorious rabble-rousers.

According to Reza, then, Jaffar was most likely just lying low. As evidence he pointed to the fact that the Laskar Jihad's parent organization, the Forum Komunikasi wal Sunnah wal Jamaah, was still operating openly, with branch offices in some seventy cities across the country, its own popular boarding schools, and a weekly magazine to spread its message. Meanwhile Jaffar was still thick with Megawati's Islamist vice president, Hamzah Haz, and other friends high in the political pecking order. Most people still tended to believe Jaffar's repeated disclaimers about a relationship, financial or otherwise, with Al Qaeda, but doubts had even emerged on that score. When you talked about a hidden force, the Laskar Jihad seemed to have most of the major bases covered.

"Jaffar come back after it get quiet, I think," said Reza. "So we need to call Jaffar." Reza picked up his cell phone and started dialing.

"You have Jaffar's phone number?"

"Sure, personal hand phone number," said Reza, smiling wickedly, as he rose and left the dining area for a quieter place outside the glass box.

I must say, I was suddenly very impressed with Norman's choice for Islamic bureau chief, and Norman seemed energized by his presence, too. But there were still a few areas of concern. Though Reza's open, honest gaze had scored highly on my bule's version of the Javanese eye test, I'd detected an area therein that my Nordic stare couldn't easily penetrate, a place protected by the man's sly humor. Also, I noted, Reza had yet to speak openly of his own political views, and to that extent remained an enigma.

"Reza seems very chummy with the radical all-stars," I said offhandedly to Norman.

"Takes one to know one," he said as he punched the dial of his cell phone. Then catching my concerned expression while his call connected, he said, "Just joking, Boss."

A few minutes later Reza returned to the table smiling and shaking his head. "Jaffar say no press interview now. Maybe next month."

"Next month," I cried—and this is where the true lunacy of a journalistic hack comes into play. In a space of less than five minutes I'd traveled the full distance between fearing Jaffar might say yes to an interview, requiring me sit down at close quarters and look him in the eye, to feeling absolutely indignant that he'd said no.

I am quite sure I appeared to Reza just then as the most fickle, mysterious bule ever to come down the pike, but at least he seemed to approve of my rapid conversion to my own reporting cause.

"Is okay," he said. "I think maybe Jaffar just get call from government people, so we keep trying—sure." He then added, his imp's grin playing at the corners of his mouth, "I fax Jaffar copy of your biosheet and phone number."

I gulped and stuttered, betraying my ridiculous nervousness, while Reza and Norman laughed and slapped the table.

"Don't worry, Boss," said Norman, "Reza's just giving you a little taste of that famous anarchist humor."

12

FEAR ITSELF

Two mornings later I rose at three-thirty, and by four Norman and I were in a taxi racing through the dark, empty streets of south Jakarta. Reza hadn't yet produced any of his famously angry men, but he'd got things off to an impressive start nonetheless by arranging a meeting with Indonesia's controversial former president, Abdurrahman Wahid. And because Wahid was notoriously disorganized, the idea was to hustle out and nab him for a talk before he slipped into the mosque for his morning prayers.

Still on baby watch at home, Reza had sent an attractive young woman from his office to guide us. Her name was Sinda. Tall and slender, she wore a tasteful jacket and trousers, and had the fresh good looks that give a man hope for the world at such an early hour.

"Now that's the kind of woman you should cultivate," I whispered to Norman when Sinda was busy discussing directions with the driver, but he only rolled his eyeballs at my sincere and helpful suggestion, and muttered comically, "Too wholesome, Boss."

The early hour added to a sense of adventure as we drove out from the city center, and the big buildings gave way to vast acreages of low-rise houses and narrow, twisting streets, where figures moved in the charcoal shadows of roadside markets, brandishing ghostly bunches of vegetables, a face flaring now and then in the flame of a cigarette lighter. But the mood quickly deflated when, rolling to a stop at a heavy wooden gate, a guard poked his head out and told Sinda that Brother Wahid had already left home to go jogging.

Jogging? He had to be kidding. Everybody in Indonesia knew that the pudgy ex-president, now in his middle sixties, was legally blind and lame from the effects of diabetes. Be that as it may, the guard thought we might intercept the elusive jogger in the vicinity of a mosque a mile or so farther on through the labyrinth. Off we drove.

Wahid is the great Trickster figure of Indonesian politics. The curious father of the post-Suharto democracy, he entered office in October 1999, riding high on a wave of reformasi euphoria, only to be impeached on competency issues less than two years later. Still in all, Gus Dur, or loosely, honored older brother, as he was universally known, remained a figure of huge esteem and affection in the Muslim community and therefore was a man of some considerable influence.

The son and grandson of famous *kiai,* or Islamic religious leaders, Gus Dur was raised a "church prince" in whom the two potent streams of old-fashioned Indonesian Islam perfectly, if erratically, fused. First, as the ex-chairman of the moderate Nahdlatul Ulama, or NU, the country's biggest Muslim lay organization, which claimed some forty million members, he had tapped the temporal power of an automatically large and adoring constituency.

But the Javanese loved him all the more for his ostensible links with what Norman called the old-time mumbo-jumbo. For millions, Gus Dur, wily, lumpish, and jokey, was the spitting image of Semar, the mischievous Javanese dwarf god, who legend said jealously guarded the dark cave at the exact center of creation,

Norman's beloved Anchor of Java—that spot, as you will remember, that lies between the cities of Solo and Jogjakarta, and moors the mundane world to the parallel realm of the spirits.

In a culture where power is seen to move mysteriously, attaching to its holder by means of a *wahyu,* or divine revelation, Gus Dur did little to discourage his mythic status. Quite the contrary. Like Sukarno and Suharto before him, he made a show of visiting Java's subterranean nexus, there to commune with the ancestral spirits amid flickering candles and the occasional side-winding snake— exactly the sort of thing that made Islamic purists spin with holy indignation but the eclectic Javanese ate with a spoon. (Gus Dur's reputation was only slightly tarnished when word got around that the tongues speaking to him in the cave on at least one occasion came not from the gods but from a tape recorder prankish aides had planted among the rocks.)

It was in keeping with his Trickster role that Wahid rose to the presidency at a moment of national turmoil that he himself had helped create. That he accomplished by beating out Madam Megawati, the heavily favored candidate in the parliamentary runoff in 1999, after wooing the vote of those Islamist delegates who were convinced on principle that a woman, though technically Muslim, could not possibly run a Muslim country. The result was several weeks of violent turmoil during which disappointed Megawati sup- porters torched government buildings and shopping centers in Solo and other Javanese cities and set hundreds of taxis on fire in tourist- friendly Bali, the aftermath of which Norman and I had experi- enced firsthand in our earlier travels.

Still in all, Wahid's Trickster energy had held the fragile democ- racy together, if at times through sheer eccentricity. Hailed as the long-awaited Islamic wise man, a moderate for all seasons, he had hardly taken office when, to the delight and confusion of many of his supporters, he left the country spinning in comprehensive com- munal violence while he embarked on an extended tour of foreign capitals.

"Genius!" one respected political commentator told me at the time in an ironic tone. " 'You see there,' people say, 'he instinctively knows that things are too hot to handle at home, so he goes overseas to wait for them to cool down!' "

The honeymoon was short-lived. The crunch came when Wahid displayed his serious side, and went after the military, determined to end its chronic abuses of power and crack its hold on national politics. Needless to say, the military did not respond with enthusiasm. And that is when senior officers moved to stymie their president, refusing, among other things, to stop Jaffar Umar Thalib and other renegades from stirring up all that trouble in the Moluccas in the spring of 2000.

Less heroic were some of Wahid's personal habits. A doctor friend who visited him in Jakarta's equivalent of the Oval Office told me she'd been startled to find the place hung with drying underwear and littered with candy wrappers, the latter a sign the president was neglecting his diabetes. An embarrassingly sloppy scandal broke when Wahid's personal masseur ran off with $4 million in government funds. Throughout it all no evidence was ever turned up that lovable old Gus Dur had knowingly participated in any chicanery, but even his staunch supporters began to have serious doubts about his management style.

Things got wild. Voted from office by parliament, Wahid refused to vacate the presidential palace, and made veiled and quixotic threats about his many followers in Java's Islamic hinterlands rising up in revolt. When the faithful failed to rise, Wahid tempestuously dumped the gasping baby of democratic reform into the lap of his vice president and successor, Megawati. Smarter than many people gave her credit for, Megawati quickly dialed back on military reforms. (As Sukarno's daughter, she was no doubt keenly aware of the fact that the military had not only ousted her father but, ultimately, helped oust the ouster, Suharto, as well.) Having restored relations with the generals, she retired behind her perpetual half-smile, projecting the image of a distant queenly mother (incidentally, her nickname, Mega, means "cloud" in Indonesian), floating above the danger and mess of decision-making as the country lapsed deeper into crisis.

And so it was that when I arrived back in Indonesia this time, in

January 2003, I'd found Indonesia plunged into one of its most confused and contentious political seasons ever as it faced pivotal presidential and parliamentary elections again in 2004. A report issued by a respected watchdog group had just come to the rather breathtaking conclusion that Megawati's government, if not the woman herself, was even more corrupt than the Suharto regime. Over two hundred mostly new political parties were actively jockeying to give her the electoral heave-ho. (And of course Abu Bakar Bashir was facing trial on charges of plotting to have her rubbed out.) Moreover, while fundamentalist Islamic parties had won only fifteen percent of the votes in the last elections in 1999, and held roughly a quarter of the seats in the assembly, dozens of newly energized Muslim groups were aggressively vying to expand their numbers, and in the process pull the political center farther toward the Islamic right.

And it was precisely therein that many observers saw the absolute greatest danger to the future of Indonesia's democracy and hence its stability—that the Islamists would engage in political jujitsu, using the new democratic freedoms to undermine democratic freedom by eventually winning enough votes to impose their beloved shariah. In short, like most times in Indonesia, it was a uniquely perilous period, when many things hung in the balance. And now, true to form, Wahid, who many considered genially cuckoo but was in fact a shrewd old fox, was planning a comeback run against Megawati, which not even former supporters thought made any sense at all.

We were still riding around in circles through the dark, mazelike lanes, looking for the jogging ex-president, and hopelessly lost, when the rising sun began washing the tumbled skyline and khaki-colored stucco walls with a delicate pinkish light the color of fresh-cut watermelon. I had suggested we call it quits when Norman, his Javanese antennae picking up signals denied the visiting bule, said, "Okay, Boss, but let's try just one more street."

And sure enough, when we turned the corner, there was the gnome-king of Indonesian politics shuffling his feet along the asphalt in the cool of the morning, supported by a sturdy aide-de-camp. Sinda immediately went all fluttery, as if in the presence of a rock star. I got pretty excited, too, when Gus Dur, huffing and puffing, cast sightless eyes on me and said, "Go wait over there behind the mosque."

Twenty minutes later the sound of feet shuffling up the alley heralded Wahid's arrival. Steered into position by his aides, he plunked down heavily in an old leather armchair that was held together with pieces of duct tape and sat there blinking and catching his breath. He had the look of an amiable old toad from a Brothers Grimm fairy tale. Not knowing how much time I had, I got to the point, asking Wahid what he thought of America's view of Islam after 9/11.

"Dark," he chortled. He then paused to unhurriedly clear his sinus passages with a series of loud, wet snuffling sounds. Learning I was from Manhattan, he made a wildly obscure joke about the seventies singing group The Manhattan Transfer, and ticked off his favorite American writers—Saul Bellow, John Steinbeck, and Chaim Potok.

"I especially liked Potok in *The Promise*," said the Muslim preacher, snuffling with special emphasis on the prominently Jewish writer, and I knew I was being spun, but charmingly.

Fixing his eyes on a spot over my left shoulder, Wahid summed up recent Indonesian political history like a chthonic David Letterman: "We had Suharto's infamous *New* Order, yah?" he said. Then there was his hapless interim successor, Mohammad Habibie, a gear-loose inventor by trade, who was remembered for "*dis*-order"! (Wahid conveniently excluded his own administration, which most tellings of the popular joke labeled "*out of* order.")

"What about Megawati?" I asked.

"*Too many* orders. Ha! Ha!"

In keeping with the local habit of changing moods like the weather, Wahid could switch on whim from lightheartedness to gravity. Frowning, he pointedly reminded me that Indonesia was not the Middle East, and said he felt Americans should have the good sense to make that distinction. Indonesia might have more Muslims than any other country on earth, but it was a secular country, not a religious state—the chief motor for Islam was in a civil society that also fostered democracy, political parties of every stripe, and cultural freedom.

"My youngest daughter paints her hair," Wahid blurted out, laughing. "Yah, sometimes red! Ha, ha, ha!"

But in the wake of the Bali bombings and all, didn't Americans have the right to be worried about people like Abu Bakar Bashir?

"Yah, ha," said Wahid, with a dismissive flap of his hand. Bashir, I was given to understand, was an historical accident—a creature churned up by Suharto's Darth Vader parenting, as it were. The dark father's brutality had forced Islamic activists underground, where they formed cells not unlike the Islamic Brotherhood in Egypt. Later, in the eighties, when Suharto felt his popular support slipping, he opened up the trapdoor and invited Muslim fundamentalists into the political inner sanctum.

"That resulted in a flourishing of Islamic hard-liners," said Wahid. "But extremists are a minority. Less than five percent would like to have the state Islamicized."

But in a country as big as Indonesia that worked out to roughly eleven million people—still a danger, I would have thought.

"Oh, yah," said Wahid. "Because the hard-liners are good in organization—ha, ha." They had financial support from rich sheiks in the Middle East, and training in ideology and tactics. But the main problem in Indonesia, he said, "is the government fears the fundamentalists. That's why it never took any action against them . . . before Bali."

Megawati was in a fearful bind, it was true. She'd been caught squarely between Washington's desire for her to step up efforts against Muslim extremists, on the one hand, and the actions of her own vice president, Hamzah Haz, who vigorously defended them. Head of the fundamentalist United Development Party, Haz hadn't only stated that he hoped the 9/11 attacks would "cleanse America of its sins," but publicly courted the radical all-stars, Bashir and Jaffar Umar Thalib, even visiting Jaffar when he was briefly behind bars. Trying to split the difference had made Megawati look unsteady.

The first foreign leader to visit George Bush at the White House after 9/11, she pledged Indonesia's support in GWOT, and then, returning home, was quickly obliged to cover her tracks. Speaking at a Jakarta mosque, she criticized the American-led invasion of Afghanistan, saying, "No individual, group or government has the right to catch terrorist perpetrators by attacking the territory of another country."

The upcoming 2004 elections, the first direct popular vote for a president in Indonesia's history, provided an opportunity to fix all that, said Wahid. A decisive leader with a strong mandate (could he really be seeing himself when he said such things?) could deal effectively with the radicals. "Not with violence," he said, "but with so-called definite actions—for example, outlawing certain organizations because they are against our law.

"But we cannot differentiate Islam from democracy because Islam is for democracy," said Wahid—spin, spin. His own political party, the National Awakening Party, worked "to strengthen Islamic society not an Islamic state." Meanwhile fundamentalist Islam was fundamentally unworkable as a state philosophy, and eventually would sink even in Saudi Arabia, which currently had the Koran as its constitution. "A constitution with six thousand six hundred and sixty-six articles. Crazy! Ha-ha-ha!"

So this was really a cultural revolution? I asked.

"Oh, yah, ha, ha, and very crucial for us. If political Islam takes over, then we go back to square one." Wahid reminded me that, way back in the 1940s, Islamists had outlined their principles for an Islamic state in a document called the Jakarta Charter, only to be overridden by Sukarno, Hatta, and other founding fathers who, though Muslim, favored a more tolerant, eclectic approach in keeping with majority Java's easygoing traditions.

Suddenly all these years later, said Wahid, "The moderates"—the country's millions of *abangan,* or so-called ID-card Muslims—"have discovered that in being lenient, being nonactive in Islamic affairs, they have given ground to those radicals."

For the government openly to repress radical beliefs, however, not only would go against Islamic teachings, he said, but would cre-

ate sympathy among moderates for militants like Bashir. It was precisely that mechanism the Americans didn't seem to understand.
Referred anger at the Bush administration and its policies in the
Middle East was already having a broadly negative effect. Even moderate politicians had blasted America as "a Godless society, a materi-
alistic society, an antisocial society, no family ties, not God-fearing,
all those things," said Wahid.

"Baseless," he sniffed. "I know America. Ha, ha, ha. I know
America! No people go to church more than the Americans. Everywhere Americans try to understand life as such and provide assis-
tance to people. Not only in material ways, but also by taking people
to their homes so they know the true American life. I can't say the
Americans have a perfect way of life but it's a tolerant way of life."

"But the view of America has darkened," I said.

"Yah, because the Americans are afraid of the radicals they
overdo some things," said Wahid—just as they had managed to over-
react to a real-enough threat of Soviet aggression in the 1950s
unleashing on American society the needless, unholy terror of the
McCarthy anti-Communist witch-hunts.

But after 9/11 didn't people have a right to be afraid? I asked.

"Yah, of course," cried Wahid. "But if Americans think all
Indonesians are extremists, or that radicals outnumber the moderates, it means they aren't seeing the world clearly."

Wahid snuffled and chortled, and observed in his friendly uncle
manner that Americans so easily forget the *realpolitik* behind the
romance of their own revolutionary mission in the world. It was a
plain fact, he argued, that the United States had a history of working
with authoritarian regimes to promote its meat-and-potatoes global
interests—in Iraq under Saddam, Indonesia under Suharto, take
your pick.

It was therefore inevitable, Wahid said, that people saw this "ten-
dency to put corporate interests first" substantially strengthened
under a president like George Bush. If such American blindness
deepened the misapprehensions about the exercise of U.S. power in
the world, Wahid warned, blinking his eyelids and staring into space,

"Then Indonesians will have big differences with the United States, including me."

Wahid shrugged. Americans talked nice on the surface about Islam being a peace-loving religion and all. But deep down there was fear, suspicion, and ignorance. "So this is the iron curtain dividing the world now," he said—a subliminal divide separating Islam from the West, and one that can't be marketed away or defeated by bombs and bullets.

While I listened to Wahid cackle and snort, I couldn't help but think that this man so many now dismissed as an archeccentric was actually talking sense. Nearly everybody I'd met in Jakarta so far was venting over a series of documentary films, recently produced and distributed by the U.S. State Department, and featuring Muslims in America speaking rosily about their lives in the Land of the Free and the Home of the Brave. Shown with fanfare by the U.S. embassy in Jakarta, the films had been widely interpreted as an insult to the intelligence and greeted with hoots and derision. Even our attempts at benign propaganda were making people mad.

Yes, Wahid almost had me, but then he spun one rotation too far. "The United States should develop the courage to combat its fears," he said, in the tradition of great Americans like Harry Truman and John F. Kennedy.

I waited for the punch line, and here it came.

"As Franklin Roosevelt said," Gus Dur intoned cheerily, raising his finger in the air, "the only thing we have to fear is fear itself!"

Fear appeared to be on holiday at the Plaza Indonesia, a gleaming upscale shopping mall in the center of town. More than forty million Indonesians may have been living in abject poverty, and several times that number struggled daily to make ends meet, but here amid the trailing red-and-white paper peonies and other decorations put out for the upcoming Chinese New Year holiday, life was sweet and cool. Families clogged pricey restaurants. Kids wearing their ball caps in reverse, in the American gangsta rapper-style, bombed around the brightly lighted concourses and filled up the video arcades. At one upscale smoke shop, you could buy a good Cuban cigar for the equivalent of thirty dollars, or what a city minibus driver made in two weeks. Norman told me there was a six-month waiting list for the latest model Porsche at the nearby dealership. (Don't you really hate when that happens?)

But the eye deceived. Indonesians of Chinese ancestry owned and operated many of these shops, as they owned and operated much of the economy in general—less than three percent of the population, they control roughly three-quarters of Indonesia's private wealth. Thus beating up on the Chinese in times of crisis had long since been a favored national pastime. They were the main victims of riots that erupted in April 1998, as Suharto clung to power, and out-and-out thugs, many belonging to private Islamic militias, had torched thousands of Chinese businesses; an estimated 1,100 people had died in Jakarta alone. The Chinese were still irrationally and deeply resented, and so I admired them for making merry when their luck was with them—it took guts to be a conspicuous consumer in Indonesia.

Though Jakarta managed to put a brave face forward in its fancy shopping malls, however, the ambient anger never failed to percolate through. Pushing through the crowds, past yet another Starbucks outlet ("Okay for the bule," said Norman dismissively), and into a local favorite called Tomorrow, I noticed that the traffic circle on the other side of the big fishbowl windows was engulfed by a throng of young people waggling picket signs and loudly decrying recent dramatic rises in government-controlled telephone and electricity rates. The youth inhabiting Tomorrow, meanwhile, seemed to be focused mainly on themselves. A dispirited-looking crew, they were dressed in strategically ripped blue jeans and hip-hop couture, the girls in unisex shirts exposing flat, bare midriffs showing off the occasional gold navel ring.

"Who are all these people?" I said.

According to Norman, I was looking at representatives of Indonesia's moneyed elite in all its glory—the sons and daughters of local business tycoons, a general or two, maybe the odd highly placed government official. "They're the young and the aimless, Boss—just like me."

"Don't kid yourself, Norman," I said. "You're not that young anymore."

"Thanks, Boss. You always know how to cheer me up."

I'd just shelled out a minibus driver's weekly salary for a light lunch and a round of chalky brown cappuccinos, when Norman's cell phone went off. It was Reza. Antonia's labor had entered its strenuous phase, and our Islamic bureau chief, now padding the corridors of the local maternity ward, was still gamely trying to direct what, thanks to Norman, we now referred to as the Radical Mystery Tour. What a guy!

Covering the mouthpiece, Norman said, "Reza says there's a big fundamentalist political rally getting started across the street at the Hotel Indonesia." Off we went.

The three-minute stroll from the Plaza Indonesia was like walking into a time warp, from the familiar, globalized world of McDonald's and Starbucks to the feisty, struggling, tumultuous third world of the 1960s. Officially opened by Sukarno in 1962, the Hotel Indonesia was the country's first international-class hotel, and a symbol of the intense nationalistic pride of a day when Sukarno, strutting in his black peci cap and sunglasses, famously told the West, "Go to hell with your aid," while he simultaneously courted the Kennedys and the Khrushchevs, flirted with Jackie (possibly even with Nina Petrovna), and alternately gave the world the business and turned on the charm.

On this day, however, a sign in the lobby announced the MEETING FOR THE DECLARATION OF THE NATIONAL SALVATION FRONT, and so Norman and I rode a creaking elevator the size of a large telephone booth up to the eighth floor and entered the Bali Room.

For the inconveniently large and certifiably claustrophobic, like me, it was a scene straight out of a birth-trauma nightmare. The room was packed to its palmy and peeling wallpaper with hundreds of sweating, jostling bodies, acrid with cigarette smoke, and throbbing with angry, pent-up emotion. Midway through the crowd, at a long table, sat half a dozen speakers basking in the sticky glare of the television lights. Holding forth at the moment, cracking a joke in a mellow, reedy voice, was a darkly handsome man in a turban and flowing desert robes. His punch line, delivered in a tone of sly calculation, sent a tremor of churlish laughter through the room.

"Habib Rizieq Shihab," whispered Norman, and despite the sloppy heat a little chill shot through me. Reza was working to set up a meeting with this outspoken, anti-Western cleric, and frankly, I was dreading it. Pundits belittled Rizieq and his organization, the Islamic Defenders Front, or FPI, as little more than a gang of common street toughs with fancy Islamic pretensions. According to inside sources, the FPI had been set up in 1998 at the behest of a senior police official who wanted to use the group as a tool to keep order in the chaos of Suharto's demise. Using Islamic youth gangs to put the stick about was a time-honored practice in Indonesia, and the cognoscenti wrote off the FPI as a typical bunch of hooligans, dregs of the Jakarta slums, who went around smashing bars and restaurants that had the temerity to serve liquor during the Ramadan holy month, while undertaking the odd strong-arm job for the cops.

But while the experts scoffed, Rizieq had used his charisma and a laser-guided orator's tongue to build the FPI into a private militia claiming some 25,000 men. However accurate the numbers, Rizieq's ability to mobilize the urban poor and fill the streets with thousands of rowdy demonstrators after the U.S.-led attack on Afghanistan had helped lead to the temporary closing of the U.S. embassy. Arrested in the general crackdown after the Bali bombings and jailed on charges of "instigating mass hatred," Rizieq was released the following month into house arrest, which the imam, as his demanding public schedule showed, was interpreting liberally.

Like the Laskar Jihad, the FPI shrewdly announced an "indefinite freeze" on its activities after Bali. But now, three months later, and with war pending in Iraq, Rizieq had recently declared that the time for diplomacy was over, and was actively recruiting fighters to battle the American infidel on holy ground. Watching him sitting there in the billowing heat, looking chic and cool in his desert gear, that distinctive voice of his vibrating like an oboe, there was something about him that struck me as feral and dangerous, and I was praying Reza would have the good sense to set up our meeting on a patch of well-traveled public ground like a hotel coffee shop.

Meanwhile it took no big-time reporting skills to see that some interesting political diplomacy was at work in the Bali Room. Seated next to Rizieq was a man widely regarded as a right-wing political kingmaker and a sophisticated former bagman for the Suharto organization. Next to him was Megawati's younger sister, Rahmawati Sukarnoputri, who'd had a falling-out with her presidential sibling and was now apparently ready to take it to the streets. Then Norman gasped and gave me a surprised elbow. "Look who's here, Boss," he said, nodding toward the man at the far end of the table.

I was thunderstruck. Sitting there, blinking his eyes patiently at the cameras, dressed in a snappy batik shirt and was Gus Dur, the man who that very morning had spoken to me of the ruinous dangers of letting the wild horses of political Islam out to ramp around in the country's politics. And now here he was seated a dozen feet from one of the most rambunctious of stallions of them all.

"Keeping your options open is a way of life in Indonesia," quipped Norman, when he saw my mouth hanging open. (When a reporter later asked Wahid what he was doing there, he reminded his questioner that he was a blind man and therefore didn't realize where his handlers had taken him. Ha ha.)

Rizieq was obviously a gifted talker. After lavishing witty praise on Gus Dur, who if memory serves had tried to have him thrown in jail on at least one occasion, Rizieq cried, "Let's take to the streets with the students!"

The preacher's smoothly haranguing words were met with angry shouts of approval and raised fists, and the room now literally rocked with negative energy. Conscious from the occasional toxic stare that I was the only bule in the Bali Room, I was edging toward an open window and some fresh air, when a voice behind me said, "You from the States?"

I turned to see an old man in a red baseball cap smiling at me from under a large gray mustache. Tjahyadi Nugroho was a Christian pastor and the leader of one of Indonesia's many tiny new political parties, a small flock grazing on the far left of the country's political acreage.

"Everybody is just so frustrated now," he said, shedding some light on the afternoon's strange chemistry. "We've come together to make common cause against the government"—groups not only from the fundamentalist right but the socialist left, Christians as well as Muslims.

Friendly and opinionated, and speaking the colloquial but dated American of my father's generation, Tjahyadi reminded me of a charming old guy you might run into down at the local VFW hall in a small West Coast town. I told him how I'd experienced the heady euphoria of democratic reform in Indonesia following Suharto's downfall. "What happened?" I asked.

"Democracy has gone nowhere," Tjahyadi said with a rueful shrug. "Everything's just completely stalled."

As he spoke, a stubby man with a barrel chest stuffed into a greasy sweatshirt was suddenly shouting out his grievances from the audience, and then Megawati's sister grabbed the mike and the room exploded in cheering shouts.

I was enjoying my conversation with Tjahyadi, and grateful to him for being nice to me. But the emotional pitch in the room did seem to be working toward a breakpoint of some kind, and when Norman sidled up behind me, and said, "Time to go, Boss," I immediately turned and followed him to the elevators. An expert in the psychology of amok, which, like road rage in America, remains an unhappy fact of life in tropical Asia, Norman always knew when it was high time to scram.

We threaded our way through the student protesters, who were lining up military-style for another assault on the traffic circle, and were reentering the Plaza Indonesia for a restorative latte, when Norman's cell phone rang. It was Reza again, this time with the happy news that he and Antonia were the parents of a brand-new baby daughter, Beatrice—*Be-ah-tree-cheh.*

"Way to go, Rez," I shouted from the background, while Norman made happy noises into the phone. But when he rang off, my faithful sidekick plunged into as deep and complicated a Freudian hole as any affecting the country of his birth.

At length and sulkily, he said, "I want to be happy for my friend, but it makes me think of my own little daughter all the way over there in Europe."

"Of course it does," I said sympathetically.

"Am I a bad person, Boss?"

"No, for chrissakes, Norman," I said. Poor guy, he needed some cheering up. "Come on, I'll buy you some sushi at that fancy bule hotel across the street and we can talk things over, if you want."

Norman nodded okay, and then added, dolefully, "I think the women have made a weakling out of me, Boss." But by the time we'd transited the pedestrian overpass above gassy and fuming Jalan Thamrin, the main thoroughfare, and found a table in Tokyo Joe's, my inquiring partner surprised me by shifting topics.

"What makes the bule so bitter?" he asked. He was remembering a red-faced old Australian businessman we'd once overheard ranting at a group of cowering Indonesian colleagues in the hotel's nearby coffee lounge in a voice that sounded like a band saw cutting through sheet metal.

"Jesus, I don't know, Norman," I said. "Too far east too long, maybe?"

Norman laughed. He knew I spoke with some authority on the frustrations of the perennial outsider, having lived from early manhood to my early middle age in Asia. "Maybe you wake up one day and realize, deep down, that you're just another bule with a bloated ego and nothing much in the way of substance to back it up. It does tend to piss you off."

Norman grimaced. "I feel that way about Indonesia—and it's my own country," he said. "I play a role, hobnob with the elite, but in the end I'm just playing a game. Bule women used to think it was cool to have an Indonesian boyfriend. But it's no longer cool to be in Indonesia. It's just frustrating and scary."

I thought what a tragedy it was when a country couldn't put to proper use its paramount resource—the young, the bright, and the ambitious. "Maybe you need to leave Indonesia for a while and try your luck someplace else."

"Isn't that copping out?"

"Not if you come back in a better position to help your country."

Norman stared dreamily in the direction of the sushi counter. "You know, when I was studying martial arts I developed this thing where, if I really put my mind to something I wanted to accomplish I just knew it would work out, and it did."

"Zen and the art of Norman?"

"Don't laugh, Boss," he said. "Like when we were on board the *Bukit Siguntang* with the Laskar Jihad. I couldn't guarantee it of course, but I just had this strong feeling that everything would come out all right."

"So is that Zen, a triumph of will, or just youth, I wonder. Youth and luck?"

"I don't know, Boss," said Norman, slipping into his funk again. "Do you think I'm overconfident?"

I looked at him, worried now that if this agonized soul-searching went chronic, Norman was going to be no damn good to me whatsoever. But if the fundamentalists could try and turn the tables in politics, I could play a little mental jujitsu on Norman.

"Too confident?" I said, stroking my chin sagaciously. "Why, I'd be inclined to say just the opposite."

"Not confident?"

"Bingo."

When Norman stared at me truculently, I felt bad and tried to blunt my verbal harpoon by saying, "Well, you know, sometimes you just can't do what you want to do where you want to do it, no matter how hard you try." I told him about a documentary film project I'd spent months trying to get off the ground. "But in the end, all that effort—*and will*—didn't triumph. Everything just fizzled. You move on."

Norman set his jaw. "Then you really didn't *want* to do it," he snapped. And from the way he said it I could tell he was suddenly feeling not nearly so depressed as before.

"Referred anger toward the father figure will get you nowhere," I said to myself, but I was secretly delighted. The Norman of old walked amongst us once more.

13

FATWA

It was the long Chinese New Year weekend and I spent the holiday trying to avoid my hotel. A flash flood had forced my favorite lodging, the elegant Regent Jakarta, to shut down temporarily, and Norman had booked me, at his usual startlingly deep discount, into a hotel favored by the foreign press corps, but on a floor badly in need of renovation. Staying there was like camping in a swamp. In the evenings, hunched over my computer, working on my notes, I was serenaded by buzzing Jakarta mosquitoes. Having levitated through layers of pollution to the fourteenth floor, they attacked woozily but no longer had the energy to bite. The night, on the other hand, was ruled by a lively race of bedbugs, which tattooed my neck and arms with ferocious postprandial welts. Meanwhile the lobby intermittently filled with banging gongs and lion dancers designed to drive out evil spirits.

And so I moved around the city, taking meals with old and trusted friends. A reunion dinner in a fashionable, dimly lighted nook with Tanya and Ramon Alwi (now released from his internal exile in the Bandas and back living happily in Jakarta) was marred by a cell phone call alerting us to the news that the space shuttle *Challenger* had crashed over Palestine, Texas. ("Palestine?! You see, it's karma!" cried Ramon, reflecting the popular view that America's technology-driven hubris invited supernatural retaliation.)

There was a long, rollicking lunch at a Japanese teppanyaki grill with Papa Des. Hulking and energetic in a luminous blue hula shirt, the king of the Bandas greeted me by throwing up his hands, and crying, "An American! You're the first one I've seen in weeks!"

But his good spirits had an edge. What he was really asking me was why Americans were behaving so spinelessly. "Of course you lost a lot of people on September eleven," he said. "Horrible! But now it looks like Osama has won the war!"

"How so, Des?"

Disturbingly, Des informed me he'd been keeping close tabs on developments in the U.S. by watching Fox News, which, through the mixed blessing of satellite TV, was now available locally. He said he was very concerned about the fearful, jingoistic tone. I suggested he might seek to balance out his menu of opinion, but he waved me off.

"The Americans seem to be going crazy," he said, and all the shouting for war was only creating more indirect support for the fundamentalists in Indonesia. "We can contain these radical people, Tracy!" cried Des. "Besides, ultimately only stupid Muslims will follow these guys, I think."

I was hoping Des was right. But when he told me over our green tea ice cream that he had it on good authority from sources connected with events in the Middle East that Iraq possessed no weapons of mass destruction, I had to laugh inwardly. Like many Americans, I was still convinced Saddam was hunkered down on his doomsday weapons, the only question being how to pry them loose—more U.N.-sponsored inspections or launching George Bush's "preemptive" war.

The next night my friend Sabam Siagian was equally agitated at America over steak and salad at the Hilton. "The United States now is not the country I knew and admired," he complained.

A director of the *Jakarta Post* and a former ambassador to Australia, Sabam had lived in the U.S. off and on for a dozen years as a journalist, a Harvard fellow, and a diplomat. But he now strongly objected to the Bush administration's recent decision to impose new antiterrorism rules requiring males visiting the United States from Muslim countries, regardless of religion or record, to register with the Immigration and Naturalization Service. Barely reported in the American media, the blunderbuss approach had created deep insult in Indonesia. Sabam and others I spoke with felt it was a foolish way to treat your friends. Looking at me fiercely over the silver and crystal, he exclaimed, "And I'm a Christian, Tracy!"

As I've said elsewhere, Sabam is a spirited man, with a tart, incisive way of speaking, and I've always enjoyed his blunt honesty. "You know, there is a perception in this country that if you're strong and rich and you listen, then you're a good person," he said. "George Bush shows the rich and powerful don't need to listen—they just do what they want."

When I switched subjects and asked Sabam about developments on the home front, he looked uncharacteristically dispirited for a moment, and then said, "I hope the resilience and common sense of the Indonesian people will prevail and translate itself into the political structure, but frankly, I don't know. Meanwhile Java is in chaos."

With that dour assessment, Sabam hoisted his wineglass and wished me luck. "Strength, Tracy, yah? It's hard but I know you can do it."

I was about to find out. Reza had scheduled our first foray into the radical camp for the following morning, and I spent a restless night among the bedbugs, mulling over what little I knew of the organization, the Islamic Youth Movement. One of many groups advocating the muscular imposition of Islamic law, the GPI, for short, also had a history of sending fighters to Afghanistan, first to kill the Soviet occupiers and now to battle the American invaders. It was reputed to run a number of clandestine camps throughout the Indonesian archipelago, where fighters trained in infiltration and sabotage, and to maintain at least informal ties with Osama bin Laden.

My feelings of trepidation amplified when, unfurling my morning newspaper, I read that suspected terrorists had brazenly exploded a bomb in, of all places, the city's National Police headquarters. After breakfast, and still unescorted by our housebound Islamic bureau chief, Norman and I arrived at GPI headquarters, a looming Gothic-style building on one of the city's car-infarcted thoroughfares. Entering the gloomy, echoing hallway, we were greeted by posters featuring the lean and hungry heroes of the day, Osama bin Laden and Abu Bakar Bashir. We were also met by two very nervous young men. One was tall and skinny, the other had a remarkably large moon face, and together they ushered us into a large outer office to await the arrival of the GPI's chairman, Suaib Didu.

To say our conversation was stilted would be to engage in wild understatement. The two men smiled vacuously at me. I smiled vacuously back at them. Norman meanwhile fiddled with his video camera, his favorite ploy for avoiding awkward situations. Then our moonfaced host brightened with sudden inspiration: "Tell us about Islam in America!" he said.

Ignorant as a lawn chair on the topic, I'd plunged into a rambling, nonsensical explanation to fill the dead air when suddenly a door at the back of the room flew open with a bang, and all four of us jumped in our seats. For there, standing stiffly in the black rectangle, was a long, angular figure pointing a rifle at us. Two thoughts flashed crazily through my head—first, how ironic it was that Norman and I were going to get nailed on our very first interview with a card-carrying Islamic militant, and stranger still, how much the designated nailer looked like the cartoon-noir character Spider-man.

Wearing a black balaclava with a heavy black mesh obscuring his face, the man moved with a menacing slowness. He lifted one jackbooted foot off the floor, held it in midair for what seemed an eternity, and then, crashing it down, shouted, "I am the commander of Islamic security!"

The alarming apparition then shifted gears, rushing a dozen paces into the room, whereupon he stopped on a dime, his weapon at the ready. It was, as I think you can well imagine, a very trying moment. But it was then, as our would-be assailant performed a neat, foot-stamping manual-of-arms drill, I was relieved to notice that his rifle was not really a rifle at all, but a long, clublike instrument fashioned from a piece of wood. Having gone through his paces, the man swiveled, thrust his weapon forward as if leading a bayonet charge, and ran full tilt out the front door.

Norman and I stared at the empty doorway as our skinny host wiped his brow and laughed. "Sorry about that," he said. "That guy's been hanging around here, sleeping in the mosque next door. He was okay till Idul Fitri"—the feast recently marking the end of the Ramadan fasting month—"then something snapped."

We were still engaged in lowering our collective pulse rate when Suaib Didu hurried through the door. A stocky man in a white shirt and rumpled necktie, he looked like an accountant late for an appointment with an important client. Apologetically, he waved Norman and me into his private office, and while the adrenaline was still pumping, I jumped right in, asking him why his group was sending jihadis to kill Americans in Afghanistan.

Up close, Suaib was a rugged-looking character, about forty, I judged, with a square head and a remarkably pleasant face. "It's a reaction to the American invasion," he said calmly. "It's not because we hate America or anything but because there's a need for peace in the world."

And killing Americans promoted world peace? I asked.

Suaib flashed an impish, gap-toothed grin, and said, "It's just something we've been doing since the Russians went into Afghanistan in the late nineteen seventies."

"Your daughter?" I asked, pointing to a snapshot on Suaib's desk of a pretty little girl of seven or eight holding a clutch of balloons. On her T-shirt was a picture of Osama bin Laden over the English words "Life Is Jihad." Stationed around the picture was an interesting collection of toy miniatures—a camouflaged tank, a mobile rocket launcher, and a passenger jet, which on closer inspection I discovered was a replica of Air Force One.

"Yes, that's my daughter," Suaib smiled, his dimples drawing his cheeks into a deep pucker. Then picking up his theme, he said: "We're not sending people to the Middle East to defend Osama bin Laden, mind you, but to defend the victims of oppression."

So his group did have ties with Osama?

"I wish," he said, again with the Alfred E. Newman grin. "We could use the financial support."

For what?

Suaib said the GPI had recently signed up 3,025 new recruits, adding to a trained militia of 20,800, who were skilled in handling weapons and the making of bombs. "But we've only been able to afford to send three hundred jihadis to fight in Afghanistan because of lack of money."

Poor GPI, I thought, sarcastically. "If your money doesn't come from Al Qaeda, where does it come from?"

"Donations," said Suaib, adding in a surprisingly confidential tone. "But you won't find any books to look at."

"Oh, why not?"

"State intelligence could use them to smear us, so we don't keep any records around. We're being closely watched."

Yes, I could see where that would be a problem, I said. Encouraged by Suaib's apparent openness, I ventured, "Tell me about your training camps."

No problem, he grinned. There was one at Bogor, less than an hour's ride southeast of Jakarta, he said, but the government had recently forced them to shut it down.

Were there others?

"Yes, all over Indonesia."

I asked him to name one.

"Makassar," said Suaib. "In the mountains."

But when I suggested I'd like to see the camp, I got the dimples again. "You have to go there blindfolded," said Suaib.

Okay, I nodded.

He grinned. "Well, then they strip you down and check your ears and everything."

I didn't mind having my ears examined.

He laughed, a little nervously, I thought. "Out of a hundred journalists who've applied, only one, from Norway, passed the initial screening."

Those Norwegians are tough, I allowed.

"Yes, but even he gave up halfway. Too cold."

"Wow, it must have been pretty cold to stop a Norwegian," I said. Suaib smiled, then frowned, allowing as how that must have been the case.

To be honest, I wondered how seriously to take Suaib. I didn't doubt for a minute that like other militant groups the GPI had sent mujaheddin fighters to Afghanistan over the years. That was a matter of record. Many groups were reputed to have training camps scattered around the country—to afford one was a badge of honor. As a rule, they tended to be small, hard to track, and with barebones facilities that could be shut down on short notice when the authorities put on the heat or the money ran out. But I also knew that all midget organizations yearn to be giants, and so my antennae went up when Suaib claimed a general membership for GPI of a half-million people. He then told me about a clandestine meeting he claimed to have had with anonymous Bush administration officials who wanted to sound him out on the threat of militant Islam in Indonesia, but he seemed involuntarily fuzzy on the details.

Most interesting to me were the glimpses Suaib, in his efforts to impress, revealed of where the GPI fit into the broader, murkier framework of Norman's hidden force. For starters, Suaib seemed inordinately proud of his associations with the military and the fact that retired TNI officers had served as trainers at his camps.

"So the military had a hand in setting up the GPI," I said.

Suaib grinned. "Another journalist asked me that and I told him he was trying to frame me."

Far be it from me to try to frame anybody, I said laughing, before asking, "Did you have any involvement in the Bali bombings?"

No, he said, but he wasn't trying to duck the question. Interestingly, he told me he'd had a long association with two of the bombers, Amrozi, the triggerman, and the ringleader, Imam Samudra. "They've been playing around with bombs for as long as I've known them," said Suaib volubly as he rotated a thumb toward the big empty spaces of his building. "They used to hang out in this compound."

A long time before Bali, Suaib said proudly, "this office helped them facilitate a change of identities," by which he meant the forging of papers.

What were they up to, changing identities, making bombs, and all? I asked.

Suaib said he was convinced the two men were getting money under the table from the police. "They bought new cars every week. But the police knew how to play tricks on them. They'd let their money run out and then offer them a big job. Neither guy knew how to build a bomb as big as the ones in Bali, though. They only knew how to blow up something the size of a truck, nothing bigger."

His allusions to the possibility of American skullduggery in Bali irritated me, and so I asked him how many Americans his group had killed in Afghanistan? (You try to be objective but sometimes, as I said earlier, you catch the heat.)

"Well, we don't kill women or children," said Suaib, adding somewhat obscurely, "and we're not allowed to kill trees."

Just Americans?

"We don't assassinate anyone just like that because it's forbidden in our religion, though given the right conditions our people can offer themselves up as suicide bombers."

"Ah-huh, ah-huh," I found myself saying idiotically, while I scribbled my notes, as if Suaib was quoting me statistics on bakery deliveries.

"Were you involved in fighting the Christians in the Moluccas?"

"Oh, yes, we worked closely together with the Laskar Jihad," he said, beaming, before he hastened to add, "but we work within the law and the Koran, not to kill innocent people."

Ah-huh.

Suaib was a very cheerful man, as fundamentalists go, but he frowned and grew uncharacteristically pensive when I asked him about the future. "Our organization has been practically banned by the government now. Many of our leaders have been arrested. That's why I'm thinking about going to Japan to study how they rebuilt their economy after the Americans dropped the atom bomb on them in World War II."

Suaib was still around when the United States invaded Iraq the following month, however, and the police pulled him in for questioning after some of his GPI members were arrested for allegedly intimidating white foreigners on Jaksa Boulevard, a popular haunt of bule backpackers not far from the U.S. embassy in central Jakarta. On this day, though, it was Suaib who was watching my back. On leaving his office, we discovered Islamic Security poised just outside the door, tense as a coiled spring, and in an attempt to head off an unhappy incident, Suaib shielded me with his body and walked us briskly to the front steps.

While our worried-looking hosts stood there waving goodbye, the masked man bolted onto the main street, brandished his weapon, and threatened drivers with a whack on the hood unless they came to an immediate halt. He then turned on his heels and, after waving our driver cordially into the traffic, snapped to attention and fired off a crisp salute.

"Islamic Security was on our side all along," I said to Norman, and I confess I couldn't help thinking it was rather sweet the way Suaib and the others tolerated their uninvited enforcer.

Ever the inquiring reporter, Norman asked, "What would happen to a guy like that in New York?"

"Security risk," I said. "We'd lock him up in three minutes flat."

The traffic in Jakarta was appalling, meaning nearly as bad as Los Angeles or Seattle. And so I tried to put to good use the hours spent stuck in taxis on smoggy thoroughfares by asking Norman to clear up such mysteries as inevitably arose during the course of our reporting day. At the present moment I was mulling over the conundrum of why, when I'd asked for the men's room at Suaib's office, our tall, skinny host had pointedly indicated the location of a freestanding faucet before leaving me be. The scene, with minor variations, had been repeated numerous times. At a prestigious Islamic university, for example, an attendant had rushed up to discreetly hand me a small bucket of water before shrinking into the background.

And thus my question: "What's with these guys shoving the water at me all the time?"

It was a rare moment when I took Norman by surprise, but I could see he was now truly and deeply stunned. "You're kidding me, right?" he said.

"I am not," I replied indignantly.

"Jeez, Boss, it's for, you know . . . washing your, uh, willy. All practicing Muslims are required to, you know . . . when they finish, you know . . ."

I was flabbergasted. How in all my travels I had failed to hoist aboard this basic piece of cultural information I will never know. Some old Asia hand I'd turned out to be. Detecting honest ignorance on my part, Norman, ever eager to explain the incult drama of his country, illustrated his point with a story. One day when they were little boys, Norman said, he and his two cousins were out playing in the park when a trip to the lavatory was indicated.

Finishing up his business, Norman's Muslim cousin proceeded to douse his privates with clean tap water. The other cousin, a Christian, was thunderstruck. "What do you think you're doing?!" he cried.

"I'm washing my willy," said the Muslim cousin, matter-of-factly.

"You're not supposed to do that!"

"Yes, I am."

"No, you're not."

"Yes, I am." And so it went, until the cousins had nearly come to blows.

"Willy-washing, Boss," said Norman, concluding his remarks, "a parable for Indonesia."

That noon we drove out to a neighborhood of sooty shop fronts and tired office buildings on the outer ring of central Jakarta and paid a call on the headquarters of the *Partai Keadilan,* the Justice Party. Though it held only six seats in parliament at the time, the organization was extremely popular with conservative Muslims for putting a squeaky-clean reputation behind the campaign for making shariah the law of the land (and a worry to those who worried about Islamic political jujitsu). I spoke with party president Hidayat Nurwahid, who told me, "In our opinion shariah is not about cutting off somebody's hand when they steal something." Rather, he said, it was a means of establishing the social discipline and welfare that the current secular political system had failed miserably to provide.

Nurwahid was a charmingly intense man in a neat brown batik shirt. He had a handsome face, prematurely gray hair, and a neat, inch-wide brush on his chin, and only blanched a little when I asked him how he would respond to charges that he was using the new democratic freedoms to drag the political mainstream to the Islamic far right.

"The West basically sees Islam as the enemy," he said, so he wasn't surprised by my question. But in his opinion improving communication was the key. "The future of Indonesia is democratic Islam, an Islam that communicates with everybody."

That sounded like slick political-speak, but perhaps I was being unfair. Nurwahid seemed sincere. There were deep grievances in the Muslim community in Indonesia, he said, as there were elsewhere in the Muslim world—over the lack of jobs, educational opportunities, and past discrimination by the government. "When the communication is better, when people know justice is for everybody, I think they will join the mainstream of Islam."

The trick was to simply make the tent bigger. There were a few misfits who engaged in violent acts, said Nurwahid, "but when people understand they aren't outcasts, they join political parties, and then nobody can stay radical for long."

The idea that the radicals could be contained by inviting them into a big tent was a common refrain among moderates and conservatives alike. (As Lyndon Johnson so eloquently put it, better to have the renegades inside the tent, pissing out, than outside the tent pissing in.) The main difference was that the tent, to Muslim moderates, was pluralistic democracy; to the conservatives it was the fixed abode of shariah.

"The best solution to poverty is not only to adopt shariah but to strengthen culture, and give people a better education," said Nurwahid. "This is what the Indonesian people want." Well, at least those Indonesian people who weren't Christian, Hindu, Buddhist, or simply religiously lackadaisical, I thought.

But I had to admit that Nurwahid had a definite point when it came to education. Public schools in Indonesia were in a dangerous tailspin. Teachers were on the whole poorly trained and abysmally paid. State funding had collapsed in the wake of the Asian economic crisis in 1997 and never recovered. In four years enrollment at public elementary schools had plunged twenty-five percent. Like elsewhere in the Muslim world, private Islamic schools had stepped in to fill the gap. And while that wasn't necessarily a bad thing in Indonesia, since the bulk of such institutions tried to provide a general education with Islamic flourishes rather than relentless religious studies, they too were generally poorly funded, badly organized, and often worked at cross-purposes.

While the last thing staunch Islamists wanted was a bunch of suspect Americans dabbling in the schooling of their kids, a number of thoughtful Indonesians had pointed out to me that education was one area where a concerted, brainy program of U.S. aid could eventually pay handsome returns and help repair the sharply negative views about the nature of U.S. influence in the Muslim world. Thanks to the efforts of Edward Masters, a former U.S. ambassador to Indonesia, and the members of the National Commission on United States–Indonesian Relations, George Bush would promise Indonesia $157 billion to improve education in Indonesia during a visit to Bali in October 2003, though Masters and his fellow experts thought the amount, if ever released, was well below what was required to do the job.[1]

---

1. See Edward Masters's testimony before U.S. House of Representatives subcommittee hearings on "The United States and Asia: Continuity, Instability, and Transition," March 17, 2004.

• • •

What I wanted more than anything while traveling in Indonesia was to give my large bule carcass as low a profile as possible. Norman, following my orders as faithfully as ever, had therefore arranged for me to speak at a conference on documentary filmmaking as a favor to an old friend who ran a broadcast institute at a new university on the Jakarta outskirts. The day after my arrival Norman proudly showed me a large ad in the vernacular press heralding my appearance, complete with full name and curriculum vitae.

"Way to keep things under your hat, Norman."

"Just trying to improve your communications with the Indonesian people, Boss."

And so, finishing up at Justice Party headquarters, we were collected by two smiling young women from the university and whisked off to campus for my gala presentation. In the car Farrah, the older of the two, looked to be in her mid-twenties, wore a pretty purple jilbab, and had a long, shapely nose in an oval face of classical Arab beauty. Chirpily, she told me, through Norman's translation, that she was studying journalism but really wanted to be a novelist or essayist. Did I have any advice for her? I burbled something inane, and we chatted along happily, until Farrah asked, "Where are you from?"

My reply, "New York," was followed by stunned silence. The two women traded furtive, frightened glances.

"New York?" spluttered Farrah, eyes downcast. "That's in America."

"Last time I checked," I said good-naturedly, and then to Norman, in an even tone, so as not to give it away: "What the hell is going on here?"

Norman queried the two women, who were now staring fixedly out the front windshield, and then said, "Word was that you were supposed to be German, Boss."

"Sorry to disappoint," I said as a silence engulfed the passenger compartment that no amount of American joshing could dispel.

Frankly, I found it highly irritating that the simple revelation of citizenship should cause full social meltdown. Or were my hosts just scared off by the media brainwashing they'd received about American baby-killers in Afghanistan?

So it was with trepidation that I walked onstage expecting to play a very tough room. Stupidly, I thought, I'd chosen to show excerpts from a film I'd made on the social upheaval in the United States in the fifties and sixties, including the story of Joe McCarthy's anti-Communist witch-hunt, the struggle for civil rights, and the youth counterculture. After those State Department films had played to such dismal reviews, I was sure anything exploring life in America was bound to bomb big time. To my infinite surprise and relief, however, both film and filmmaker were enthusiastically received.

Though one friendly young woman in Islamic dress mildly objected to the inclusion of graphic archival photos showing the lynchings of black men in the South, the boys guffawed and whistled appreciatively at the images of partial nudity briefly revealed in a hippie body-painting scene. And in general the idea that the all-powerful United States had suffered its share of tumult and tragedy seemed to convey a message that in the historical sense at least their own huge, multifaceted country was not alone in its struggles. The chairman of the department presented Norman and me with memorial trophies, but I modestly declined the further honor of encore performances at other institutions.

Even Farrah warmed up. Maybe it was the friendly, laughing reception we received, or possibly she'd managed to convince herself that, since I looked the part, I really was German after all. In any event, when I'd finished speaking with one of our admiring fans, she leaned in and whispered, in surprisingly serviceable English, "Would you like to meet Abu Bakar Bashir?"

When my mouth opened but no words came out, Farrah explained: "I come from Bashir's village. I know his wife."

"Sure, please give it a try," I said. Farrah said she would and promised to call me. I never heard from her again, but I took her gesture as an encouraging sign that, if you manage to stumble on the right approach to things, you at least stand the chance of creating the basis for improved communications.

Each of us is whispered to by his or her own unique set of fears, and only a fool claims any kind of superiority in that department. Yet the next morning, when I sat on the veranda of the Freedom Institute, an elegant white bungalow in an upscale residential neighborhood a few blocks from my hotel, Norman's display of nerves was really getting on my nerves.

"Relax, will you," I said as he sat in a plastic patio chair nearby, stiff as a department store mannequin. "This guy is on our side."

But I knew what was eating him. I was waiting to speak with Ulil Abshar-Abdalla, the young Muslim activist whose championing of tolerance and reform had won him a large and devoted following, a reputation in intellectual circles as the Martin Luther of Indonesia, and of course that death order, or fatwa, from disgruntled fundamentalists. Specifically, Norman didn't like the way the house sat in a narrow flowering garden open to the street, where we'd be sitting ducks for any demented spirit contemplating a drive-by execution. And so he was up and nervously pacing the patio when Ulil joined us.

Relaxed and outgoing, Ulil had a square, open face, gold-rimmed glasses, and wore the unofficial uniform of what Norman referred to as the "Gap activist"—a neatly pressed madras shirt, white cotton pants, and open-toed leather sandals.

I told Ulil I was intrigued by the idea, recently set out by Tom Friedman, the foreign affairs columnist for the *New York Times* and a veteran Middle East watcher, that either Islam was going to have a war within its own civilization, by which he meant a rigorous sorting-out of its values, or there would surely be a war between civilizations, namely Islam and the West. I was curious to know how well Ulil thought the template fit Indonesia.

Ulil smiled and shook his head. Americans might not know it, he said, but that struggle was already going full tilt, not only in Indonesia but throughout Southeast Asia. "If you go down the street to the universities, the campuses are filled with a very vibrant debate about democracy, pluralism, human rights, and minority rights. So the clash of values is occurring. If we, as an Islamic society, can pass this exam, so to speak, and reform our tradition, I think the larger global clash can be avoided."

"In other words, you don't rule it out," I said.

Ulil smiled puckishly. "Yes, if the Islamic world is completely hijacked by Osama bin Laden, and we are totally isolated from the outside," he said, "or the world we live in is the world of Osama and of Pat Robertson and Jerry Falwell, then a clash is inevitable."

So Ulil agreed that it was dangerous for dyed-in-the-wool Islamists to be playing politics?

"It's definitely a problem," he said, "because it sacrifices religion for narrow political purposes. But this is a process we must go through to reach democratization. I mean, as long as we Indonesians are successful in creating a system that can accommodate all political forces in society, and not sideline Islamic elements, I think it's good. What we need now is to create an inclusive system to bring the extremist Muslims into the mainstream politics."

The big tent again, in its democratic guise. "That's what the Islamist politicians say, too," I said.

Ulil shook his head again and smiled—I didn't understand. "It all depends on how you define the system," he said. "First, there's no such thing as an 'Islamic system' already in place. We have yet to invent it. Yes, Islam has a history of fourteen hundred years, but that's just history. I understand why Muslims are so preoccupied with politics of identity. But the obsession with identity . . . or the Caliphate, a Pax Islamica that transcends national boundaries . . . is so pathetic in most cases it just jeopardizes the essence of religion itself."

He went on: "The democratic process is the Islamic process for me. So when you consolidate democracy and establish a solid system that is inclusive, the name doesn't matter. What counts is the essence."

I said as how I could see now where such views would get him into hot water with the fundamentalists.

Ulil smiled a big, confident smile, even puffing out his chest a little. "Yes, I wrote a column in the newspaper that unfortunately earned me a death fatwa."

As Ulil spoke, I looked up and noticed that Norman had disappeared. Out on the big open lawn a calico cat was stalking a bird in the distant hibiscus tree.

"But what I was doing," Ulil continued, "was simply reiterating old ideas we've been discussing for years."

"Like what, for instance?"

"I said that Muslims should be clear in making the distinction between the core of Islam, which is universal . . . and the Arabic element, which is not an Islamic thing but just a garment that embodies Islamic tenets and teachings. This is crucial because for some Muslims the line is blurred."

For Ulil to question the Arabic origins of Islam, which for many were hardwired into the Koran, and therefore inseparable from the religion, had been bad enough. What had driven his critics crazy, however, was the argument that, in effect, God should keep his nose out of the conduct of civil society.

"The fundamentalists claim God prescribes a complete and comprehensive law in detail on everything, including public and private matters, which is ridiculous. There is no 'God-provision' on how we should conduct our elections, for example. Islam enjoins us to live and benefit from human achievements no matter what the religion."

I admired Ulil for showing such panache in the face of danger, but I wondered out loud if he wasn't being a little too cavalier. He flapped his hand dismissively. The fatwa had come from a low-level group chasing after some easy publicity, he said. Even Hidayat Nurwahid, Ulil's political alter ego, who had publicly disagreed with every point he'd raised in the offending column, had stepped up to rebuke the death-dealing clerics.

"So you're saying all the media attention about the fatwa has been overblown?"

Ulil thought for a moment and in thinking grew subdued. "Well, what really concerns me is that, technically speaking, you know, anybody who believes in a fatwa can execute it. So this is dangerous for me, I think, yeah."

I wished Ulil luck, and then rose to go, just as Norman, having missed our entire conversation, came sauntering up the driveway to collect me. "Where have you been?" I asked.

"Checking the security perimeter, Boss."

"That would explain the magazines?" I said, pointing to a couple of glossy tabloids rolled up under his arm.

"Neighborhood newsstand, Boss—traditionally important listening post in Indonesia."

14

RIZIEQ

I was heartened by my meeting with Ulil and his colleagues, and the knowledge that such sharp minds and courageous spirits were engaged in a struggle that the vast majority of Americans weren't aware was even being waged. ("They fought while we slept," was the phrase that strangely though not inaccurately came to mind.) When it was over, though, it was my turn to take over from Norman in the heebie-jeebies department. Our meeting with that mercurial America-hater, Habib Rizieq Shihab, was set for that afternoon, and not on neutral turf, as I'd been praying for, but at Rizieq's compound in one of Jakarta's more grimly militant slum neighborhoods.

And so when the pong from our taxi driver's farts forced Norman and me onto the pavement outside the Hard Rock Café on booming Jalan Thamrin, I was suddenly overcome with a powerful, life-affirming urge to consume a bacon cheeseburger. The restaurant was nearly empty, its big, open space clanging with heavy-metal music at a volume anticipating a mob. When I beckoned our waiter and asked him if he wouldn't turn it down a crank, however, he replied with a wink and a smirk that he couldn't help me out—you see, like, the music's, like, preprogrammed, dad.

He was a lanky Indonesian fellow with the looks of a young Keith Richards—long, wild hair, with something lodged in it that may or may not have been a small tree branch. If the anti-Western jihad did not exist, I decided, this slouching, cooler-than-thou scarecrow was the reason it would have to be invented. Normally, confronted with such annoying rigidity from a representative of McWorld, I'd have gone ballistic. On this day, however, facing the very real possibility of less benign inflexibility from Jihad, I behaved like a model global citizen. I waited patiently for my burger to arrive and when it did, I took a bite the size of a small horseshoe. I then shook my head from side to side, and said, "Um-mmmmm."

"How is it, Boss?" Norman inquired.

I flashed a thumbs-up sign, and said through bulging cheeks, *"Scruhm-shous!"*

But I could tell Norman didn't really share in my delight. That was because he hadn't yet received his order, and I knew from past experience that nothing got under his skin like the thought of special privileges being accorded to the *bule*. I could see the storm clouds breaking over the foothills of amok when his burger finally arrived, and he immediately ripped off the bun and clucked his tongue in disgust.

"What seems to be the problem there, Norman?" I asked wetly as I washed my fries down with a large, delectably foamy root-beer float.

"I ordered pickles," said Norman, speaking through clenched lips. "This burger has *no pickles.*"

Norman summoned our waiter again, who sauntered over with his long, sly grin. Whatever Norman said in Indonesian, Scarecrow shot him a look easily translatable as, "Chill, dude—I mean, like don't have a coronary or anything."

Amok! Norman's eyes flashed with liquid heat, cutting through the trappings of the ambient rock culture like a molten kris, and the emissary from the Land of the Cool wisely scurried off to get his boss. It was a thoroughly impressive performance, and one clearly requiring comment. And so with the saintly aplomb of a man who routinely blows his cork once a week while reporting from the field and twice as often in highly stressful situations, I tsk-tsked and said, "Relax, Norman. It's only a pickle, for chrissakes."

"It's the principle," he muttered.

"The pickle principle?"

Norman sniffed, refusing to dignify my remark with a reply as he stared sulkily into the big space where decorative guitars were hung like Christmas. At the next table, meanwhile, a corporate bule in a fancy shirt and silk necktie, who had come in from one of the big office towers nearby, was sharing with his local staff the riveting details of a recent adventure on golf links where it was unlikely any of them could afford to play. They smiled and nodded over their cheeseburgers and generally did a good job of pretending to be enthralled.

Norman shot me a disgusted look, as if he might be reevaluating his alliance with our wonderful worldwide consumer culture, when a polite, clean-cut manager appeared with a peace offering in the form of a plate of make-up condiments. After administering a brief but pointed lecture on the art of customer service, Norman sent the man away. He then displayed one of his truly noble attributes, namely self-correction. Laughing reproachfully at his now-vanished sour mood, he posed a conundrum for the ages: "Can you have the Hard Rock Café in an Islamic superstate," he said in a tone of mock contemplation, "or only the rocks?"

After lunch we hopped a cab on Jalan Thamrin, and despite the comforting burger feed, my head was beginning to spin with dark images of hostile robed figures, full of knives and teeth. But I wasn't all *that* worried. I mean, Rizieq might be a firecracker, I thought, but, hey, we had our Islamic bureau chief, Faisal Reza, who, finally released from baby detention, was scheduled to be on hand to sort out such complications, Islamic or otherwise, as might arise.

But when I said, "So where are we hooking up with Rez?" Norman stared out the window and murmured, "The baby's sick, Boss. She turned yellow last night. They had to take her to the hospital."

I felt the cheeseburger return on me slightly. "So Reza will *not* be joining us?" I said, struggling to maintain an even tone.

"You are correct, Boss."

I could hardly blame Reza for putting his family first of course, so as usual I blamed Norman. I said, less evenly now, "And there was a reason you were withholding this information from me?"

"Didn't want to worry you, Boss?" ventured Norman.

"Am I correct in assuming, then that we are still operating on a strict need-to-know basis here?"

"Correct, Boss."

I said no more—anyhow, it was too late to pull out now. And so, as we drove on in edgy silence, my interior worry demon was up and prancing on its hind legs. When we reached Rizieq's neighborhood in the northern part of the city, we got out of the cab on the main artery road, the crush of cars spewing plumes of hairy black smoke, and walked into the tightly networked backstreets. The gas fumes were so thick on the ground here, and so amplified by the intense heat, that I was suddenly feeling a little woozy, which under the circumstances may have been a blessing in disguise.

The neighborhood seemed profoundly unwelcoming. When Norman stopped and asked a fat middle-aged woman in a nylon jogging suit for directions, he got a glare and a wordless finger pointed deeper into the tangle of streets.

"Friendly," I said.

"Very homey," replied Norman.

It was also a little surreal. Turning a corner, we came upon a playground that looked like something out of a Palestinian settlement on the West Bank—a dusty patch of earth, a dilapidated, riderless seesaw, and no children. In the next instant, I found myself galumphing down a narrow alley between buildings, like a balky bule heifer in a chute, and then after a seemingly interminable wait (only about ten minutes), I was sitting cross-legged on the floor of a small outdoor study, staring across a low wooden desk at Habib Rizieq Shihab. Small, animated, and crisp in his snowy white kaftan, despite the obnoxious heat, the preacher was younger than I'd remembered him from the Hotel Indonesia. Looking to be in his late thirties, he had a well-trimmed black goatee growing from a boyish, unlined face the color of dark honey.

Unsmilingly, he asked in halting, schoolboy English, "What is your name?" When I said Tracy, he cracked a wolfish grin, as if he couldn't believe his luck. "You are Mister *Cray-zee?*"

"It's, uh, Tracy," I stammered, chuckling with false good humor, while the perspiration collected at my hairline. A large, curved scimitar hanging on the wall over the imam's head stressed the importance of displaying good manners.

"Oh, *Tray-zee, Tray-zee,*" chuckled Rizieq, watching clinically as the globules of sweat began to ski-jump the length of my nose and splatter on my open notebook. In a voice that sounded more like a command than a welcome, he said, "Relax, Mister Tray-zee!" and then added, grinning archly: "Where you come from, *Ah-mer-ee-ka?*"

"Yes, uh, America."

"You stay in *Ah-mer-ee-ka?!*" he cried. Having asked the question, he now feigned surprise by my startling admission of citizenship.

"Well, actually, uh, New York."

"Ah, New York!" He looked over at Norman, nodding his head slowly up and down, as if he now had the complete mental picture, chockablock with polymorphous Western deviltry. Frowning, Rizieq dropped his English, ordered Norman to translate, and then fixed me with a sudden stony look. "Why have you come here, *Mister Cray-zee?*"

Good question, I thought. "Well," I began, in an honest-seeker-of-knowledge tone, "many Americans, including myself, don't understand Islam as well as we might, and . . ."

The conciliatory crap didn't fool Rizieq for a second. "That's because America doesn't *want* to understand Islam!" he cried, cutting me off in midsentence. Eyes flashing, he added, in a truculently self-satisfied tone, "Even if you try and explain something to someone who doesn't really want to understand, they will refuse to understand!"

Things were getting off to a bad start. But from painful experience I knew that the absolute best way to whip up a fine bloodlust in an otherwise hostile interviewee was to come off as a whinging cream puff. So purely as a matter of self-preservation, I shot back, interrupting Rizieq as he had interrupted me: "Well," I said, firmly, "*I* want to understand."

It seemed to work. Rizieq stared at me blankly for a moment, and then blinking benignly, said, "Okay, so you want to hear my vision, is that it?"

"Yes, please."

"The Hotel Indonesia vision, or the whole thing?"

"The whole thing, please."

Long or short, it was generally the same. "Indonesia's problems are rooted in a moral crisis that has resulted in economic and social crises," said Rizieq. "Nothing changes if the morals don't improve. To accomplish that I think everybody in the world would agree the right approach is a religious approach."

Rizieq spoke confidently, with a taunting, sibilant precision; it was like finding yourself in a dream listening to a story told by a king cobra. I was absolutely fascinated by the way the man rolled his *r*'s dramatically, and how his tongue lovingly caressed the word *Islaaaaam,* as if reluctant to let it go. "In Indonesia the majority is *Islaaaaam,* so *Islaaaaam* is the right solution for us."

That was very logical, I thought—and a recipe for untold bloodshed. What about the Christians in the Moluccas, the Hindus on Bali, or the non-Muslim ethnic tribes scattered throughout the country? Wouldn't they all fight to death rather than be ruled by Muslim law?

"Any country in the world," said Rizieq, "will be guaranteed safety and prosperity if the majority of people have good morals. And if the majority lives well, the minority will be protected."

But what about the millions of secular Muslims who rarely if ever saw the inside of a mosque—what if they didn't want to go along?

Tough cookies. "Our goal is to make shariah the law for the majority and the minority," Rizieq said flatly, with a sharp little thrust of his jaw. That would happen, "whether others like it or not, whether they agree or not—so our morals will stay intact."

Rizieq swung his torso around, pressing a button on the wall behind him, and a buzzer sounded deep inside the adjoining building. However irrationally, I was bracing myself for the arrival of the infidel removal squad when a door opened and a male attendant pushed a teapot across the floor on a lacquered tray. Rizieq intermitted his lecture long enough to pour the tea into thimble-sized cups and then set one before me, saying, "Tray-zee, Tray-zee, Tray-zee, *selakan, selakan*—please, please."

It's even hard for me to fathom, as I now sit peacefully at my writing desk in Manhattan, how much this small gesture of hospitality caused my spirits to soar. But soar they did as Rizieq picked up his earlier train of thought. "Indonesia will become a republic of the mafia in five years," he said, chortling darkly. "What crime doesn't exist in Indonesia? Which government body is clean? None! They're all involved in protecting the bad guys!"

Why? "The main culprit is that the governments of the Islamic majority states, including Indonesia, think anything from the West is good, superb! They open the door as wide as possible, so Western culture has been able to infiltrate very easily into our society . . . through various media in this globalized era."

Then in English, "You understand, Mister Tray-zee, yeah?"

Yes, I said, I'd have to agree that the media did go overboard on occasion.

Rizieq paused to encourage me in another cup of tea, and then continued: "So the question now is how to get a government that accommodates shariah Islam. If a government doesn't accommodate us they will have to go. And if the government that replaces them is similar they'll have to be replaced, too."

"Until?"

"Until we get what we want!"

Possibly wandering the suburbs of the Stockholm syndrome, I found myself unexpectedly warming to Rizieq. (As writer David Margolick has pointed out, "[R]eporters are disconcertingly adaptable.") Yes, he was actively recruiting volunteers to defend Saddam Hussein in the event of a U.S.-led war. His boys had stalked Americans on the streets of Jakarta and Solo. But you had to respect his intelligence—plus, in that flowing desert getup of his, he had an undeniable charisma.

His vision was certainly romantic enough. No matter how irrational it might sound to Americans, Rizieq's militant brand of Islam was really part of what *New York Times* correspondent David Rohde has neatly described in general terms as a "romantic liberation movement . . . that combines Islam's powerful call for social equality with a critique of Western corporate imperialism and the corrupt Muslim elites who benefit from it."

But Rizieq, while obviously sympathetic to the worldwide Islamic revolution, was himself content to save Indonesia from the satanic advances of global consumer culture, with its emphasis on things like fast food, easy pleasures, and modern tax accounting. And because he'd never been linked in any way with Al Qaeda, Jemaah Islamiyah, or the Laskar Jihad, Rizieq as a public figure rather eloquently made Sidney Jones's point that to be militant and angry didn't mean you automatically bowed down to Osama. There was in truth a fine line separating groups that spouted anger and hate and those few that struck out violently, and oftentimes it wasn't at all clear who or what flipped the switch. That was all the more reason, I supposed, for trying to understand the true personality of radical Islam rather than getting hung up on labels.

Seeing as how I am a bit of a romantic myself, or perhaps it was because of the mind-warping heat, I found myself briefly entertaining the quaint notion that Rizieq, this America-hating preacher, and I, men from starkly different worlds, might actually succeed in reaching across the chasm of ideas, upbringing, and values that separated us, for a meeting of the minds.

So I said, "Surely at some point, if only as a matter of mutual self-preservation, Islam and the West have got to reach some kind of accommodation, don't they? I mean, what's the solution?"

"Very simple," said Rizieq in a cordial tone. "Let the Muslims do shariah properly. When you force Islam to follow capitalism or the democratic system, there will be a collision. That's not even globalization—it's Americanization! So let's not bother one another and everything will be hunky-dory."

Hunky-dory? I looked over at Norman, who shot me a querulous look, as if to say translators are susceptible to stress, too, you know.

Seeing as how Rizieq and I were getting on like a house afire, I thought this might be a good time to put forward the question that good conscience, here at the end of a blind alley on militant turf, compelled me to ask. I told Rizieq that I understood his premium on morality. Broadly speaking, who could disagree? (My mind also flashed with a glimpse of the world the way he saw it—a place where McWorld, with its promise of never-ending consumer comforts for the lucky, was not a recipe for liberation, but a false world in which downtrodden Muslims suffered while the West got fat greasing its collective chin with bacon cheeseburgers.) But did Rizieq really think the bombing of the two nightspots on Bali, killing all those innocent people, had advanced the cause of Islamic morality in the world?

I smiled as I spoke, but I could tell the fun part of the interview was over. The imam's cheeks took on a ruby-red glow, as if I'd swatted them with a badminton racket, and he chuckled sardonically—*heh, heh, heh.* "The bomb is the answer, is that what you want me to say?"

"What I want you to tell me is if, in your opinion, Bali became a target because it was perceived to be a place of low moral fiber."

"For me, it's not a moral issue, it's a political issue," he cried, his eyes dilating with anger. "It's dissatisfaction with what America is doing in the world today!"

And what exactly was America doing? I asked, displaying my journalist's talent for posing the infuriatingly dumb question.

Rizieq grew apoplectic. America supported Israel in the humiliation and suffering of the Palestinian people! America attacked innocent Muslims in Afghanistan! It was now moving on Iraq against the wishes of its own allies! Did I need reminding that the ringleader of the Bali bombings, now in police custody, had expressed his remorse for killing so many vacationing Australians when it was vacationing Americans he'd set out to murder?

"I don't condone the attacks, mind you," Rizieq went on, hotly. "But I know why they happened."

Why?

Rizieq glared at me, as if dealing with a particularly moronic student of Koranic scripture, and then cried, as if nothing could be plainer, "Because America doesn't listen!"

"Oh, right," I said to myself, "and you're aces in the listening department." Small of me, I know, but I was tired of being harangued. I started to put my notebook away, and said something fatuous like, "Well, we certainly have something to learn from you and thank you for your time."

But Rizieq motioned me to stay put—not so fast, Mister Crayzee. He then sat up ramrod straight, buttoned the top button of his kaftan, and unloaded perhaps five minutes of scorching invective on Norman in Indonesian. When he was finished, he told him sternly, "Now you tell him that straight."

Norman translated: "You must understand that the existence of Osama bin Laden or the Bali bombers is just a reaction of disappointment to the evil America does to the world of Islam. That evil results in people who want to teach America a lesson."

And now I have to tell you that from the earnest boyish way he seemed to hang on every word of Norman's translation, his mouth slightly agape, it occurred to me that Rizieq was sincerely trying to take this opportunity to get his message across to an un-listening American. "If you don't want another Osama bin Laden there is an answer," he said a little pleadingly, I thought. "Stop your American arrogance! As long as America behaves arrogantly there will be thousands of Osama bin Ladens!"

"So the solution is not to go after Osama bin Laden or other terrorists?" I asked perversely, but Rizieq was perfectly straightforward.

"It's not that," he cried. "Stop the American arrogance! Stop the evil acts! If that happens I'm sure there won't *be* another Osama bin Laden."

The key, according to Rizieq, was for America to listen up, wise up, and see itself as others saw it—a nation committed to a double standard. America was poised to invade Iraq after Saddam Hussein had violated U.N. resolutions. At the same time, the U.S. had sent Israel billions of dollars in foreign aid, and then stood by and watched as Ariel Sharon pushed the Palestinians around and defied a different set of U.N. resolutions. (I could have pointed out that the nature of these resolutions, at least technically speaking, was not the same, but under the circumstances I felt it would be a waste of breath.)

"America has come to only recognize the attack on the World Trade Center and the Pentagon and the attack on American embassies abroad as terror," said Rizieq. But in his view it was essentially a problem of semantics. If America didn't speak the language of compromise, it had to expect messages written in the grammar of terror.

"Forget about the radicals, the hard-liners!" said Rizieq, his voice vibrating smoothly now. "Even the most moderate Muslim groups, if America pressures them, will become radical. The problem is not whether there are radicals or moderates but whether there is pressure or not!"

His argument was simplistic of course, but I could see his point. On the other hand, hypocrisy is a two-way street, and it always killed me the way nearly every anti-Western radical, Islamic, Communist, or otherwise, I'd ever talked to face-to-face, Rizieq included, liked to say it was the U.S. government they hated, not the American people. But unless I was badly mistaken, weren't those ordinary American individuals Rizieq's Islamic Defenders had attacked in their "sweeps" and tried to run out of the country?

Interestingly, though, I found Rizieq's answer again shrewdly logical. "If American citizens are being thrown out of a Muslim country, you must understand it is simply so they will go back home to tell their president, 'Look, we were visiting this country, doing business, enjoying our vacation, whatever, and just because of you and your policies there is a problem.'

"If the Indonesian people say that to your President Bush, he will not listen. If Americans can't get their own president to listen to their problems, then they should change the president!"

Sweat had saturated my notebook, and the pages were puckering and threatening to bleed ink. I was really feeling drained by the heat now, but I summoned the energy to point out that our democratic system might not be the best, but at least we did have the opportunity select our top leader every four years.

To my surprise, Rizieq bobbed his head, as if listening intently. (Perhaps he was seeing himself in a future political role?) Then things suddenly took an unexpected turn. The great firebrand paused, frowning in thought, and then flashed his even white teeth in a luminous smile.

"I think *you* should be president, Mister Tray-zee!" cried Rizieq.

I stared at him in disbelief. He'd been haranguing me about America's sins for the past hour, and now he wanted to nominate me as the Viking candidate for president from north Jakarta?

"The president should be somebody who listens," Rizieq went on to explain, "and not a warmonger! He should be a man of persuasion. If that were the case there would be no problem!"

That was a hugely debatable point as well of course, but my audience was now over. Rizieq apologized, but it was time for him to go say his prayers, and without further ado, he rose, whipping the tail of his kaftan behind him with a practiced flourish the way I remembered seeing Peter O'Toole do it in *Lawrence of Arabia*, and then walked Norman and me out to the porch where we'd left our street shoes. As we winged our way up the alley, Rizieq stood on the stoop, waving us goodbye. "You are welcome anytime, Mister Tray-zee," he cried. "We will help you. Our gate is open to you twenty-four hours a day!"

Well, that is the fascinating thing about the reporting life. You go in expecting to get nailed and come out having been nominated for president. But others failed to see the humor or irony in my encounter. Later, I shared the story of Rizieq's enthusiasm for running me for president on the good listeners' ticket with a prominent Jakarta pundit. He laughed sarcastically, and said, "You see how naive and dangerous these people are?"

I laughed to be polite, but basically I didn't think it was all that funny. There was little doubt that Rizieq, like other militants operating on the boundaries of the law, presented a threat to Indonesia's struggling democracy. But then again so did the country's corrupt democratic politicians and the other elite members of Norman's hidden force. (How big a danger the FPI presented outside Indonesia was also a matter of debate and degree. Despite its bluster, the FPI would by this time of writing only ever dispatch a dozen or so recruits to Iraq, though Rizieq, in another interesting variation on his house arrest, would travel there in April 2003 on what he billed as a humanitarian mission and get himself promptly socked with another jail sentence.)

As for Habib Rizieq Shihab, the man, I must say that he struck me as being neither particularly malicious, nor crazy, and in the end no worse a listener than many people I've talked to. And please don't take this the wrong way—but had I been in Rizieq's shoes, I'm not sure I wouldn't have seen the world exactly the same way.

15

DEAD MEN WALKING

On the evening of October 9, 2002, three men sat in a car parked at the elbow-bend of Jalan Legian, the crowded, lively road to Kuta Beach in Bali, and eyed their "white-meat" targets with a sort of gleeful reptilian hate. As the ringleader, Imam Samudra, later told police, "I saw lots of whiteys dancing, and lots of whiteys drinking there. That place—Kuta, and especially Paddy's Bar and the Sari Club—was a meeting place for U.S. terrorists and their allies, who the whole world knows are monsters."

Samudra and his men were hardly alone in their hatred of the Sari Club, however. Seen by foreign tourists as the apotheosis of the Bali "cool," and in fact an entrepôt for clubby casual sex, both free and paid-for, it had earned a bad name with many ordinary Indonesians, who saw it as a "whites-only" bar that denied entry to "the dark-skinned," as Norman put it, unless you could produce a foreign passport, or belonged to a favored group of prostitutes and gigolos. Exceptions were made for Indonesian women escorted by a bule male. As for local males: "Forget about it," said Norman, who had been turned away at the door one night in 1999.

"I once blurted out that someone should blow the place up," he later told me, remorsefully, but it was an opinion widely shared, and by then of course widely regretted.

After casing their targets a final time, the Bali bombers swung into action. At nine P.M. on October 12, a man named Ali Imron (who, like others on the team, hailed from Java's Islamic heartland) rode his motorbike past the U.S. consulate on a broad, tree-lined street several miles from Kuta, slowing down long enough to drop a small parcel in front of the building. An hour later "Arnasan" pulled up in front of the Sari Club in a white Mitsubishi van and parked it there. Then at eleven P.M., "Idris" punched a number into his mobile phone from a remote location and the sidewalk outside the U.S. consulate erupted. Inside Paddy's Bar, a suicide bomber, "Jimi," simultaneously blew himself to particles, sending panicked patrons rushing for the exits, and toward the one ton of explosives in the parked van, which now went off. As Maria Ressa points out in her comprehensive book *Seeds of Terror,* the blast proved "so fierce it ruptured the internal organs of the people in the area"—and in the blinking of an eye one of Bali's most famous corners, an entire city block, had vanished into rubble.[1]

Chillingly, as Ressa notes, Imam Samudra stated in his police confession that Bali had been attacked symbolically, "so that Muslims understand that . . . whether they agree or not . . . there are a handful of [us] who feel called to revenge the barbarity of the Coalition Army of the Cross and its allies"—meaning mainly the United States, most NATO countries, Australia, and Japan—"toward the

---

1. In addition to the examples of pointed testimony found in Ressa's book, see "The Bali Bomber's Song," *Tempo,* February 18–24, 2003, as well as the consistently thorough coverage of the Bali attack to be found in the magazine's English-language edition.

Islamic State of Afghanistan, which resulted in tens of thousands of casualties in September, 2001."[2]

News of the Bali murders, involving Jimi, GWOT's first known Southeast Asian suicide bomber, rocketed around the earth's plangent media-sphere as usual, but hit with particular force six hundred miles due north, in Jakarta, Indonesia's largest bule enclave and home to many of its hundreds of American and European branch corporations. Not unreasonably, vulnerable expatriates feared the enemy would next go after the city's hotels and office towers, which extremists had long since identified as symbols of the West's corporate "occupation." When word came through Western embassies of a "definite credible threat" against the three thousand students attending Jakarta's three large international schools, a mood bordering on panic set in. "I mean, now we were talking about the kids, for chrissakes," one American father told me. "And every parent could see in their mind's eye all those schoolbuses lined up and stuck in the morning traffic like sitting ducks."

To get a better feel for how the bombings had provoked a siege mentality in the foreign community, I paid a call on the Australian school's kindergarten campus, a trim white building up a leafy hill on a backstreet in south central Jakarta, where I spoke with Penny Robertson. About my own age, Penny had a strong, handsome face, brown as a hen's egg from the sun, smiling brown eyes, and a pleasing, down-to-earth Aussie manner. She had helped found the Australian schools in both Jakarta and Bali, and had been quickly on the scene in Kuta after the recent blasts.

"It was devastating," she said. "I mean, Bali was the safest place in the world, wasn't it? We all had our Christmas holidays there. Our senior kids hung out at Paddy's Bar on the weekends. No worries." Then suddenly her students were combing the small local hospital

---

2. Preliminary estimates by international human rights groups put the number of civilian casualties from the U.S.-led action in Afghanistan at between 3,000 and 5,000 as of this writing; radical Muslim groups used figures that appeared to peak in the neighborhood of 200,000 dead, or approximately twice the number killed when the U.S. dropped the atomic bomb on Hiroshima.

in Denpasar, Bali's main city, unzipping body bags and searching for a classmate's mother who had gone missing in zero hour at the Sari Club.

"It took forty-eight hours but we finally located all our students," Penny said. Thank God, they were all safe, if badly traumatized. "Interestingly, though, it was nothing compared to the fear that went through the community in Jakarta. Everybody here felt that absolutely nothing was being done to stop the radical Islamic element from gaining the upper hand" in a sprawling, essentially defenseless metropolis of thirteen million people.

The Megawati government's desultory response to Bali hadn't helped. Initially, officials rushed to pin the bombing on Al Qaeda— "hoping to place the blame on foreigners, not Indonesians themselves," as terrorism expert Zachary Abuza has noted. Meanwhile Megawati's internationally embarrassing Islamist vice president, Hamzah Haz (who, by the way, turned down my repeated requests for a conversation), warned against connecting the dots to his friend and ostensible political ally Abu Bakar Bashir.

As credible suspects were rounded up, and the evidence pointed to Jemaah Islamiyah, if not Bashir himself, international security firms specializing in the emergency relocation of embattled corporate types suddenly found themselves doing a land-office business. Threatened with a mass bule evacuation and the prospect of hemorrhaging foreign investment, the Megawati government moved belatedly but with rare speed nonetheless to tighten security against a foe that key officials had until only the day before yesterday refused to acknowledge.

Penny laughed. "It was then of course we learned that the 'definite credible threat' was neither definite nor credible," she said— a painful first lesson in the unreliability of "wartime" intelligence. The international schools, which had been shut down in an ad hoc security blitz, quickly reopened. Parents, who'd packed up their households to return to Sydney or Melbourne, had, in the resilient, get-on-with-it Aussie manner, unpacked and stayed on. Now, three months on, the trauma of Bali lingered in personal stories edged with loss, regret, and even a bitter humor, like the one Penny remembered a friend telling her about fleeing the conflagration with her ten-year-old son. "Mum, Mum, that man hasn't got an arm," the boy had cried as they ran for their lives down the Kuta road. "Oh, don't be so stupid!" said the mother. "Not everybody has arms!"

It was an unusually bright, smog-free day in Jakarta, and Norman and I decided to drive the short distance through the leafy and commodious streets of Kebayoran Baru to visit the home of the Faisal Rezas and see how the new baby was getting along. For a man committed to the cause of social justice, Reza's house was surprisingly posh. Long and narrow, it sat on the edge of a small ravine and had a cool and pleasant feel. The interior was inviting, too, dark and sparely elegant, with large windows shuttered against the afternoon sun and vintage Italian movie posters on the walls.

"Not bad for an anarchist, eh, Boss," said Norman as Antonia, vivacious in a red batik frock, her long, raven-colored hair flowing over her shoulders, rushed onto the driveway to greet us in the Italian style, with kisses and hugs and benedictions. The rest of the family was considerably less buoyant. Beatrice, the baby, was still yellow from jaundice and sleeping in her tented crib under a therapeutic blue light. Suffering from a severe case of stomach cramps, Reza sat on the balcony out back smiling wanly but looking exceedingly green around the gills.

The cramps, according to Norman, were my fault. Two nights earlier I'd prevailed on Reza to break away from his household duties long enough to back me up at a dinner with a formidable Islamist politician at my hotel, leading Norman to diagnose Reza's problem as case of "five-star diarrhea" aggravated by the class contradictions inherent in forcing Reza to consume fancy hotel victuals, thus separating him from "solidarity with the people."

Having been made to feel ridiculously guilty, I reached into my shoulder bag and handed Reza a packet of Pepto-Bismol chewables.

Thanks to my previous interventions in his alimentary misadventures, Norman had developed a certifiably religious devotion to the big pink tablets (replacing his early allegiance to a local product that looked something like a small charcoal briquette and manifestly did not work). The word on the bule miracle cure had spread quickly. Reza flapped his hand appreciatively, and placed one of the pills on his tongue, innocently, as if receiving a communion wafer.

Medications administered, we gathered around the patio table and got down to business. Reza told me he'd managed to contact a leading Islamic militant, reputedly one of Abu Bakar Bashir's chief lieutenants, who might be able to slip us in to talk with the emir in his jail cell at National Police Headquarters. But the man was insisting on a cash payment for talking to me, a hundred U.S. an hour, and so I had to say no. I've never paid for an interview or access to a news source and wasn't going to start with a commercially minded militant.

Maybe we could find a "free radical" in the Bashir camp, Norman suggested, and Reza nodded in assent. He thought he could surely arrange something by the time Norman and I returned from our impending trip to Bali and the three of us embarked on our tour of Central Java in ten days' time.

As we talked, the house beyond the screen door filled with friendly voices—Antonia's bule colleagues from the linguistic institute where she worked as a translator. When cameras flashed around the crib and Norman went in to offer his photographic expertise, Reza and I lapsed into a languorous state. We were smiling at the pleasant commotion over Beatrice when Reza casually pointed to one of his daughter's admirers, a tall, bulky man whose outline was visible through the screen door.

"Jewish," said Reza in a low voice, and my antennae shot up immediately. What was this, I thought—why would Reza, a Muslim, suddenly take such pains to single out a Jew from among his other guests? Being so skeptical is a terrible thing of course, but from Reza's secretive manner I couldn't tell whether he thought being Jewish was a good thing or not, and the question troubled me.

The screen door suddenly opened, and the man stepped onto

the balcony to join us. He had sandy hair, a sparse sandy beard, and the scholarly pallor and shyness of the professional translator. To break the ice, I asked him that famous American question (which turns out to be a favorite one in big, multicultural Indonesia, as well), "Where are you from?"

"Well, that depends on who's asking," he said as a cryptic smile played at the edges of his mouth. The fellow then asked me to guess. There was something familiar about his mixed accent but in the torpid heat of the afternoon I couldn't untangle it, and I shrugged my shoulders.

"I'm Israeli," said the man coyly. "My friends here know it"—he beamed affectionately at Reza—"but they don't say. And I don't tell anybody on the outside."

"I don't feel so bad now," I said.

The Israeli arched an eyebrow and, a little edgily, asked, "What do you mean?"

"Well," I said, "I thought I was taking a chance coming here as an American, but an Israeli—I admire your guts!"

The man laughed. "But I'm an American, too, you see. At least I have an American passport, so I don't have any problems with the government here."

"Are there many courageous Israelis in Jakarta these days?" I asked.

"There's one more, but he travels on a Canadian passport," said the man. "So we're both covered!"

We laughed again, and I felt particularly good because I now realized that this quietly adventurous man had counted on Reza to keep his secret, and Reza had kept the faith. Sometimes all it takes is a flashing moment, and I knew then that, results of my rudimentary Javanese eye exam notwithstanding, I could safely trust Reza with my life.

The screen door opened again, and Norman stepped out at gunpoint—well, really at squirt-gunpoint, as Reza's toddler son, Gillie, up from his nap, was now directing guests onto the balcony with a large plastic weapon, and generally stirring up havoc in a disarming Italian-Indonesian sort of way. Amid the happy chatter that followed, Norman opened his wallet and passed around complimentary tickets for a cocktail party to be held at a Jakarta hotel that evening to raise money for the Bali bombing victims.

Reza eyed his coupon with inscrutable interest, and then looked up at me and asked me, "You go to party tonight?"

"I don't know, I might," I said, blathering on about how I hated cocktail parties but seeing as how it was for Bali and all, well . . .

"So you go or not?" Reza repeated insistently.

Suddenly I grew wary. "You seem very curious, Reza," I said. "Tell me, what's it to you whether I go or not?"

"Maybe he's going to bomb the place," said Norman, with a nervous laugh. Reza joined in, emitting a low, reedy chuckle, and then after a pregnant paused continued to press his question: "So you go or not?"

Now his infernal persistence made me angry. This was Indonesia, where everything shifted like the tides, and wondering if I hadn't jumped too quickly to my private vote of confidence in Reza, I snapped, "So what if I *do* go?"

Reza smiled serenely. "Oh, nothing, nothing," he said, blithely waving away my concern. And now it was my turn to laugh, sheepishly, as I realized the old bule had been completely hoodwinked.

"Relax, Boss," said Norman, grinning broadly, "it's just a little of that anarchist humor again—we hope."

By the time Norman and I arrived on Bali, the resort island was once again the safest place on earth, at least as far as any immediate terrorist threat was concerned. The bombers had hit and run, and in spite of their initial reluctance, Indonesian authorities had moved surefootedly, arresting Imam Samudra on November 21, 2002, after some fancy technological sleuthing involving the tracking of cell phones and ATM records. With the help of investigators from Australia, the U.S., and Japan, there were already two dozen suspects in custody. Mounting evidence had privately convinced police investigators that Jemaah Islamiyah was the culprit and Bashir was directly linked to the attacks. And even though the JI warlord believed responsible for overall strategic planning, Riduan Isamuddin, alias Hambali, was still at large, it was assumed by intelligence officials in the region (quite optimistically as it turned out) that, as one senior source told me, JI's "back" had been "broken."

Bali faced some murderous problems nonetheless. Daily tourist arrivals, the bellwether of the local economy, had plummeted from the usual nine thousand a day to less than seven hundred. Desperate hoteliers were offering many of the island's fifty thousand rooms at fire-sale rates just to keep facilities operating and staffers at work. And so it was inevitable, in a place where tourism employed nine out of ten wage earners, that people talked ominously of a "second bomb" going off, meaning the social explosion that might come when and if the money ran out and large numbers of Balinese returned broke and grumbling to their villages. Megawati's government was encouraging the Balinese to diversify into "agribusiness," but few thought it a realistic plan. There were now three million Balinese, or twice as many as in 1960 before the foreign tourists started coming in big numbers. Hurling semicitified locals back at the land was no solution. Bali had become a tourist Mecca, and the island would now literally live or die by tourist.

Deeper tensions troubled the island, as well. Tear-shaped Bali has been Indonesia's great Hindu oasis ever since newly arrived Islam began challenging the Hindu orthodoxy on Java some eight hundred years ago. That confrontation, setting rajah against sultan, eventually helped bring about the collapse of the heavily Indocentric Majapahit dynasty and sent Hindu nobles south seeking refuge. Since my last visit there three years earlier, however, Bali's Hindu majority had slipped from ninety-three percent of the local population to eighty-three percent, and the sudden demographic shift amplified widespread fears that the island was being "colonized" by Islamic fundamentalists from Java who, financed by ultra-orthodox Saudis and Kuwaitis, might ultimately seek to win by peaceful means what the JI boys had failed to do with their bombs.

The Balinese had good reason to feel vulnerable. Ever since tourism exploded in the 1980s, as the Western economies reached new heights of affluence, enabling plumbers from Adelaide, roofing contractors from Houston, and the much-abused Japanese "salary-men," and their families, to fund brief, trip-of-a-lifetime interludes in paradise, the impact on traditional Balinese culture had been nothing short of breathtaking. In the early nineties, places only slightly off the beaten tourist track were often linked to the outside world by a few old-fashioned crank-style telephones. "Now kids watch MTV and think the lifestyles they see there, doing what you want without limits, equal 'freedom,' " my Balinese friend Gusky Suarsana, a prominent local businessman, told me. And so along with the good jobs and brighter lifestyles had come some ugly side effects, which included sharp rises in drug and alcohol abuse, teenage pregnancies, prostitution, and AIDS, and a general weakening of the important existential safety net of village tradition.

Hindu activists were feeling particularly exposed. When I visited a local psychiatrist and community leader, Professor Doctor Luh Ketut Suryani, at her clinic in Denpasar, and asked how the night-club bombings had influenced the Balinese psyche, she looked at me with an engaging smile and said matter-of-factly, "People think the dead are following them."

A large, handsome woman with fierce dark eyes, Dr. Suryani went on to explain that survivor guilt, a standard feature of Western psychiatry, was compounded in Bali by the local belief in the workings of karma. Many of her patients really were convinced that the bombings symbolized heavenly retribution for the sins of lives past and present. Many also privately interpreted both the impact of Western-style tourism and the recent influx of Muslim fundamentalists in the same light. And Dr. Suryani did not disagree: "Maybe God *is* punishing us for what we've allowed to happen here," she said. "Bali is a small island and beautiful. We've tried to change from mass tourism to quality tourism but unsuccessfully. And so what we have now is amoral tourism," by which she meant the hedonistic, drunken, bungee-jumping, spring-break-type hijinks that centered on frenzied clubs where the traffic peaked at three and four o'clock in the morning. "Prostitution, striptease," she said. "People building hotels near temples. The old balance between human beings, God, and nature is totally upset."

Now Suryani, like others, worried that capitalism and Islam, each seen to be belligerently un-Balinese in its own uniquely powerful way, were slowly pushing the local psyche to a breakpoint. "The Balinese are not aggressive people," warned the doctor. "It's hard for them to stand up for themselves. They won't speak out till we're in crisis. But if they feel their self-esteem damaged they will react and then it can't be stopped."

Was she predicting communal bloodshed in Bali? I suspected the good doctor was, quite understandably, feeling a little overwrought, but I could see her point. While Bali was still the strongest local economy in the country in terms of fundamentals, the statistics are really secondary when you're talking mass psychology, aren't they? One day Sarajevo was a tourist haven, too, hosting the Winter Olympics in 1984, and the toast of the world; a few years later, it was in a state of brutal ethnic meltdown in an evaporated multicultural Yugoslavia, and fears and rumors and old complexes had prepared the rationale. These days the international micro-scene did not automatically encourage optimism.

Still in all, the Balinese are a highly adaptable people, and it seemed to me they were, in general, banking on the global consumer culture, with its promise of jobs and better-managed, forward-looking lives, to overwhelm the forces of Jihad. Radical Islam had sucker-punched Bali in the cruelest way imaginable and briefly traumatized the world in the process, but locally it was McWorld that was still clearly calling the shots. Even Solidaritas Bali, the private support group Norman and his friends had helped organize after the bombings, had failed to rouse sustained enthusiasm for erecting a permanent memorial at Bali's Ground Zero in Kuta; by March 2004, new commercial construction was reported sprouting from the banana grove marking the grave of the Sari Club. Meanwhile Paddy's had been reincarnated a hundred meters down Jalan Legian as Paddy's Reloaded in what the media predictably touted as a "symbolic act of defiance."

Judging by my immediate circumstances, I should have fallen into a happy coma in Bali. In his inimitable style, Norman had managed to acquire for us a lush cream-colored villa not far from the

Kuta strip, with two tasteful, airy apartments separated by a full-sized swimming pool, a large patio, and a full kitchen staffed by six smiling Balinese women—all for the ridiculously low price of a hundred dollars a night. But after a week on Paradise Island, I was ready for a symbolic act of defiance myself.

Thanks to my own stupidity, the great annual pilgrimage to Mecca was under way, which meant that local Muslim leaders of consequence were unavailable, and so reporting from paradise took on the quality of wading through a very large vat of warm molasses. One morning at breakfast, as I watched the warmth rise in wavy lines above the blue mirage of the pool, and our kitchen ladies, glowing with silent, perplexed smiles, had gathered around a balky toaster as if waiting for it to emit a signal from the Great Beyond, I decided, so suddenly it surprised me a little, that I wanted off Bali as soon as humanly possible.

The Defender of Java, who had also been troubled by the Bali doldrums, picked up my mental signal, instantly. "Bring on the jihad, Boss?" asked Norman.

I nodded. Better to head for the Islamic heartland, where radical fires were said to burn hot and bright, I thought, before both of us went stark raving troppo.

"There's a flight for Jogja tomorrow at five A.M.," said Norman.

"We're on it," I said.

16

LAIR

The sun was barely up when we arrived in Jogjakarta, and from our taxi I could see the new day glowing around the bluish margins of the city's encircling volcanic bottomlands. It was indisputably lovely, even for an alleged fundamentalist hotbed, I thought. What was really unusual, though, was the high level of human traffic energizing the streets. Despite the early hour, the broad grassy borders along the highway into town were already streaming with hundreds of people—men in prayer caps with kaftans billowing out behind, women in their frumpy, nunlike habits, and the kids dinging along as miniature, manic versions of the grown-ups.

As we drove, the human flow swelled to a torrent, and then suddenly diverted itself into a large roadside mosque, where the courtyard, big as a lake, was already filled to the brim with worshipers. And then there was all the livestock to consider. "What's the deal with the goats and sheep?" I asked Norman, in my customary trenchant style, as I pointed to the ubiquitous clumps of poor little spindly-legged creatures dotting the roadside and straining meekly at their tethers.

"It's the day of the slaughter, Boss," said Norman matter-of-factly, and then of course I remembered. This was Id al-Adha, the Muslim feasting holiday celebrating the end of the annual pilgrimage to Mecca with a final submission to God in the ritual slaughter of farm animals.

How auspicious, I thought as I suddenly grew gloomy again.

But it was not in fact a particularly auspicious time in Central Java in any event. The area's two fabled court cities, Jogjakarta and Solo, represented the collective consciousness of Islam in Indonesia, and right now the psyche was sharply split. On one side, you had the old-time religion, Javanese Islam—infused with the island's original animistic thinking, with its demons and shamans, its magical spells, and its basic beliefs in good and evil, all richly marbled, broadened, and complicated by the thousand-odd years during which Hindu and Buddhist kings and priests had ruled the roost prior to the coming of Islam. Then, after the decline of the Majapahit dynasty triggered the last great Hindu exodus to Bali, around the time Columbus was leaving Spain on his ill-starred mission to find the magical Spice Islands, Central Java gave rise to the Mataram empire with Islam as its chief political organizing principle.

The other half of Java's Islamic mind developed much later and was considerably more austere. Nature abhors a vacuum, but man in his spiritual life yearns for simplicity, and by the beginning of the twentieth century that desire had taken the shape in Indonesia of a movement, inspired by thinkers and doers in the Middle East, to "purify" the religion of Mecca by returning it to a Koran-thumping fundamentalism. "That created friction between traditional Muslims and the puritans," Jadul Maula, a leading Islamic thinker and activist, would later tell me. "So the radical groups we have now, Bashir, Jaffar, and the others, are just the latest in a long line of 'purification' Islam, which demands that the Koran be taught literally."

Okay. And so today the old-new struggle for the soul of Indonesian Islam, between the literalists and the old-time romancers, you might say, was once again putting strains on Java, and by extension its two old rival Islamic principalities. Now separated by an hour's drive along a modern concrete highway, Jogja and Solo were at the center of the militant new incarnation of Islam that had emerged full-blown after the suppression of the Suharto years. Jaffar Umar Thalib's headquarters were located in an Islamic boarding school on the leafy outskirts of Jogja. And the epicenter of the epicenter, at least as far as the media, intelligence officials in the region, and the Indonesian police were concerned, was Ngruki, that ragged little satellite town near Solo, where Abu Bakar Bashir had his pesantren, Al Mukmin.

Which side, Javanese Islam or Islamicized Java, had the momentum on its side? That is what I had come to Central Java to find out.

First, however, I found out about the Jogjakarta Hyatt, where the lobby was decorated for tourist-friendly Saint Valentine's Day with big red paper hearts with frilly white borders. I had to hand it to Norman—he'd really outdone himself this time, scoring two deluxe rooms at only fifty dollars a night. Mine was located on the ground floor, with a big glass door opening onto a cozy stone patio where a black butterfly the size of a squash racket was busily seducing a brilliant red hibiscus. In the middle distance shafts of sunlight filtered through a stand of trees, beyond which I could see the dappled greensward of the adjoining golf course.

The place was gorgeous—too gorgeous, in fact. As my friend Habib Rizieq Shihab had proudly reminded me in Jakarta, it was just such fancy Western-style hotels in Central Java that his Islamic Defenders had targeted for the "sweeping" of American visitors. And so after making sure the patio door was tightly locked, I drew the curtains with extreme prejudice, and shoved a bulkily upholstered armchair into place as a barricade. It was then, while leafing through my guest information packet, which included coupons for the first fifty balls free at the hotel driving range, that I discovered I'd been registered under the name of "Mister Norman Wibowo."

"Can't be too careful, Boss," said Norman when I found him occupying a table in the main dining room, a spacious light-filled atrium overlooking an Olympic-size swimming pool and formal tropical gardens. I smiled inwardly, realizing that, released from the spell of Bali and back on sacred soil, the Defender of Java was now fully revived. I had just one further question: "If I'm you," I said, "then who are *you?*"

"I'm the new Faisal Reza," Norman said proudly. Reza wouldn't need his name around the Hyatt, he reasoned, since he wouldn't be staying with us—our Islamic bureau chief had eschewed my offer of posh circumstances, preferring instead to preserve his "man of the people" status by bunking with politically correct friends in town. And as Norman astutely observed, a good Muslim name was a terrible thing to waste.

It was then that the old Faisal Reza, fresh off the plane from Jakarta, joined us over coffee. And I cannot tell you how reassuring it was finally to be in the presence of a man who I now had every confidence would know how to keep two questionable Christians, Norman and me, out of hot water while we did our duty in the Islamic heartland. Smiling his bashful smile, Reza hitched up a chair and, officially released from his household duties by Antonia, I could see he was raring to go.

For starters, Reza had managed to arrange an interview on the spur of the moment with Pakubuwono XII, the ceremonial ruler of the Javanese court at Solo, and someone I'd long wanted to meet. Not only was the eighty-year-old sunan, or king, a living link to Java's mystical Islamic past, but he was also known as a famous ladies' man and something of a card into the bargain. (The sunan boasted half a dozen official concubines, with whom he'd sired at least thirty-seven children, though if I understood Norman correctly, he was by no means faithfully polygamous.) Not surprisingly perhaps, the sunan also happened to be the liege lord of the Clan Wibowo.

"After sunan," said Reza, ticking off the agenda with his look of choirboy innocence, "we go Ngruki"—there to pay a call on Abu Bakar Bashir's alleged academy of terror. I winced inwardly at the thought, but tried to put things in perspective by reminding myself that stealing a peek inside the inner sanctum of fundamentalism was exactly why I'd come here, and every inquiring hack must occasionally take his medicine if he wants to satisfy his curiosity. (As I think

I've said earlier, I often regret not having gone into a more predictable line of work, but at age fifty-three I had to face the fact that
I was pretty much otherwise unemployable.)

And so, an hour later, I found myself in the back of a gleaming
beige sports utility vehicle, racing through the flat, crowded streets
of Jogja and out onto the highway to Solo. Behind the wheel was
our hotel driver, a bluff, pudgy man with gold-rimmed glasses and
the fat bejeweled fingers of a head eunuch. To my surprise and
Norman's chagrin, mild-mannered Reza immediately set to teasing
the fellow with such barbed questions about the local political scene
that Norman gracefully stepped in to keep things nice and friendly
by distracting us with a story.

During his brief career as a jet-setting movie star (so far at least
he was only ever in the one acclaimed art-house flick), he said, he'd
been hurrying to make a location shoot at the royal palace in Solo,
when he boarded a plane in Jakarta and found himself seated next to
a chipper old man with an inquiring eye, who smiled and asked him
affably, "So you're going to Solo today?"

Being in the movies and all, Norman was eager to nip in the bud
any designs a nosy old codger might have on starting up a conversation, so he replied frostily, "Well, if this is the flight for Solo, then I
guess I'm going to Solo, aren't I?"

Hardly had the words escaped his mouth, however, than Norman spied something on the old man's briefcase that made his blood
run cold—the royal crest of the house of Solo! To a man whose
father's family still ranked as minor court retainers from the days of
pageantry and glory, and whose secret Javanese name lay buried in a
local vault there, engraved on a sacred kris, this could mean only one
thing: Norman had just gravely insulted the very man, the Anchor of
Java in its human form, whom he was sworn by the oath of his
ancestors to defend to his dying breath. To say he was mortified
would be putting it rather mildly.

Luckily, the sunan didn't seem to notice. Instead, he appeared to
be absolutely mesmerized by the flight attendant's shapely rump,
which he assiduously studied, to-ing and fro-ing in the aisle. Once
they were airborne, His Excellency invested the remainder of the

flight in the ultimately unsuccessful bid to persuade the young woman to agree to favor Norman with a date.

Norman is an excellent storyteller, and we were all laughing at his comic misadventure as we zipped across Java's broad central plateau, its emerald-green fields encircled by nodding palms and ringed in the hazy distance by a coronet of blue volcanoes. But the whole atmosphere quickly shifted once we hit Solo. The city seemed even shabbier and more sun-baked than I remembered it from my sojourn there three years earlier; its dusty morning streets were sparsely peopled, and carried a sense of quiet desolation. As the low whitewashed buildings, with their corrugated tin roofs and rusted iron gates, ticked by, Reza turned to me and smiled enigmatically. "Now we are in center for terrorism," he said.

The way he pronounced it, *teh-rhor-rhee-zhum,* rolling his r's for emphasis, made it sound particularly menacing. Reza then helpfully reminded me that the big bomb used to blow up the Sari Club on Bali had been manufactured in a rented building down one of Solo's side streets.

The sunan turned out to be a spry, birdlike man in a striped polo shirt, and our audience was surprising and full of laughs. For one thing, we met in the coffee shop of a local hotel, which the king said he preferred to the Kraton, his sprawling, spookily threadbare Dutch Revival palace down the street. (Though, if you ask me, I think it had mainly to do with the attractive young women who were waiting tables at the hotel.) When I asked His Royal Highness what he thought about Jemaah Islamiyah operating at the heart of Javanese Islam, the sunan told me sharply that Islamic fundamentalism was a profound misunderstanding of Javanese traditions.

"Islam here is not the same as Islam in the Arab world," he said, arching lively eyebrows and tilting his head so he could look at me down the barrel of his shapely aquiline nose. "We here in Java never wanted to perfect Islam but to adapt it to our universal culture. If you really want to follow the Koran, you have to follow God. You want to follow Muhammad? Muhammad is an Arab—he's not Javanese!"

At that moment the sunan had been on the throne for fifty-seven years, but had in fact ruled for only a couple of weeks. That was mainly due to the talent of the Solo royals for making bad political choices pretty much ever since they'd established their capital in 1745. One important turning point came in 1825, when the sultan of neighboring Jogja led a revolt against Dutch colonial rule and Solo's elite sided with the Dutch. They did it again in 1945. Shortly after Pakubuwono XII was enthroned as king on August 14 of that year, the Japanese Imperial Army surrendered to the Allies, and the Dutch returned to reclaim their former colony, occupying Solo for use as a garrison town in their campaign to crush the Indonesian partisans. Once again, Jogja offered spirited resistance, while the Solo royals welcomed Dutch officers by throwing a lavish palace reception. When the Indonesians won their independence fight in 1949 and the partisans took control, Solo was unceremoniously stripped of its political autonomy and its playboy king, increasingly squeezed for funds over the years, began steering his long course for the coffee shop.

As our conversation proceeded, I must say that the sunan did not appear to have really clicked to the potential dangers of militant Islam. There was one particularly lively moment, however, when our waitress made the mistake of bending down in front of HRH to pick up a spoon that had fallen to the floor. In a movement I thought very fast for an eighty-year-old man, the sunan snatched his cigarette pack from the table and hurled it sidearm, striking the woman square on a large rounded ham and producing a sharp thwacking sound.

While Norman and Reza dissolved into schoolboy giggles, however, I did not join in the hilarity. That was because I was too busy keeping an eye on a local journalist named Rashid, a veteran of the Solo terrorism beat, whom Reza had invited along to guide us into Abu Bakar Bashir's lair in Ngruki. All the while I'd been listening to Norman's translation and taking notes, I could see him studying me from across the table with a crafty, hooded gaze. When I turned to look him squarely in the eye, however, he would purposely maintain eye contact for a full second, smirk, and then wagging his head as if at some private joke, look quickly away. (Javanese eye exam score: zero.)

And so I was struggling to stay focused on the sunan as he

worked toward the climax of his political philosophy. "Look," he said, blinking the royal peepers coolly, "it all boils down to sexual libido. Why do you think all those Indonesian maids are sent over there to Saudi Arabia?"

Flashing a gleeful, here-we-go-again grin, Norman decided to draw the sunan out with a little gentle humor. "Sir, tell me, can you still travel overseas at your age?" he inquired. The question elicited a tart, birdlike expression.

"Of course," said His Royal Highness, "if you pay for my air ticket . . ."

"But you still like it there, overseas?" Norman persisted.

The old man eyed him quizzically. "You're talking about the red nipples of the foreign ladies now, right?"

The sheer outlandishness of the remark sent Norman and Reza into renewed paroxysms of laughter. Even Rashid gathered his small, troutlike mouth into a sour grin, and then glared in my direction, as if daring me to laugh. Not wishing to offend, I managed a weak smile, but to be honest I was pretty seriously freaked out by this time. All I could think of was: This is the guy Reza's picked to lead us into the belly of the beast?

When the interview was over, and the sunan made a trip to the washroom, Norman, loyal swordbearer for the Viking interloper, took advantage of the jocular mood to ask Rashid if there was any problem in me, a foreigner, paying a call on Bashir's pesantren, what with the U.S.-led coalition about to lay waste to Baghdad and all.

"No problem," said Rashid, before cracking a wolfish smile and adding portentously: *"Inshallah*—if God wills." When he followed up this rollicking witticism with a sardonic laugh, I could feel various bodily valves open and shut as they battened down for emergency action.

I shook hands with Pakubuwono halfheartedly and said good-bye. Back in the car, Norman observed in a tone of ironic pride, "That's my king, Boss."

"I never would have guessed," I said, distracted and miserable.

"Yeah," said Reza, looking out the window and cackling dryly, "and sunan don't give a shit about *teh-rhor-rhee-zhum.*"

• • •

Terrorism was all I could think about now as we drove Solo's dusty, sun-fried streets. Seeing as how it was too early to head for our rendezvous in Ngruki, Norman suggested we stop for a bite to eat and discuss final security procedures for visiting the reputed headquarters of Terror, Incorporated. Rashid smirked but said okay, and then curtly guided our driver to a restaurant, a long, low establishment open to the street, where clapped-out vans and minibuses spewed diesel smoke at the diners.

There were five of us around the table, including our driver, who persisted in cracking forced, unfunny jokes and talking loudly. Ever the gracious host on my expense account, Norman ordered enormous quantities of food—a spicy corn soup, a braised tofu dish with red chile peppers, fried chicken, lamb *saté,* and the ubiquitous Indonesian fried rice, *nasi goreng.* As the others ate heartily, I loaded my plate without hunger and choked down a few bites, lest I show the inquiring Rashid how jittery I was.

But in the never-let-them-see-you-sweat department, I was a wretched flop. The day was beastly hot of course, and the added factor of nervous tension plus all that spicy food had fired my sweat glands to new heights of perspiratory achievement. I was mopping my face with a handkerchief when Rashid looked up from his soup and asked, "Why do you sweat so much?"

There was that smirk again. "It's the soup," I said lamely. "It's very hot—you know, spicy."

Rashid snorted derisively, as if he thought that was pretty rich. "I'm eating the same soup as you but I'm not sweating," he said. A few seconds later he looked up from his bowl, and said probingly, "You're not Jewish, are you?"

I looked at Norman, who was translating our conversation, and saw the flicker of fear in his eyes. Before I could stammer out the correct answer, Norman beat me to it. "No," he said, answering for me in Indonesian. "His ancestors were Swedish—he's a Viking, can't you tell?"

"I thought because he is so big and bulky he might be a Jew," said Rashid. He flexed his arms, making his pectoral muscles jump under his T-shirt, and grinned sourly.

In spite of the unfriendly circumstances, I couldn't help but chuckle to myself. I was thinking how amused my best pal back in Manhattan, Robert Schonfeld, would be to hear that the Jews had a reputation in these parts for being such musclemen. But the spasm of humor faded quickly as I sat there, trying to appear enthusiastic about my food, my fear floating on sweat, and Robert's parting words rang in my ears. "Don't go looking for trouble," he'd told me as I was literally on my way out the door to the airport, "and if it finds you, turn around and run as fast as you can in the opposite direction. Those guys over there will cut your throat, smiling."

I looked over at Rashid, who was smiling, archly and into his soup, and the thought of running, or at least canceling the afternoon tour, did make a determined sprint across my mind. But of course friendly advice from back home doesn't often fit the circumstances in the field, and I knew in my gut that running just wasn't on. After all, Norman had quit a good job, laying his future on the line to accompany me; in spite of his own considerable misgivings, he'd devised the protocol for Operation Enduring Tracy, which required him to go in first to check any premises deemed questionable and see if it was safe for the American bule to enter. That was courage. And whatever I was paying Reza, it clearly undershot his commitment to our mission. No, having come this far, having asked so much of my guys, I simply could not chicken out now.

I was choking down a spoonful of rice when Norman pressed his earlier question with Rashid: "Is it safe for an American to visit Ngruki?"

Norman was still talking, but Rashid looked dead at me. "What are you so afraid of?" he demanded sarcastically, flashing a sharklike grin. "What does your imagination tell you you're going to find at the school?"

"I'm not from around here," I said. "You tell me."

Rashid grew openly impatient, drumming his fingers on the table. "It's just a bunch of kids," he said in a mocking tone. "You're afraid of kids? Besides, I've already told them a foreigner is coming."

"An American?"

"A foreigner. If they ask you where you're from, pick a country, any country you like. Just don't tell them you're from the United States."

That part made me feel even less easy. In all my years of reporting I've never once assumed a false identity to further a story; it always seemed so unsporting to do so. Today wasn't about principle, though. I stood as fully prepared as the next man to lie through my teeth to save my skin or even to prevent something really uncomfortable from happening. The real problem was that I happen to be a bad liar, one of the worst, and I knew beyond any doubt whatsoever that I'd be tripped up on a technicality as soon as I opened my mouth.

"What country am I from? Well, ah, I mean, ah . . . Canada!" I was sure to blow it, whereupon curved and cruel blades would be drawn.

We finished our meal. While the others sauntered out into the sunshine, toothpicks dangling from their mouths, I hung back with Norman. As we pretended to pore over the bill, I said, "I'm telling you right now, Norman, I don't like the way that guy looks at me."

"I know, Boss," Norman said. "He's got the shifty eyes."

Out on the sidewalk, meanwhile, Rashid had stopped and was looking back over his shoulder at us, working his toothpick into his gums. Norman saw him, too.

"Don't worry, Boss. I'll go into the school with him and check it out first. If it doesn't look right, we leave. Period."

As he spoke, his nostrils flared and his eyes glittered with Javanese steel. The Defender of Java, back on ancestral ground, was gearing up for battle. "If he thinks he's running this show he's sadly mistaken," said Norman.

Norman then marched resolutely outside and straight up to Rashid, who he grabbed by the elbow and looked directly in the eye. Whatever was said, the atmosphere inside the van was as silent as the tomb as we headed for Al Mukmin.

17

TERROR HIGH

Ngruki was a virtual magnet for paranoia. By the day of our visit the international media had succeeded in painting a picture of Abu Bakar Bashir's pesantren as a radical educational factory where, as one TV correspondent put it, instructors "inculcate hatred for non-Muslims and breed new recruits" for Jemaah Islamiyah and Al Qaeda. That image grew amid great hubbub shortly after the Bali bombings when police entered Muhammadiyah General Hospital in Solo, where Bashir had taken refuge on a respiratory complaint, and arrested the gasping, wheelchair-bound emir. The ensuing melée resulted in injuries to Bashir's outraged supporters, thus leading to further headlines in the Indonesian press about the barbarity of the cops and by implication their ostensible sponsor, President Megawati and her ostensible guarantor, George W. Bush.

The picture of Al Mukmin as an incubator for an anti-Western hatred wasn't wrong, mind you. Not by a long shot. But personally I find that it always pays to remember, especially in our all-news-all-the-time electronic age, that journalism remains an exceedingly blunt instrument. Terrorism experts now obligingly rolled before the TV cameras in the U.S. and Europe dourly rubberstamping the idea that Mukmin was Southeast Asia's "Harvard of suicide bombers," in spite of the fact that suicide bombing had so far been successfully tried only once in the region, in Bali, and the bomber had not attended Al Mukmin. Neither was there any solid evidence that Al Mukmin was in fact training foot soldiers for Al Qaeda; JI was perfectly capable of training its own foot soldiers for its own purposes. "Well, they're all terrorists, right?" a well-regarded former international TV news anchor said to me over dinner one night, offering a brisk and tidy example of how easily fear and ambition can help conflate the facts in a sort of "Damn the details, we're at war, man!" mentality.

The fact of the matter is that Al Mukmin's alumni rolls did include some indubitably dangerous characters. There was Fathur Rohman al-Ghozi, for example, who was touted as Jemaah Islamiyah's master explosives expert. Wanted for bombings that had killed the Philippine ambassador to Indonesia at his Jakarta residence in August of 2000 and twenty-two people in Manila later that same year, al-Ghozi was eventually nabbed in the Philippines in January 2002, with 1.2 tons of bomb-making materials in his possession. (Sentenced to seventeen years in prison, he would die under mysterious circumstances in a gunfight with Philippine Army rangers on the southern island of Mindanao after escaping a Manila jail in July 2003 with, some sources said, the help of the Philippine military.)

By far Bashir's most notorious protégé was Hambali, Jemaah Islamiyah's operational mastermind, and that rarest of terrorist birds—a central figure who, according to intelligence officials in Washington and the region, was an actual living, breathing tactical link between JI and Al Qaeda. Yet another veteran of the mujaheddin campaign against the Soviets in Afghanistan in the 1980s, Hambali is said to have deeply impressed fellow Islamic warrior Osama bin Laden with his penny-pinching flair for stretching terror budgets. His organizational skills evidently wowed Abu Bakar Bashir, as well, since it was Hambali the emir chose to serve as his right-hand man when the two men were living in exile in Malaysia in the

1990s. And according to the *Far Eastern Economic Review,* Asia's leading newsweekly, it was Hambali's success in overseeing guerrilla
operations in the Philippines and Indonesia after Suharto's downfall
that had made him the man to call when Al Qaeda was "looking to
Southeast Asia as their new stronghold."

Thus, by 2001, Hambali was ready for prime time. Allegedly
authorized by Al Qaeda to call the shots on his own (intelligence
officials later pegged him as No. 4 and the only non-Arab in the Al
Qaeda hierarchy), and angered over the misfired New Year's terror
blowout in Singapore, he made the pivotal decision to switch from
zeroing in on Western embassies and other symbolic "official" targets
to the fattest "soft target" of them all, in Bali; Hambali then allegedly
upped the ante by persuading traditionally easygoing Southeast
Asian Muslims to offer themselves up as suicide bombers. It was a
fairly textbook case of a local terror organization cooperating on a
plan with Al Qaeda that served the strategic aims of both (what
Zachary Abuza has ingeniously called "terrorism by Rolodex")—
and perhaps unusual only in that the plan was successfully conceived
and coordinated in the body and soul of a single double operative.

In some ways, then, Hambali made an even more appealing villain for the international media to follow than the venerable Bashir.
For one thing, he was not merely menacing but missing—still on the
loose after Bali, he was believed, with good reason, to be looking for
his next opportunity for a deadly strike. Now dubbed the new
"Osama of the East" in some press accounts, Hambali was believed to
have arranged for promising pupils from Solo to do "postgraduate"
studies in training camps in Afghanistan and the Philippines. And
here of course is the point: Sending Indonesians overseas for training
was, once again, not the same thing as filling the ranks of a centralized
Al Qaeda with Indonesians. Jemaah Islamiyah didn't have to be
directly in the pocket of Osama to be plenty dangerous on its own,
acting independently or lining up with Al Qaeda or other terrorist
groups as its local interests dictated. In the end the media implication
that Islamic terrorism was all-Al-Qaeda-all-the-time smacked of little more than a reassuringly comprehensive fiction masking a more
complex and harder-to-manage reality.

If the devil lives in the details, as they say, then the details regarding Jemaah Islamiyah's top boss, Abu Bakar Bashir, were particularly illuminating. For one thing, Al Qaeda could be said to be a mere teenager of an organization compared to JI, which had its informal beginning when Bashir and a colleague, Abdullah Sungkar, founded Al Mukmin way back in 1972. (Sidney Jones and her team of terrorism detectives would eventually turn up documentary evidence pinning down JI's "official" founding to January 1, 1993.) Of Yemeni descent, Bashir and Sungkar were devoted followers of Darul Islam, a movement that gained prominence in the turbulent 1950s by promoting the establishment of a shariah-based state in Indonesia. The pair's popularity grew, in essence, from their role as fiery right-wing talk-show hosts, exponential Rush Limbaugh types, who used a radio station in Solo, later dubbed "Radio Ngruki," to send their extreme but brainy views out across the hamlets and fields. Before long, devoted listeners and students, jazzed up on calls for jihad against the godless Suharto regime, had formed themselves into a secret society they called Jemaah Islamiyah, which means, loosely, "Islamic community." [1]

Bashir and Sungkar's radio career abruptly ended in 1978, however, when the two men were arrested for subversion and sentenced to nine years in jail. Released on appeal after four and undeterred, they continued proselytizing until 1985, when this time they managed to duck an impending Suharto crackdown and flee to neighboring Malaysia. And it was then that these two small-time preachers from Indonesia took their fundamentalist franchise international. Their timing was excellent. Enlivened by the rise of the radical ayatollahs who had replaced Shah Reza Pahlavi's corrupt and

---

1. Suharto investigators claimed that Sungkar had gone so far as to install himself as military governor of a shadow Islamic state, though considering the source, the charges were never widely believed in Indonesia, and the rest of the world simply didn't care. Whatever was up, the name Jemaah Islamiyah provided excellent deniability, since it could be argued to describe just about any group of Muslims anywhere, and hence so vague as to be meaningless, which is exactly what Bashir insisted when the police started putting on the heat after the Bali bombings.

gaudy regime in Iran with a shariah state in 1979, Islamic fundamentalism was enjoying a burst of renewed popularity all across the
Middle East and Asia. Out from under the Smiling General's heavy
thumb, it was a relatively easy matter for Bashir and Sungkar to
attract enough converts and money to begin knitting together a
broad underground network. By the time Suharto belatedly went
the way of the shah in 1998, the two old partners in radicalism were
able to bring the heart and head of their now relatively much larger
and better-organized operation back home to Ngruki. Sungkar died
in November 1999, and Bashir went on to acquire rock-star status
among Indonesia's increasingly fervent militants. By then it would
have been clear to anyone who really wanted to look closely, though
few of us had reason yet to do so, that Jemaah Islamiyah was no mere
Al Qaeda proxy.

There were hundreds of private Islamic schools in Central
Java—most espousing some form of moderate Islam. Only a relative
handful, like Al Mukmin, expressed a rock-ribbed radicalism. So
why didn't the Indonesian government simply go ahead and put the
troublemakers out of business? you ask—as some in the Bush
administration had quietly pressed Jakarta to do. Part of it was politics, of course. President Megawati and her allies feared stoking a
hostile response in the Muslim community as a whole by appearing
to shutter schools in an educationally starved country without solid
proof of criminal activity. For anyone who genuinely cared about
fostering a civil society, it was also a thorny problem of political
theology—how to respect principles in a still-wobbly democracy
while maintaining control.

Working at the heart of that dilemma, government prosecutors
continued to insist they had insufficient evidence to indict Bashir
for having had a direct hand in either Bali or the thwarted Singapore
conspiracy. That was despite the fact that captured Al Qaeda capo
Omar al-Faruq had reportedly been singing like a canary for his
CIA interrogators, and was said to have directly fingered Bashir for
helping to organize both plots. But such ostensibly damning evidence was strictly inadmissible in the crucial court of Indonesian
public opinion, and for one simple reason: The Americans had

refused to allow Indonesian investigators to talk directly to al-Faruq, insisting instead that they rely on CIA transcripts. And so while U.S. officials shook their heads over the sad state of the criminal justice system in Indonesia, most fair-minded Indonesians were simply unwilling to accept the "trust us" approach from the Americans, particularly in light of their own long history of forced confessions under Suharto. The truth meanwhile appeared to be lodged unsteadily somewhere between the two opposing camps.

And it was precisely because of that mixed and shifting picture that I'd felt duty-bound to sit down with Bashir, look him in the eye, and draw my own conclusions. But that wasn't going to happen now. Try as he might, not even the resourceful Reza could manage to get me in to see the emir as long as he remained in jail. Instead, he'd arranged for me to speak with the *ustad*, or principal, who had taken over Bashir's duties at Al Mukmin.

Technically a suburban village, Ngruki was in reality a poor, gritty tangle of ramshackle houses hemmed in by low cinder-block walls. And so, ten minutes after leaving the diner in Solo, when we turned off the main road into an intricate system of alleyways, each one narrower than the last, I could see Norman's eyes dart nervously, and I knew what he was thinking—one glance at the area's incult geography was all it took to tell you that any hope of a speedy escape, should escape be necessary, was completely out the window.

A final turn brought us into a bumpy lane a few inches wider than the car. Our driver, not nearly so jolly as before, nosed gingerly along lest he rasp his shiny new door panels against the rough stone walls, and then rolled to a stop when the street abruptly ended at Al Mukmin's big front gate. Three young men sitting on campstools, posting the guard, raised their heads and fixed us in a collective scowl.

"Wait here with Reza, Boss," said Norman. He then moved to join Rashid, who was already inside the compound and trading sly grins with an anorexic-looking fellow in a sarong and a prayer cap. When Norman offered his hand in greeting, the man suddenly went snake eyes, squinting at Norman's outstretched paw but refusing to shake it. Rashid then smirked in the direction of our car, while Snake Eyes, renewing his smile, wagged his head approvingly, and my imagination supplied the dialogue:

"You got the American in the car?"

"Yeah, he's in there all right. What a sucker!"

But that wasn't it at all. Quite the contrary, in fact. When Norman sauntered back to car, cool as a deputy sheriff, he stuck his head in the open window and said, "The head guy isn't here, Boss."

"Where is he?"

"Dunno. Still watching the goats get whacked, I guess." Whatever the case, Snake Eyes was adamant: No strangers were going to be allowed to roam around the premises without word from a higher authority. I sighed and made some perfunctory to-do about having come all this way only to get stopped at the gate. How damnably ironic! Secretly of course my heart soared like an eagle—but prematurely. For it was precisely at that moment a short, potbellied man flew past us on a motorbike, and Reza was out the door in a flash, shouting, "Hey!" and waving the rider to a stop. After a minute or two of friendly, laughing conversation, Reza returned, and said matter-of-factly, "That man head of terror school. He say, 'Okay, you come in.' So let's go!"

Involuntarily ruing the excellence of Reza's connections, I gingerly stepped inside the gate and presented myself for inspection. Snake Eyes stepped back and involuntarily dropped his jaw, as if regarding a visitor from a distant planet. Then without a word, he slipped through a small half-door in one of the flimsy prefab buildings nearby, on his way, I was convinced, to alert the goon squad that an extra-large Christian had just offered himself up for vivisection.

We walked on. The main school building was large and white, and sat about a hundred yards away at the far end of a dusty little main street flecked with quartz crystal that flared and sparkled in the blazing sun, and had the look of a showdown scene in a Clint Eastwood Western. Moving forward slowly, hands at my sides, no false moves, I hastened to aggressively remind myself that I was by no means the first foreign journalist to tramp this road. But of course, with Rashid's menacing behavior, and all the media hype about the run-up to war in Iraq, my worries were hard to shake.

But here is the good thing about being an addicted observer—you can always find something of interest to focus on, which is what I did now. When we reached the front steps of the school and I bent down to remove my shoes as custom required, I couldn't help but notice that the dozen or so pairs of cheap plastic sandals scattered around the base of the stairs all had interesting little pictures or symbols of some kind etched in ballpoint pen on their insteps. When I took a closer look, however, my heart gave a thump—the little symbols were in fact crude renditions of the Holy Cross and the Star of David.

"So students can always step on them," said Reza brightly when he caught me gawking.

"Ah ha," I said. I was feeling myself overcome with renewed numbness, when a young man of about sixteen suddenly stepped forward to greet us. He was dressed in an impressive green flannel blazer with a school crest over the pocket, and had a shy, smiling face with rashes of acne crowning both cheeks. That he'd been quickly pressed into service as our guide was evident from his partially slicked-down cowlick and the wrinkled training clothes underneath his snappy jacket.

"Welcome to our school," said the boy, bashfully pumping my hand in a big, looping fashion, as if remembering a lesson in Western etiquette. Good manners, I was to learn, were strictly emphasized at Al Mukmin, along with math, history, science, art appreciation, language arts, English and Arabic, and of course strenuous amounts of Koran and jihad.

"I will be happy to show you anything you want to see," offered the boy, who said his name was Dudin.

"Anything?" I said in a kidding tone. Frankly, after the sandals and that fuss at the front gate, I was surprised and relieved to have been so cordially received—plus, one look at Dudin told me he was no terrorist. If anything, he looked like a young Tiger Woods modeling the green blazer awarded annually to the winner of the Masters Golf Tournament.

"Well, there is one rule," Dudin said, quickly searching my face, as if fearing I might object, as Norman translated: "We have to ask permission before entering somebody's dorm room. That's for privacy."

"Understood, Dudin," I said, and off we went on our campus tour. Though relatively new, the main building, with its endless acreage of white ceramic tiles and fissured, whitewashed concrete, was built in a style reminiscent of the ready-made dilapidation perfected by Soviet architects during the Cold War. But media reports that Al Mukmin was scrupulously free of the ornaments of Western culture were simply wrong. True, there was what American students might consider an appalling absence of machines dispensing chips, candy bars, sodas, and bottles of designer water. On the other hand, Al Mukmin's large inner courtyard was fully occupied by what appeared to be a regulation-size basketball court with backboards decorated in the unmistakable red-white-and-blue design of our own National Basketball Association. (If a study has not been conducted on Michael Jordan's contribution to the war against terrorism it should be commissioned forthwith.)

While we paused to watch a scrimmage in progress, I made a few mental coaching notes on the need for better defensive screening and rebounding after the shot, in case I was asked for my opinion. (I wasn't.) Dudin meanwhile told me that Al Mukmin had two thousand students, half high school and half elementary school. There were eight hundred girls, he said, and perhaps so I wouldn't get the wrong idea, he was careful to stipulate, "They have their own dormitory."

I learned from Dudin and others that the curriculum was indeed varied but focused principally on seeking *tawhid,* or "unity with God," in the community of other Muslims. That meant submission to the principles of the Holy Koran as enshrined in the dictates of the shariah. And of course the tool of submission was jihad, the battle against whatever threatened "Islamic perfection" or whoever sought to misinterpret or tread on the religion. No names were named, but you could safely assume "America" or "George Bush" would satisfy any pop quiz.

For red-blooded high school students, however, the threat to

Islamic purity not infrequently arose much closer to home. As an article in *Tempo* magazine explained: "[If] a student is caught writing letters to the opposite sex, the student is deemed to have committed a major offence," and forced to do manual labor around the campus while he (or, theoretically, she) pondered the downside of hormonal surge. And if that was grounds for a scandal, the article went on, "imagine what happens to those who are caught dating, having pre-marital sex, stealing or consuming liquor." I imagined. The correct answer was not the lopping of offending bodily appendages, though, but simply getting expelled from school and having to go back home to face the music with your mortified parents.

We proceeded up a broad stairway. Walking the second-floor gallery, circling the basketball court from above, I was surprised to come upon a blackboard devoted to English conversation phrases to remember: "I am pleased to make your acquaintance," "Don't mention it," and so on. A few paces farther along a group of boys, dressed in clean white shirts, their hair neatly combed, were lollygagging at the railing and giggling nervously at the sight of a huge foreign guest. "Excuse me, fellas," I said as I passed by, to which they immediately and enthusiastically replied in English, "Don't mention it, Sir!"—"You are very welcome, Sir!"—"After you, Sir!"

I am of course naive. But at that precise moment, rightly or wrongly, my whole impression of Java's alleged Terror High changed irrevocably and for the better. I am now at the age where I find such respect for elders surprisingly refreshing, and wondered, a little absurdly, I supposed, how I might have been received were I visiting a typical American high school. But a wealthy Indonesian business-man whose opinion I respect assured me a day or so later that it was not an outlandish question. He had in fact recently moved to Cen-tral Java from Bali, in a loving father's hope of protecting his son from the resort island's pervasive drugs, sex, and rock music culture.

For many Indonesian parents, the pesantren (or its day-school equivalent, the madrassah) is the only option. Islamic schools gener-ally take in pupils regardless of their ability to pay tuition; if they simultaneously whip the kids into shape for life's hard slog, well, so much the better. In a country with a crumbling public education

system, where a religious schooling often represents the only reasonable alternative, striking the right balance between personal freedom and community responsibility is an adventure fraught with
even more peril than in the United States. (Our two countries had a
lot to talk about, and education, as some of America's Indonesian
experts have suggested, is a good place to start.)

"You still think this is a school for terrorism?"

We had finished our tour, and were loitering near the basketball
court, waiting for the delinquent head man to show, when Rashid
surprised me by speaking in English, a language I hadn't realized he
spoke.

I laughed. "It's hard to know, isn't it?" I said. "But I'll admit I
didn't know what to expect. That's why I had to come and have a
look, I guess."

Rashid nodded. "The people here are radicals in their heads," he
said, touching his forefingers to his temples, "but not in action."

My reporter's nose told me he was probably right as far as Dudin
and his pals were concerned. They struck me in the main as a bunch
of typical teenagers—meaning, likable, curious, malleable, hero-
hungry kids, looking to fill in the blank tablets of their future with
high ambitions and big dreams.

Did the school recruit and train terrorists? Well, it seemed fairly
clear that nobody was openly majoring in bomb-making or sniping
techniques. And the plain fact was that most graduates of Al Mukmin eventually entered society as government workers, doctors,
lawyers, soldiers, even journalists. On the other hand, many did
become Islamic clerics, who went forth to spread the word of the
Prophet in its austere *salafi* format. And of course there was that
worrying handful of undeniably dangerous alumni who had been
implicated in dastardly deeds in the Moluccas, Singapore, the Philippines, and now Bali.

How did Rashid explain that? "All I can tell you is that I met
Bashir almost every day from the time of the World Trade Center
attacks on," he said, and he was convinced from the emir's demeanor

that he didn't know any of the Al Qaeda hitmen, Singapore plotters, or Bali bombers personally, despite the testimony of al-Faruq and at least a few of the thirty-three JI suspects then behind bars in Singapore who had also incriminated Bashir. On the other hand, Rashid said cryptically, "Bashir does have a lot to hide."

He didn't want to go into the details, but when I pursued the point with other friends, the picture that emerged of Bashir was that of the spiritual "linchpin" of a mixed and shifting religious society with an active paramilitary auxiliary. That is to say, Al Mukmin was legit, at least on the surface. It was perfectly possible to attend the school and not know what, if anything, was going on in the highly secretive background. What was going on? Speculation centered on a group of hard-core individuals I mentioned earlier, who dabbled in clandestine activities that included running terrorist training camps and plotting attacks, sometimes in league with Al Qaeda, often not, while securing funding from elements in the military and industry in return for certain favors. At the same time, this relatively small, well-organized band of brothers was not infrequently at odds with itself. (Abu Bakar Bashir, knowledgeable sources believed, had opposed Bali on tactical grounds; Hambali and others, who had opposed Bashir's "moderate" approach, had been willing to go full throttle for Islamic revolution, whatever the cost.)

And therein lay the confounding dilemma for the United States and its allies in conducting the war on terrorism. "[T]he Ngruki network," as Sidney Jones had noted in one of her excellent reports, "is far wider than the handful of people who have been accused of ties to al-Qaeda and includes individuals with well-established political legitimacy for having defied the Soeharto government and gone to prison as a result."[2] Putting the heat on Abu Bakar Bashir, whatever his exact degree of involvement in JI's nefarious deeds, had already made him a hero among many moderate Muslims; to go after others without solid evidence risked creating an entire pantheon.

---

2. See the International Crisis Group's *Indonesia Briefing: Al-Qaeda in Southeast Asia: The Case of the "Ngruki Network" in Indonesia* (8 August 2002), available online at www.icg.org.

"The challenge, both for the Indonesian government and the international community," Sidney's report concluded "is to be alert to the possibility of individuals making common cause with international criminals, without taking steps that will undermine Indonesia's fragile democratic institutions." Don't overdo the Al Qaeda threat or you'll miss the bigger picture, Sidney had warned me over lunch in Jakarta, and having made the effort to journey to Al Mukmin, I thought I understood a little better now what she'd been driving at.

The sun was dipping low over the backboards in the courtyard, and we were still cooling our heels, waiting for the headmaster to arrive, when I asked Dudin, "What year are you in school now?"

"Junior," he said, his eyes fixed on his wiggling toes.

"One more year to go, then," I said. "What will you do when you graduate?"

Dudin looked up and flashed a big smile. "I want to join the Justice Party," he said, adding that he was impressed with its clean reputation and commitment to good works. When I told him I'd met the party leader, Hidayat Nurwahid, in Jakarta he looked at me as if I'd told him I'd recently shared a coffee with the Prophet himself. "Aha!" I said. "So you want to be a politician?"

"Yes," he said, nodding more energetically than before.

"Well, you're a handsome kid and obviously smart, and that's a big advantage for a politician." As Norman translated, Dudin beamed a flustered smile and then grabbed my hand and shook it in his eager, looping way.

"Now let's get the hell out of here," I said, turning to Norman. He agreed. So did Reza. It was clear by now that the head man had stood us up, but Reza said, "Is okay"—he still had a few radical aces up his sleeve, people who might shed further light on Bashir and his works.

And so we left the compound, relaxed and smiling, and climbed back into the car. This was not the first time, as the attentive reader will know, that I'd greeted an encounter with radical Islam with palm-sweating trepidation only to be released to the street the unharmed recipient of unanticipated cordiality. It had happened in Jakarta with Suaib Didu, the redoubtable Habib Rizieq Shihab, and others. It wasn't wrong to be afraid of course, given the long ledger of murders and kidnappings that had befallen foreigners in the Muslim world in recent years. But I also had to admit to myself that, as a pretty typical American, my fears were at least occasionally exaggerated, just as old Gus Dur had stressed to me when I'd spoken with him on that dewy morning in Jakarta two weeks earlier.

And here is how I explained the situation to myself: There was absolutely no doubt that genuine bad guys stalked the territory, and deserved to be hunted down like the cruel dogs they were. At the same time, however, it struck me as equally important that young men like Dudin and his friends be given as broad a menu of options for their individual pursuits of happiness as possible, if only to make them less susceptible to the agitated dreams of Pax Islamica.

And suddenly, viscerally, I was more than ever convinced that George Bush had set America on a devastatingly shortsighted path when on September 20, 2001, he'd declared, "Either you are with us, or you are with the terrorists." The black-and-white surety of such a statement really is shocking in its ignorance of the realities of a world where, as my realistic colleague, the writer Ian Buruma, notes: "It is perfectly possible for a practicing Muslim to be against the United States intervention [in Iraq], free-market capitalism, sexual freedom and the importing of Hollywood movies without being a theocratic revolutionary."

In combating terrorism, as in other areas of communication (war being communication by other means), I have always suspected that the medium is an inescapably important part of the message. Dudin and his pals, and the teachers and students I met at other heartland schools, only served to confirm and deepen that prejudice.

The highway back to Jogja was straight and smooth, a band of silver concrete slicing through the countryside, cleaving the rolling hills and flat pasturelands, everything glowing with golden light in that moment of the day the filmmakers rightly call the "magic hour." The mood inside the passenger compartment, meanwhile, was one of happy exhaustion. Norman, crammed into the jump seat in the rear, had already dozed off, and was emitting soft, staccato snores. Sharing the backseat with me, Reza stared glassily out the window, his heavy eyeglasses reflecting the glorious scenery, while he smiled at some private thought.

Eventually it was the Islamic bureau chief who broke the silence. "Yah," he began with a dreamy sigh, "I invited to visit United States . . . for conference in Los Angeles . . . on social justice."

"Terrific," I said. Reza spoke his English gamely, but his habit of leaving out the tense confused me. I took him to mean that his trip lay in the future, and immediately I pictured Reza and I tramping Manhattan streets, strolling through Central Park, marching up Fifth Avenue, while I pointed out the tall buildings and historic landmarks. "You've got to come to New York, Rez, so I can show you around," I said. "You will stay with us of course."

But I had misunderstood. The meeting had already taken place, in the spring of the previous year, and Reza had not attended. "Why not?" I asked.

"Yah," said Reza slowly, as if getting the English syntax ironed out in his head before he spoke. A friend—who or how well-placed he didn't say—had told him he was on a list of suspected terrorists and agitators to whom the U.S. State Department would automatically deny entry visas.

I was outraged. How typical, I thought, leaping to the conclusion that some sort of Kafkaesque snafu had resulted in a situation where even with Suharto gone from power, the U.S. government was still denying visas to individuals who had helped turn out the dictator in favor of a democratic experiment the U.S. government had publicly endorsed. Crazy! Leave it to the geniuses in Washington to keep a democracy fighter like Reza from visiting the Land of the Free and the Home of the Brave.

But it wasn't that simple. Reza told me that as far as some people were concerned he *had* been a terrorist bomber.

"You were suspected of planting a bomb?" I asked incredulously.

"Yah," said Reza. "Is true." He adjusted his glasses and for a brief, shameful moment the image of this gentle man squatting on a floor, tinkering with the innards of a bomb, flickered through my head, and I wondered if he really was an anarchist, after all. I turned to glance at Norman, who was wide-awake now, his mental antennae fully extended.

"Tell me about it," I said.

It had started on the night of January 18, 1998, four months before the Suharto government fell. "The bomb exploded in apartment building—public housing for poor people," said Reza. The village name meant "highland" in Indonesian, he said, and he smiled at the lofty name for such a crummy slum neighborhood. Nobody was hurt in the blast.

On television the next day, the police produced a jumper cable, a car battery, and a computer loaded with documents they said pointed to the existence of a dangerous underground organization—the People's Democratic Party, or PRD. They immediately launched a manhunt for Reza and his fellow party members. "So you did not in fact plant the bomb?" I felt guilty for asking the question, but I felt obliged to set the record straight.

"No," said Reza, shaking his head and smiling. "The bomb belonged to the police but we got blamed."

I believed him—of course. Deep down, I not only trusted Reza, but I had come to appreciate in my dim bule way what he was trying to do for me. In spite of the baby's arrival, Reza had fought hard to get me access to the right people—the people he thought could give me a broad and balanced view of the Islamic landscape. Truth, not spin, was his interest, and he had put his credibility on the line to vouch for me. He was that kind of man.

"I'll look into this immediately," I said. If a wrong had been done, we'd try and get it cleared up pronto.

But Reza waved me off. "Someday maybe," he said. Right now, though, he had no plans to go to the United States. Besides, U.S. Immigration was currently busy screening Indonesian males as potential terrorists, regardless of their backgrounds.[3] Better to let things cool off first, Reza thought.

---

3. While the U.S. government does not divulge the contents of their terrorism watch-list, sources indicate it may include the names of as many as 85,000 persons.

Outside the windows the sun was dropping behind the hills as we pelted on toward Jogja. On our left we passed a series of low single-story buildings spread out in the yellow-brown landscape like a temporary college campus.

"You know what that is?" asked Reza.

"Military?" I said.

Reza nodded. "Kopassus headquarters," he said, and he then fell back into a kind of percolating silence, as if the sight of the Special Forces garrison had stirred a deeper pool of memory. At length, he sighed and said: "We believed people power could bring us democracy." After all, Reza and his colleagues had seen a housewife, Cory Aquino, ride the People Power Revolution all the way to the presidency of the Philippines in 1986, after longtime dictator Ferdinand Marcos had been forced to flee the country. It took a long time for similar conditions to occur in Indonesia, but then in 1996 a series of riots suddenly broke out in major cities around Java.

"We analyzed those riots," said Reza, and he was surprised. "Ordinary people, mainly the urban poor, were fighting the military with sticks and stones and Molotov cocktails. We thought if we could organize a million people, change was sure to come. So we went to live in the slum neighborhoods. We slept in the mosques. We organized."

It was no picnic. After three decades of Suharto most people still found it constitutionally impossible to step out of line. So the PRD went deeper underground, infiltrating the student movement. That and the unexpected economic crisis that hit Asia in 1997 provided the necessary spark. Suddenly, revolution had stopped being hard work and became exhilarating; democracy in its molten form was on a roll. (Norman was now stepping in where necessary to help process the mounting flow of Reza's English.)

"Things escalated day by day," said Reza. "The police knew they had to stop groups like us or Suharto was finished. So they faked the bombing case to break our relationship with the students who were generally against the use of violence. They said the students weren't to blame. The PRD was the *provocateur.*" He smiled at his use of the infamous word.

"We were hiding every day now," Reza said. Everybody used false names—Reza had five. His favorite was Abdul Aziz, the equivalent of John Smith. "I got that one from reading the newspaper," he said. (Imam Samudra, the Bali bomber, eventually used the same name.) "We had five secret offices in Jakarta where we published statements attacking Suharto."

Then things suddenly got dangerous. In February 1998, Kopassus agents arrested Wiji Thukul, a well-regarded poet and democratic activist, and he vanished without a trace. In mid-March, a day after Suharto had been reelected by his rigged parliament to yet another five-year term, Reza was arrested on the street and thrown blindfolded into the back of a van. His abductors tortured Reza every day for a week, using fists, and something Reza called the "electric stick," which made his limbs jump crazily and sucked the air from his lungs. Every day, his interrogators pressed him for the names of other party leaders.

"I didn't talk," said Reza, blinking innocently and then adding with his wicked smile, "But I did give them some wrong information. So they got angry and beat me up again." Reza then changed his story, insisting he wasn't interested in "regime change" at all but only in forming his own religious party. "Shut up!" his jailors screamed. "You're from the People's Democratic Party. You're a Communist!"

On the physical side of things, meanwhile, Reza's tormenters showed some real ingenuity. They made hairline cuts on his arms and legs with a razor blade and then squeezed the juice of a fresh lemon over them. They put Reza's feet underneath a low table and sat on it, happily swinging their legs like kids playing on a fence. They stripped him naked, placed him on a large block of ice, and then punched and kicked him—to "warm up" his blood, they said.

As Reza talked, darkness fell quickly. In the distance the lights of Jogjakarta twinkled with a refrigerant quality, blue and cold white, and I suddenly shivered in spite of the tropical heat. "They hung me by my neck and took me down before I died," said Reza, rounding out the anatomy of his torture.

After a week of nonstop beatings, his jailers removed Reza's hood. "I looked at my hands and legs, and it was nothing but blood, blood, blood"—dried of course, and under the skin in the form of massive bruises. But at least he could now see where he was.

"It was just like the movies," said Reza. "My cell was maybe two meters by two meters—there was a container for water, one for poop, and a cot for sleeping." The guards kept the air-conditioning going full blast day and night to ensure a chronic state of discomfort. "And every morning they called to me, 'Hey, dog! Wake up!' They passed a bowl of rice and a cup of water under the door. So maybe I *was* like another species of dog."

Reza even did the jailhouse equivalent of howling at the moon. He knelt down on the concrete floor on all fours and cried, "Allah Akbar . . . Allah Akbar," and though he had never considered himself a religious Muslim by any stretch of the imagination, and had rarely gone to a mosque, it comforted Reza to hear the sound of his own voice shouting out the name of God.

Reza had been behind bars for two months when one day his captors told him he was going home, and then beat him savagely— in honor of his release, they said. They gave him the equivalent of ten dollars in Indonesian rupiah, a new set of clothes, and a ticket for the high-speed train so he could travel to Madura, the island off the Java coast, where his mother lived. On seeing her son alive, Reza's mom fainted dead away out of sheer motherly happiness. Then an hour later the police knocked on the door. They had a warrant for Reza's arrest and orders to take him back to Jakarta to stand trial for sub-version. It was the old trick of releasing a prisoner, who then myste-riously disappears back into the system. (And here's what really boggles the mind: Quite apart from the gothic cruelty of the Suharto police state, think about the incredible misappropriation of manpower and resources required to keep thousands upon thou-sands of people under thumb, and for much of the time with at least the indirect financial support of the United States.)

Reza went to Jakarta, but not with the cops. Tipped off by a neighbor, he had managed to slip out his mom's back door in the nick of time. Once back in the capital, Reza threw himself into helping organize the final round of antigovernment riots that were now gathering lethal momentum against the Suharto regime. And then on May 21, 1998—the day that many had dreamed of and few dared imagine finally came—the Smiling General, doughy-faced and smiling a last enigmatic official smile, announced his resignation before the TV cameras.

We were approaching the city limits now, and Jogja offered itself as an enlarging wafer of light on the near horizon, when Reza said moodily, "I still don't know why I was released." Of the twenty-three activists abducted in Reza's group, only nine survived to tell the tale. Of the other fourteen, one was found dead, buried in a shallow grave in a forest back down the road we'd come, near Solo. Five years later, the others were still missing and presumed dead.

A few weeks after Suharto's demise, Reza summoned up the guts to march into military police headquarters in Jakarta and demanded an investigation from the new government. (This was despite the fact that the mere sight of a police or military uniform induced in him bowel-swizzling feelings of panic.) Eventually, a special tribunal was set up to look into Kopassus abuses, and eleven military officers were put on trial for kidnapping. "They all got eight months," said Reza, "but nobody ever actually went to jail."

As for Reza, the charges against him had never been officially dropped, and thus technically he was still an enemy of the state, a suspected terrorist-bomber at large. He smiled his clever smile—well, that was Indonesia for you.

"And can you guess what the name of the kidnapping group was?"

I shook my head.

"The Rose Team," he said.

I looked into Reza's eyes the way I had that first night over our spaghetti dinner in Jakarta, and though the streetlights of central Jogja flared and faded around us, now I could see that the little question mark I thought I'd detected behind his smile had gone missing. In its place was a flat, transparent gaze without a hint of mirth or irony.

Reza gulped, pushed his glasses back on his nose, and said, "I don't agree at all with the Bali bombers and what they did. But I know exactly how people like them feel. I know how angry they are. They're reacting to the same atmosphere of injustice in this society." He was not afraid of what terrorists might do to his country, he said flatly, but how chronic injustice might eventually lead to something even worse.

Having finished speaking his piece, Reza instructed the driver to pull up at the next corner so he could hop out and make his way to his politically correct lodgings somewhere along the darkened side streets. Headed back to the Hyatt, Norman and I traded astonished looks. "Jeez," said Norman. "I knew Reza was arrested and everything but that's the first time I've ever heard the story. Reza trusts you now, Boss. You should be flattered."

I was. I also understood why I'd been getting such a respectful, if not always warm and fuzzy reception from the radical all-stars we'd encountered in our travels. In the struggle against Suharto, which was in reality Indonesia's great, blistering Homeric poem, those who had risked their lives opposing the government, and paid a high price for it in many different ways, shared the respect of old comrades in arms, even if they found themselves separated by ideas and occupying opposite ends of the political spectrum. In effect, Reza's jail time and torture had won me an audience and an openness I could never have mustered on my own, and I felt incredibly grateful to him.

I also realized how foolish I'd been in my adolescent choice of fears. When I got back to my room at the hotel, I immediately pulled the armchair away from the patio door, the one I'd stupidly put there to keep out imaginary intruders, climbed into bed, and slept like a baby for the first time in many nights.

18

THE MELLOW AND THE BRAVE

The next morning, on my way to the bathroom, I came upon a startling mystery. Bleary-eyed and woolly-headed, I couldn't for the life of me figure out why or how somebody had scattered such a large number of pinto beans on the floor of my room during the night. When I bent down to puzzle over them, however, I noticed the beans had multiple kicking legs. Well, this was old Java, after all, and while I'd slept peacefully in my bed, a large-scale invasion of garden beetles had apparently been thwarted by the intervention of some hidden force.

When I begin to have such semihallucinatory thoughts, it is a clear sign I've reached that inevitable low point in every journey when, wrung out and road weary, I sorely want to go home. My melancholy was amplified when I flicked on the TV and saw a crowd estimated at a hundred thousand people clogging my neighborhood across the world in Manhattan, marching on the United Nations to protest the now-presumptive inevitability of America's preemptive whacking of Saddam Hussein's Iraq. CNN meanwhile had been abuzz with word from

Washington on yet another round of theoretically impending terrorist attacks that would put the nation's capital and New York once
again in the bull's-eye, and Homeland Security officials had jacked
up their color-coordinated antiterrorism alert to the penultimate
Code Orange.

And suddenly it hit me: Here I am, I thought, standing in this
cozy, well-appointed hotel room at the reputed center of Asian terrorism, in my undershorts and T-shirt, presiding over the fallen beetles, and watching golfers stroll languidly up the fairway, while back
in the good old USA a kind of mass hysteria appears to have set in. I
paused briefly to consider the extreme weirdness of my situation,
and then I reached for the phone to call home.

Toshiko was engrossed in the final quarter of an NBA game on
TV, and everything was fine, she said in her even-keeled, daughter-
of-samurai-warriors way. But frankly, there was something below
and beyond the words that I didn't like. On further questioning, my
wife finally confessed that she had been dutifully following government security guidelines, filling the bathtub with water in the event
the municipal waterworks were taken out, and shopping for a sturdy
flashlight. When she asked me if I had any duct tape stored among
the tools and spare lightbulbs in the utility closet, I got scared.

"That does it," I said. "I'm coming home right now."

"Now you listen to me," Toshiko said firmly. "You just stay
where you are and keep focused on your work. Everything's fine
here."

When I hung up I felt foolish for having caved into my fears like
that. Then inadvertently locating *Barney and Friends* on a local TV
channel, I watched the hulking purple dinosaur prance and burble
goofily in Indonesian, and I realized, not for the first time, mind you,
that the media biz to which I'd arguably devoted the best years of my
life wasn't always totally helpful in forming a realistic picture of the
world. (Did I just hear somebody use the phrase "gross understatement"?)

Worries about home had nevertheless put me in a dark mood,
which is normally an excellent excuse for acting lazy and stupid. But

Reza wasn't about to let me dog it for a minute. One of the areas I'd been eager to explore before my malaise set in was the question of where Indonesia's women stood in relation to key questions about the Islamic future. Accordingly, Reza had piled on the interviews, starting on this gray and humid morning with a woman named Hindun who taught Islamic law and Arabic at a large pesantren in the Jogja suburb of Krapyak.

It is a simple but unassailable fact that in the Islamic setting it is the men who tend to hog the media limelight, and various public opinion polls suggested that in any event men and women pretty much shared the same views. Nearly three-quarters of all Indonesian men and women sampled, for instance, were on record as favoring the adoption of some limited form of shariah law. Roughly half of those polled felt a woman should always be accompanied by a male relative when traveling outside the home. Less than a quarter felt women should be allowed to work on the outside, and again men and women appeared to be in perfect sync on the issue. Was it possible that Muslim women in Indonesia were really prepared to go along with the fundamentalist program in lockstep, as the polls seemed to suggest? That is what I had wanted to know.

But not today. Today, as I say, was soupy and dismal, and as we drove across town in the wilting heat, I was inwardly churning with thoughts of rebellion. You could drag a reporter to an event as Reza was doing now, I thought stubbornly, but you couldn't force the reporter to report. Very unprofessional of me, I know, but that's exactly how I felt.

And Hindun matched my gray expectations to a tee. Only twenty-eight, she wore the gray, tentlike frock of the devout Muslim matron, her face a plump oval framed in a bloodless gray jilbab. Dressed in my standard reporting uniform, a navy blue cotton T-shirt and khaki pants, I was sweating like a leaky radiator, and it made me uncomfortable just to look at her. But there she sat, hands primly folded in her lap, smiling a flat gray smile.

Preparing myself to endure the unendurable, I asked Hindun to tell me about her school. In halting English, she began to listlessly tick off a stream of dull gray statistics: "Our school has an enrollment of fourteen hundred students, half boys and half girls, half junior high and half senior high . . ."

Lord save me, I thought, as Norman, recognizing a treadmill to oblivion when he saw one, jumped up from the sofa, mumbled some flimsy excuse about having to check with some guy about a thing, and flew out the door.

"The girls have a six P.M. curfew, the boys, eleven. . . ."

Fighting to keep my eyelids from clanging down, I decided to ask one last question before finding my own excuse to bolt. "Tell me," I said, "what's your view on adopting Islamic law here in Indonesia?"

Based on the polling numbers and her conservative demeanor, I fully expected Hindun to duly endorse the idea. But I was very much mistaken. To my surprise, the question appeared to kindle a spark behind all that heavy fabric. Hindun's English markedly improved, and she spoke up firmly and with a hint of wry humor flickering in her eyes.

"Well, the funny thing is, when people talk about shariah law, you know, the first thing they want to do is use it to discriminate against women."

"Oh really?" I said, perking up my ears.

"Yes. They tell us how women should have to stay in the home, or have to wear the veil. And why is it, do you suppose, the first thing they try to promote is polygamy?"

She clucked her tongue and gave me that same smile my wife gives me when I have once again done something to confirm my lifetime membership in the Big Dumb Guy Club. On Java, Hindun said, many men liked to stay home and play around with their pet birds, the bird being the symbol of the soul in Javanese tradition. "If the women have to stay home, too," she murmured with unanswerable female logic, "who is it exactly who's going to earn the living?"

"But you yourself wear the jilbab," I said.

"Of course and for me it's just something I do, like watching television—a tradition, not a law." Nowhere in the Koran did it specifically state that a woman had to cover herself, said Hindun.

Her mother had never worn a scarf, for example. "And as far as I know, the Prophet wasn't interested in discriminating against women," she said with a knowing smile. "He was trying to create social harmony."

So what was the big attraction of shariah for people who didn't happen to want multiple wives or to turn traditions into law?

"People support shariah because they're frustrated with conditions in this country," said Hindun. But for her money, it was much better to deal with social issues head-on. "Many people still believe that when women get married they have to serve their husbands. Power is still in the hands of the husband—how many children they will have, how they will be educated."

So why didn't more women object? I asked.

"Women get less information than men," said Hindun. "At night men go to the library or discussion groups at the mosque, and women can't leave home. Few women can read Arabic, so they're stuck with the narrow interpretation of the Koran they get from whoever their leader happens to be"—almost always a man.

There was that knowing smile again. "That is why," said Hindun, "I've established a group of men and women who meet at night and discuss reproductive rights."

"Wow," I said. "The fundamentalists can't like that very much."

Hindun shrugged. Yes, she often got phone calls from irked imams ordering her to put a stop to her scandalous business. "They worry men and women in one place like that after dark are maybe doing free sex or partying."

I must have appeared scandalized by Hindun's explicit language because she looked at me and laughed. I smiled sheepishly and said, "I only meant that it sounds dangerous. Have you ever thought of giving it up?"

"No," said Hindun firmly, flashing a look unmistakable to any New Yorker—*get serious*. "These people get stuck on a symbol and ignore the core of our teachings. Our Koran supports reproductive rights and they try and hide it, but if you look it's there in the verses."

"But in America we always hear that the fundamentalists are getting more and more powerful," I said.

"Are they?" said Hindun, with that impish twinkle in her eye. "Maybe at the intellectual level, yes. But at the grass roots I don't think so—they're too strict. They don't allow people to live their lives." And particularly in Java, with all its overlapping cultural layers, it wasn't that easy to impose a single formula erasing all others.

Norman breezed back through the door, and just in time to create a moment of supreme social awkwardness. Grabbing his camera, he insisted that Hindun and I scrunch together on the sofa so he could snap our picture. As we did so, the big overstuffed cushions gave way under the weight of my body and Hindun and I briefly bumped fannies. Flushing, I feared I might have breached some Islamic statute, but Hindun was more interested in reminiscing about a brief visit she'd recently made to New York City on a teacher exchange program.

Worried about rumors circulating in Indonesia of widespread Muslim-bashing after 9/11, and of course the dangerous image of New York they saw on imported TV dramas, both Hindun's parents and her in-laws had tried to talk her out of going. But Hindun wasn't the kind to scare easily.

"Oh, it was very exciting," she said, "but . . ."

"But what?"

Hindun smiled shyly, and looked down at her hands, "Well, I really wanted to see a mafia gangster but New York wasn't like the movies at all. I was disappointed about that part."

Next on the agenda was Ruhaini Dzuhayatin, a lecturer in sociology and the director of the Center for Women's Studies at the State Institute of Islamic Studies in Jogjakarta. Light poured in high stained-glass windows as we sat talking in Ruhaini's university office. Dressed elegantly in a turquoise-green pants suit with a diaphanous headscarf, she smiled the same shrewd smile as Hindun when I asked her if she agreed Indonesia was becoming increasingly dominated by males.

"In the past this society had much more space for women," she answered. "Now ironically democracy has given the fundamentalists the opportunity to enter the political arena so they can say politics is not a woman's place. What they're really saying of course is they want to install shariah law, meaning there's no room for women at all!"

I jokingly told Ruhaini to please not be afraid to speak her mind, and she laughed delightedly. "When the fundamentalists tell me they're protecting us, I tell them, 'You're restricting us! Why don't you go think about cutting off people's hands instead and leave women alone?' "

"And what do they say?" I asked.

Ruhaini smirked, but charmingly. "It's always, you know, 'We have to start with something simple that people will understand.' And that's where the danger starts. You witnessed for yourself what happened in the Moluccas. All the fundamentalist groups had relations with military factions, so they could physically threaten people."

"So you fear the fundamentalists will use the same tactics to start threatening women?"

"Since the Bali bombings, the fundamentalist groups have lost some of their support from the military because of the bad international reaction," said Ruhaini. "It also lessened support for shariah law, and so for now it's more comfortable for us to talk to them. We don't know how long it will last, but this is the right time to convey our message."

"And what message do you have?"

"We've got to change our educational system. The way we teach history now, for example—it's really the history of trauma. My daughter came to me a while ago and told me that religious ideas are what we have to fight for. I moved her to another school."

I asked Ruhaini if she agreed that lack of formal education was the main cause of women's acceptance of shariah.

Surprising to me, she shook her head emphatically no. "That's the fascinating thing," Ruhaini said. Indonesia had plenty of brilliant women, graduates of top universities, who'd gone on to graduate studies, even studied aboard—women who then joined a fundamentalist group.

"Is part of it a question of romance, then?" I asked, trying to test a hunch. And I must say that as much as any other person I'd spoken to on this trip, Ruhaini and I seemed to be communicating on the same wavelength.

Her eyes brightened immediately. "Yes, that's part of it," she said, savoring the idea a bit. "It's the romance of the golden age of Islam."

Ruhaini then leaned in over the table and, in a confidential "get-this" tone, said, "Last year Islamic women from a local university here marched on parliament in Jakarta to demand the institution of shariah. They were demanding the reinstitution of polygamy because they argued that's the best way to end prostitution. They even formed a Polygamy Party!"

Ruhaini laughed and clapped her hands, then told me she'd struck back by publicizing the results of an authoritative public opinion poll showing eighty percent of Indonesians were against polygamy.

"I guess you showed them," I said.

She shook her head again. "No. They said, 'You got those results because you interviewed people who don't understand Islam.' So we're really operating within a difficult framework here. The fundamentalists don't really want to think about things intellectually, academically, or critically."

Ruhaini had demonstrated some critical thinking, however, when she organized a campaign to legalize prostitution, which fundamentalists insist on seeing as perhaps the darkest symbol of the nation's moral crisis. "They burn the brothels," said Ruhaini, shaking her head, "when sexually transmitted diseases are spreading out of control!"

I couldn't help but admire Ruhaini's guts, and as our conversation drew to a close, I felt compelled to share a bit of secret knowledge. I hadn't told anybody, not even Norman, the title I had in mind for my book—*Allah's Torch*—for fear its meaning might be misinterpreted. What did she think?

"I think it's great," she said enthusiastically. She got the point immediately and without explanation—the torch of Islam was meant to bring enlightenment, but in the wrong hands could also be put to destructive ends.

Then she had a secret for me. "You know," she said, smiling coyly, "working at the Islamic Institute requires us to wear the jilbab, but when I was studying in Australia I went uncovered. I'll show you!"

She jumped up and disappeared behind a bank of gray metal lockers clustered in the middle of the big shared office. The noise of a metal door banging shut prompted Norman to look up from his camera gear. He raised his eyebrows and smiled, as if to say, "What's up now, Boss?"

But I grew edgy. What if Ruhaini emerged from behind the cabinets scandalously bareheaded? What if some self-appointed religious cop should wander in and catch her in the act? What if she lost her job . . .

I needn't have worried. When Ruhaini returned, she thrust a passport-size photo at me across the table. "That's me without the veil!" she said, and I'll be hammered if she didn't look totally different. The face in the photo was that of a typical college girl, with bright eyes and raven-colored curls, less grand in a way than Professor Ruhaini in her green Islamic chiffons, more of a girl-next-door. "The veil for me is part of tradition, not a religious thing," she said, enjoying my surprise. "And I still love my jeans!"

It was late afternoon now, and a day that had started in gloom was ending in mellow sunshine, when we pulled onto the hard-packed earth of a courtyard belonging to the Institute for Islamic and Social Studies to meet its chairman, Jadul Maula. A smoldering intellectual presence, Jadul wasted no time in telling me what a pathetically damaging job he felt the Western media was doing in covering the struggle against radical Islam.

"A reporter from a big American paper came here a couple of months ago and her first question was, 'How come Indonesian Muslims haven't done anything about there being so many terrorists here—why haven't the moderates spoken out?' "

He looked at me with an expression of utter contempt at the memory. "To me," he said, scratching his chin thoughtfully, "that's an angry statement. I told her Muslims in Indonesia have fought extremism every day since the beginning of the twentieth century—in the marketplace, in the schools, in the mosques. Where were you?"

He laughed sardonically and stared at me in a challenging manner. "Look, I'm not a beat reporter anymore," I said, explaining that I was just a guy traveling around trying to make some sense out of Islam, which few people in my country seemed to understand, perhaps in part because of the media.

Jadul appeared to like my tortured explanation. He looked a little tortured himself. A tousle-haired chain-smoker, in a black T-shirt and faded blue jeans, he reminded me of one of those French intellectuals you see in the old foreign art-house flicks—a man from whom one could reasonably expect the Indonesian equivalent of words like "jejune."

"Where's it all headed?" I asked, displaying the razor-sharp intellect for which I am known.

Jadul winced. He laughed. He winced again. He examined the glowing tip of his unfiltered cigarette. How to put this so a reporter who claims not to be a reporter can understand? We were sitting on a bamboo platform at the back of the yard under a single electric bulb. On the wall behind us a painting in throbbing acrylics depicted a man on a surfboard, with flowing blond hair and an aggressive lantern jaw, barreling toward us through the banzai pipeline.

"Most people discovered Islam in Indonesia after the Bali bombing," said Jadul, "and it's limited to what the media tells them. The truth is Islam has been around since the seventh century, and all the many different kinds of Muslim 'experiments' make up Islam in Indonesia. One of them, the one that came in at the beginning of twentieth century from the Middle East, came to purify Islam and return it to the original teachings from Mecca."

Just then an airplane flew directly overhead, drowning out our conversation. "That's the rich people passing by," said Jadul, holding his cigarette between pinched fingers and cracking a thin smile. The courtyard was dark now as the wailing chorus of the evening call to prayer rose around us in the soft night. Norman told our driver, who had parked nearby, to turn down the heavy-metal music blaring from the car radio so we could hear ourselves think, and Jadul went on: "So you see, it's a long historical process. We have Communist Islam, which focuses on social justice. We have big moderate groups—the NU and Mohammadiya—which focus on a tolerant, multicultural agenda. Each group has its own logic and way of dealing with things. And now the media, which plays a big role in all this, come along and is only capable of seeing this struggle in terms terrorists and antiterrorists."

Certainly Jadul wasn't suggesting that concern with fundamentalism was wholly a media creation? I asked.

He smiled and examined the tip of his cigarette again. "Of course not," he said, as if tempted to say, "How jejune," before he added: "But the plain fact is we've been fighting extremist Islam here a long time and we've developed cultural mechanisms for dealing with it. The approach that the media is taking, concentrating only on the existence of a terrorist network in Indonesia, corrupts and weakens moderate Islam's natural defenses."

The more the media harped on the momentum of extremist forces, for example, the more money flowed in from rich patrons in the Middle East, helping the radicals to vastly improve communications, which in turn created a siege mentality about the encroachment of Western values, ripping the scabs off old wounds and humiliations.

I wasn't sold on Jadul's argument that the media was so overwhelmingly culpable—after all, it wasn't the media that was manufacturing the bombs or cutting people's throats. But I did like his idea that Indonesia had the ingredients within itself to fix itself, and it was heartening that so many Indonesians—Ruhaini, Hindun, Ulil, and others—I'd talked with seemed to recognize this concept, which was overlooked by so many who didn't happen to be Indonesian. When I asked Jadul what steps Indonesia might take to boost its natural immune defenses, however, he stuck to his antimedia guns.

"My suggestion is that the mass media look at Islam in Indonesia as a plurality among the radicals and moderates," he insisted. "They should look at how Islam has developed historically," he added, with a dismissive wave of his tobacco-stained fingers and a final smirk. "But they won't of course! The media is completely ahistorical!"

I shook hands with Jadul, who was lighting up another cigarette, and said goodbye. Back in the van I asked Norman what he thought. "On the whole, Boss," he said, "I prefer these mellow Muslims— even the ones who behave like tortured Frenchmen."

That evening we—Norman, Reza, and I—found an appropriately mellow place for dinner in a rambling, Dutch-style villa in the center of town, where the seating was done according to musical preference. "Country Western or Indonesian?" inquired a young woman when we walked in the door. To our left, we could hear the gamelan orchestra tuning up in the empty Indonesian section, making the usual pleasant tinkling sound like a car wreck.

"Country," we said in unison, and followed the woman to the right, down a flight of stairs and into a cozy dining room with a grotto at one end lush with tropical lilies. At the other a local trio was playing "Your Cheating Heart" in a sly, swaying tropical rhythm. All the tables but one were occupied by groups of braying European aid workers.

"Uncivilized bule," snorted Norman with princely hauteur. But he quickly forgot about the unruly bule when he discovered the large open kitchen was staffed entirely by attractive young women, pert in their crisp white uniforms and old-fashioned floppy red chef's hats. They *were* exceedingly cute. And so was our waitress, a young woman with pouty bee-stung lips and a kewpie doll face, who said she was half Javanese, half Balinese, "Just like Sukarno."

"Gggrrrrrrrr," said Norman as we watched her sashay back into the kitchen with our order. "A blend of the regal and the animal. *Sassy!*"

We settled in. Norman and I each picked up a handful of magazines from a big side table and were idly leafing through them, while Reza, who told me he'd slept very badly the night before in his windowless borrowed room, entered into a trancelike state. Norman snapped his fingers, trying to bring him out of it, but he didn't flinch. For five minutes our Islamic bureau chief was a rapt traveler of another dimension. Then his eyes popped open.

"Ah, refresh!" said Reza, smiling his crafty smile, while he stretched his arms luxuriously above his head, and beguiling smells wafted from the kitchen. Cinnamon and cardamom. Ginger and cloves. Reza stuck with the Indonesian blue-plate special, which arrived on a rattan tray wrapped in banana leaves and tied with a rustic cord, while Norman and I loaded it on Western-style—roast duck in tangerine sauce, gargantuan deep-fried prawns, and homemade ginger ice cream, and then ordered seconds on the prawns and ice cream, all of which our waitress delivered with languor and efficiency.

Playing hard-to-get with Norman, Miss Pouty Lips even flirted with me, practicing her limited English. I did not mind.

Pout. "Where you come from?"

"New York."

Pout, smile, pout. "Oh, big deal, yeah?"

I looked at Norman for guidance. *"Very sassy,"* he said, approvingly.

"Danger," cautioned the Islamic bureau chief, grinning wickedly.

It was a thoroughly mellow, relaxing evening, and one whose enjoyment is hard to match for amiability, playfulness, sly innuendo, humor, and innocence anywhere but in Old Java. Dinner lasted a little over three hours, and by the time it was over, and though I had another full week before I was scheduled to fly back home, I was suddenly feeling nostalgic again, not for my own big, erratic mother country this time, but for big, erratic, endearing Indonesia.

19

WILD HORSES

The next morning I was just plain sick. I jumped out of bed as usual, but something was radically wrong. My body was listing badly to starboard, and when I took a few steps I crashed heavily into my repositioned armchair, badly stubbing my toe. Climbing into the shower, I felt so dizzy I had to grab the towel rod to keep from going down again. There is nothing more worrying for the traveling hack than to be sick on the road, and I thought frantically, What the hell is going on here? Stroke? Tropical brain disease?

I continued to fret as I wobbled my way toward the main dining room, where I spotted Norman sitting at the far end near the big windows. Tacking unsteadily toward his table, I collapsed in the chair opposite and said reflexively, "So how's it going this morning, Norman?"

"I don't feel so good, Boss," he moaned. "How do I look?"

"Like Elvis," I said.

Norman brightened through his malaise. "Really?"

"Yes, in his Las Vegas period . . ."

"Meaning what?"

"Meaning little green and puffy, pal." And this was God's honest truth. His face was strangely bloated, and a forelock of his normally neatly coiffed hair was plastered to his forehead like a spit curl.

"I feel really dizzy," he said disconsolately.

Bingo! On hearing the word "dizzy," I am ashamed to say I felt suddenly and remarkably less miserable. (As I've said before, there is something truly creepy in human nature.) When I told Norman that I, too, was feeling wildly off-kilter, he cried, "I knew it!" and jumped to a perfectly plausible conclusion for Central Java: "That half-Balinese waitress last night—she bewitched us!"

"You were bewitched all right," I said. "But I'm afraid it had more to do with the MSG than witchcraft." Remembering our many courses, I suddenly realized that the food had been absolutely laced with the suspect seasoning, particularly those big, irresistibly tasty prawns. But in the battle between science and romance, the latter will forever be the stronger. Elevating his eyebrows, while his fingers sprinkled invisible powder onto his eggs, Norman insisted on having been poisoned by our beautiful waitress, and would entertain no argument to the contrary.

When Reza joined us, fresh from another night in his windowless room, he reported himself to be in tiptop condition, and further congratulated himself on having had the wisdom to avoid the obviously unhealthy Western menu.

"Power to the people," said Norman.

"Capitalist decadence strikes again," I said.

Reza laughed good-naturedly, but I could tell he was all fired up. That was because this morning he had a special treat in store. He'd arranged for me to meet with a man named Irfan Suryahardy Awwas, who ran a fundamentalist group called the Majelis Mujahidin or, in its more elaborate English title, the Council of Mujahedeen for Islamic Law Enforcement. The MMI was interesting for several reasons. Set up during the heady days of the Spice Islands jihad in 2000, it was at least on the surface what it said it was—a loose coalition of fundamentalist groups advocating the peaceful and democratic adoption of the shariah. Its leadership roster, on the other hand, seemed specifically designed to raise the pulse rate of any sober-minded terrorism detective. First, the MMI's founding father was none other than Abu Bakar Bashir, who had been elected paramount leader at the organization's inaugural convention. Another board member, and Irfan's older brother, was Fikiruddin Muqti, alias Abu Jibril, alias Mohamed Iqbal bin Abdurrahman, the putative head of one of Jemaah Islamiyah's two paramilitary wings, and at the moment behind bars in Malaysia for his alleged plans to turn Southeast Asia into a pan-Islamic state.

Irfan was a remarkable figure in his own right. Described variously as a "member of the Ngruki inner circle" and among Bashir's "top lieutenants," he was a hero of the anti-Suharto student movement who was found guilty of subversion in 1986 and sentenced to some very hard time. Today, in addition to his MMI directorship, he oversaw a publishing operation that churned out a steady stream of books, magazines, and newsletters decrying satanic America and the Zionist enemy. According to Zachary Abuza, who labeled MMI "a who's who of Southeast Asian terrorism," Irfan Awwas ranked among a handful of Jemaah Islamiyah officers who "remain at large" and "live openly in Indonesia." Other sources stipulated that Irfan might not technically be affiliated with JI but was nonetheless intimately familiar with the ins and outs of its militant agenda.

Normally, the prospect of encountering such a high-caste fundamentalist would have produced in me a standard case of the willies. But the MSG overload had left me so cotton-headed that it was impossible to focus on anything long enough to attach my fears. And so we drove through Jogja's pleasant, flowering side streets and a few minutes later pulled into the driveway of a Dutch-style villa, where a gate was pulled shut and locked behind us. When we got out of the car an old man in a prayer cap and wearing bottle-thick spectacles was tickling a feather duster over an outdoor display case filled with books and video disks claiming to document Christian atrocities in the Moluccas. Invited inside, we sat down on a couch covered in blue Naugahyde, as if waiting to take our turns in the dentist's chair, while Reza and Norman buried their noses in newspapers from a nearby rack.

The mood was not enhanced by Irfan's arrival. A handsome man, with a large round face, a head of glistening black hair, and dressed in a turquoise tunic buttoned up to his neck, he had the boldly charismatic look, I thought, of a young Mao Zedong—and of a man who had swallowed something exceedingly sour for breakfast. As he sat down heavily in his chair, it became apparent that his dyspepsia was linked to a "white paper" on terrorism, which he proceeded to lambaste without introduction.

When I innocently asked, "Oh, and what white paper is that?" Irfan churlishly explained that the Singapore government had recently published a report alleging that the MMI was a "reincarnation of Darul Islam," the early group espousing an independent religious state in Indonesia that had inspired Abu Bakar Bashir and, according to the Singaporeans, had later morphed into Jemaah Islamiyah. I thanked Irfan for alerting me to the existence of this interesting document, and I said I'd be sure to pick up a copy when I visited Singapore on my way back to New York.[1]

My ignorance appeared to irritate Irfan, though I couldn't blame him if he was feeling the heat. Sidney Jones had also recently identified him in one of her reports as being closely linked with Abu Bakar Bashir and, by implication, the mind if not the means of JI—a group Irfan continued to insist publicly did not in fact exist.[2] In any event, our conversation was not getting off to a promising start. Still fuzzy from the MSG poisoning, I made the mistake of lobbing Irfan a softball, asking him if he would explain to me where his group fit within the constellation of Indonesia's Islamic groups.

"I've been asked that question too many times," he said curtly,

---

1. I did get a copy in Singapore (also available online at www.mha.gov.sg as *White Paper—The Jemaah Islamiyah Arrests and The Threat of Terrorism*); based largely on the testimony of the thirty-three terrorism suspects then behind bars in Singapore jails and public domain accounts, the report did contain a few points I would question, including a weakly made link between JI and Laskar Jihad, but there was nothing about Irfan's group that struck me as inconsistent with my own reporting.
2. See the International Crisis Group's *Indonesia Backgrounder: How the Jemaah Islamiyah Terrorist Network Operates* (11 December 2002).

and then demanded, his voice edged in suspicion, "What is your purpose for coming here?"

It was pretty simple, I said. I wanted him to tell me what MMI had in mind for Indonesia. Perhaps he'd be kind enough to share his views with me on why and how shariah law should be imposed on big, culturally diverse Indonesia?

"We offer Islam as an alternative," he said snappishly, "just as other groups offer alternatives to build Indonesia for the future." Then warming to his topic, he added: "Our belief is that Islam is the best choice. It's been around in this country for many years so there's nothing new about it—and it covers all the human needs."

If I wasn't mistaken, I said, there seemed to be a lot of disagreement even among Muslim groups about just how or to what extent to adopt Islamic law. How did he propose ironing out such differences?

"We invite other groups to bring their alternatives and discuss the best solution," said Irfan. "But even though we are trying to do this in a democratic manner American propaganda comes into play!"

"Propaganda?"

"Yes, propaganda! America accuses anybody who wants to implement shariah law of being a terrorist." You could see the heavy hand of America in the new antiterrorism legislation Indonesia's parliament had recently passed. It was based, he gave me to understand, on an all-too-familiar logic: "If Israel slaughters Palestinians their excuse is self-defense. But if Palestinians defend themselves they are terrorists!"

He smiled at his neat tautology. "It's true—the American government has never said they hate Islam. But we'd rather have them say it, if they'd stop killing Muslims."

So solving the Palestinian problem was the key to solving Indonesia's problems, was that it?

"The main problem," Irfan said, still seemingly perplexed by my American thickness, "is that America uses democracy as a device for imperialism. The problem starts when one country wants to control another country."

Didn't Indonesians bear any responsibility for their political future? I asked.

"Indonesia carries a huge burden," said Irfan, "but none of our elected leaders has a vision to build Indonesia without foreign help. There is therefore every incentive for them to become morally corrupt."

In Suharto times, Irfan said, accurately enough, the government came up with a bright new plan every five years, while Suharto and his cronies stuffed foreign money into their pockets. "But the Indonesian people were never asked for *their* opinion. In our view, finding solutions by going back to religious beliefs is far more objective and wiser than what the secularists have been doing all this time—because patently secular logic has no values behind it."

The MSG was wearing off now, and I was looking forward to saying goodbye to Irfan, but I couldn't let our conversation end without asking him what he thought of Abu Bakar Bashir's arrest.

"Tragic," he said, clucking his tongue. "The police arrested him before they could prove their case."

What about the people who supplied evidence against Bashir—Omar al-Faruq and the others?

"Pressure from the United States," Irfan sniffed. "It's obvious. Basically people want to convict him for wanting to create a new Caliphate, an idea that's been around since the time of the Prophet. It's the same charge that was brought against him under Suharto. Now all these years later, they're still trying to put him on trial for what goes on in his mind, not his actions."

As a parting shot, Irfan said he had a message for America. "Even in Indonesia the Americans were never our enemies!" he said. "And this is coming from a person who the Bush administration considers a terrorist! We can have global peace very easily."

That sounded good to me, I said. What did we have to do?

"The American people just need to take a hard look at the crimes that George Bush is committing toward Islam," said Irfan, adding with a final searching look, "I hope I can count on your integrity in reporting this accurately."

"I shall so report," I promised.

Now that I have done so, however, I would also be remiss if I didn't tell you that I sensed something disconcertingly furtive about Irfan's operation. It was nothing more than a personal feeling, mind you. But while Irfan and I were talking, a tall, wiry young man in a military-style tunic rushed in the front entrance and, seeing me sitting there, quickly ducked into a side room, where he and another man dressed in fatigue pants proceeded to eye me through a crack in the door before eventually slamming it shut.

Irfan caught me staring at the men. "Many foreigners come here," he said, chuckling dryly. "They come here safe and they leave safe."

And of course I, too, rose safely and walked back out into the sunshine safely, more clearheaded than when I came in. And therefore I couldn't help but wonder if that was something that really needed to be said.

One of the truly crazy things about the life of a foreign correspondent is the wild assortment of events a day can throw at you. Two hours after leaving Irfan, I found myself at the royal palace in Jogja, sipping strawberry juice with Prince Joyokusumo, the sultan's younger brother. Ever since I got the idea of returning to Indonesia, I'd wanted to talk with the head man, Hamengku Buwono X. Unlike the rakish sunan of Solo, the sultan of Jogjakarta was an active player in the life of the nation, and the reasons for that were at least partly historical. While the royal court at Solo was treating the Dutch occupiers to that famous palace reception during the war for independence, Hamengku Buwono IX, the current sultan's father, had refused to deal with the Dutch at all; locking himself behind palace walls, he had become a mighty symbol of resistance for the rebel fighters. The upshot was that after the revolution, while Solo was effectively reduced to an ornamental satrap, Jogja was accorded special status as a self-governing district, something like a small American state. And now, the son, Hamengku Buwono X, carried on the family business with a special flair.

While he too ruled, ceremonially, as a Javanese king, the sultan managed his city-state's daily affairs as an elected and highly popular governor, with the clean hands, moderate Islamic credentials, and reputation for keeping the lid on extremist violence that many thought might one day make him a good choice for president. I'd first met Hamengku Buwono in 1999 and had found his remarks on Indonesia's future so thoughtful and illuminating that I simply wanted to see, I suppose, how this quiet, unruffled man at the center of things was holding up under the threat of a resurgent Islam.

So why was I invited to lunch by his brother? I was wondering precisely that and strongly suspected I'd been shunted off as a courtesy to the B-team, when Prince Joyokusumo gave me a tour of the sultan's birth home and began plying me with dutiful factoids. A large fleshy man in a formal coat and sarong, he reverently showed me a small bedroom off the vestibule where he said the sultan had been born in the late forties. He reminded me that the name Hamengku Buwono means, in Norman's translation, "He on Whose Lap the Universe Sits."

Entering the vast, fusty parlor, with gamelan music tinkling archly on a nearby stereo system, the prince led Norman and me to a small, round table, where he asked us to choose our seats by juice preference, each place setting featuring a different local concoction—honeydew melon, orange, banana, watermelon, or avocado. Ever the rebel, Norman chose the bright green avocado.

"Very homey for a palace," whispered Norman as we drank our juices through a straw and looked around. To our right was a large formal dining pavilion opening onto an inner garden, with a long, European-style table seating twenty-four, a tick-tocking grandfather clock, and portraits of the royal forebears lining the walls. On the left was a modern kitchen, like something out of a Julia Child cookbook, featuring a generous fridge, neat Formica counters, and a gleaming microwave.

"All Islamic influence in the Kraton is embedded in its symbolism," said the prince, and I nodded politely, looking forward to a tedious time of it. Joyokusumo proudly produced a coffee-table book on the subject of the palace, and had been showing me the picture of a gold artifact in the form of a goose, which he said symbolized sensitivity—one of the key attributes of the sultan. I yawned inwardly. He pointed to the stag—"The sultan has to be energetic and clever," said the prince. Next came the peacock, for "stature," and so on through the animal kingdom.

Then the prince said something that made the hairs on the back of my neck stand up on end. "The sultan is the commander of the militia of course," he said, "but he is also the leader of the battle within."

The battle within—I still don't know exactly why, but the way the prince said it reminded me of the medieval rendition of Jesus Christ as "The Warrior Who Fights Forever," and I felt a telltale shiver race up my spine, not from the previous night's MSG overdose, but from that hidden spot in the psychosoma from whence the gods broadcast their signals.

I was suddenly all ears. "Tell me more," I said.

"Well, we call it Jihad Akbar," said the prince, smiling benignly, "the battle against mortal ambition. That means the sultan is the leader of jihad, both without and within, as well as the servant of God who manages religious affairs and within that also explains the civil society concept in which the leader is Muslim but can embrace any other religion."

In other words, said Joyokusumo, "The sultan strives to be the perfect being. He lifts his sword not to kill mortal ambition but to control it."

He had my undivided attention now. As we continued to work on our juices, he referred to another page in his book, a photograph of the royal parasol, a large piece of equipment the size of a picnic table umbrella but finished elegantly in lacquer with dozens and dozens of razor-sharp pleats.

"This parasol is inscribed with the ninety-nine names of God," said Joyokusumo, "and ensures the sultan is always under His protective aura as he strives for a divine quality. All the names are tied together by the one central pole that symbolizes the highest name, which the sultan dares not emulate, which is *Allah Akbar.*"

What Joyokusumo was describing to me of course was the concept of the Greater Jihad, and the man who leads it, with all the cosmic bells and whistles as decreed by Javanese tradition. I was fascinated, and it suddenly dawned on me how dramatically the soul of Javanese Islam differed from the original desert religion. I could now understand how Jogja's early rulers had out of practical necessity used Islam as a defense mechanism against the invading Dutch, and yet by imbuing it with the promise of secret powers had created a spiritual bulwark, as well—the sort of "vital mystery"that man of symbols, the psychologist Carl Jung had talked about as giving colonized cultures the "pride and the power to resist the dominant whites."

Contrary to my expectations, lunch with the prince turned out to be an absolute delight, and a long one, stretching from noon till nearly four-thirty. Interestingly, Joyokusumo said he'd found the fundamentalist preoccupation with adopting shariah an odd goal for a true Muslim to aspire to, since in contrast to pursuit of Islam's highest level, *hakikat,* or true self-mastery, "following *shariat* so strictly is a sign of only the very fundamental stage when the individual cannot control himself, has no self-mastery, and must be constrained by rules."

Himself a member of the national parliament, Joyokusumo turned briefly to Indonesia's political turmoil, concluding, "Everything is on a very short fuse now."

And so what was going to happen?

"Only God knows," said the prince. "But why don't you ask the sultan when you see him on Monday?"

People speak of the fog of war to explain the confusion that overcomes observers on the active battlefield, but for me, a middle-aged writer trying to make sense of a phantomly war against a chamelonlike enemy, I'd reached the stage when too much information, not too little, fogs the brain. In a single day I'd had encounters with a firebrand and a prince, been subjected to the rhetoric of the Lesser Jihad, and the high symbolism of Javanese Islam. But beyond that it got complicated. For some days now I had been aware of a condition building in me, which Norman had accurately diagnosed as "radical overload."

And what had I learned? As I sat there in my hotel room, up to my eyeballs, informationally and emotionally, I don't honestly think I could have said. All I knew was that I was feeling drained and a little hopeless. But of course this was mystical Java, and I was poring listlessly over my fat notebooks, when an answer to my confusion appeared at my door in the form of a wise and well-plugged-in interlocutor, whom I'm obliged to refer to as the Insider.

I started by asking my guest about Irfan and the MMI. On the surface, he said, MMI was in fact a clearinghouse for various fundamentalist Muslim groups, all sharing a common interest in applying shariah law. Fine. But within the MMI were a handful of "wild horses," the operatives with a hidden agenda, hidden even from other members.

"For example?"

"Well, it's the kind of thing you see in action on college campuses right here in Jogja," said the insider. "Militant groups organize, emphasizing the democratic process. But all the time they exert subtle psychological pressure on recruits to take more radical stands"— slowly proceeding with indoctrination, so as not to stampede the colts.

He then looked me in the eye and said flatly, "Irfan, in my opinion, is involved in terrorist training." [3]

Didn't that prove the point that the Indonesian government was in some form of denial, just like the Washington insiders said? If there was a dangerous fifth column at work, why didn't authorities bear down until they got the goods on it?

My guest smiled at my American naiveté. What the Americans and others always overlooked was the basic math. Indonesian Mus-

---

3. Zachary Abuza puts it equally bluntly: "MMI is clearly part of the regional Jemaah Islamiyah network," he notes in his book *Militant Islam in Southeast Asia,* suggesting a cloak-and-dagger operation further obscured by the fact that the group "does not keep membership lists and thus it is impossible to accurately guess the size of its membership."

lims were willing to be preponderantly neutral. The radical organizations were prone to internal discord. There was dissension at this very moment inside the Jemaah Islamiyah, with its more militant members threatening to break away and form their own organization.

"That's typical in radical organizations," said the Insider. "We have conflicts and eventually split up. There is the larger goal of creating the Islamic state, of course. But methods of struggle differ, and the tactics, especially violent ones, raise contradictions among groups. I think that's what we're seeing now."

"It strikes me it's highly dangerous just to let the process run its course," I said—particularly when there were now so many opportunities for disgruntled locals to tie up with the international terrorism bazaar.

The Insider nodded. Yes, criminals were dangerous anywhere. But what Americans also always seemed to miss was a far greater danger. In the end you what you really had to fear was the effect that endemic poverty, lack of educational opportunities, and crooked courts and cops would have on society. Solving those problems was a matter of basic governance that could not be imposed at the point of a gun or a sword, but had to be nurtured from the inside out. Alleviate the glaring social ills and you help remove terrorism from the equation.

The Insider was not alone in his thinking of course. The idea was widespread in Indonesia that the U.S. could do itself a huge favor in the Muslim world if it pursued an evenhanded solution to the Palestinian-Israeli problem more aggressively, doled out aid more creatively, and meanwhile kept its mouth shut if all American officials had to say was how much respect they had for Islam while the U.S. military dropped bombs, accidentally or not, on innocent Muslim civilians. "Draining the swamp," the experts' term for improving conditions in the Muslim world, would, in the opinion of many people I talked to, work marvelously in a place like Indonesia that already had a solid record of development to build on—if only our two countries could do a better job of communicating on the same wavelength. People like Bashir or Jaffar or Habib Rizieq wouldn't disappear entirely, the idea ran, but they would become increasingly marginal.

Such arguments generally struck me as a little too pat and gauzy for their own good, and given the complexity of the world's terror map, I wasn't entirely persuaded. On the other hand, you had to admit the U.S. wasn't exactly doing a bang-up job of winning hearts and minds in the Muslim world at the moment, and at a minimum the Insider had given me that gift for which every inquiring hacks yearns—a picture frame to place around raw information that allows you to evaluate it anew and with at least some sense of coherence. For the time being that was plenty. I thanked my guest for coming, shook his hand, and then watched him quietly slip into the hallway, still surprised at the little miracle that had brought him to me in the first place.

20

JAVA MAN

The next morning at breakfast in the sun-splashed atrium, Norman looked over at me with a pained expression, and said, "My whole immune system is breaking down, Boss."

And to be honest he did look like a man who'd run a gauntlet, and not very successfully, either. The MSG-induced puffiness had subsided now, but his right eye in particular was a road map of angry red veins, as if someone had just removed their finger from it.

"Okay, Norman, tell you what," I said, "seeing as how it's Sunday and all, I suggest we confine our activities to something relaxing—like trying to track down our old shipmate from the Moluccas, Jaffar Umar Thalib."

Reza had been forced to return to Jakarta to tend to his domestic responsibilities, but his enthusiasm had been contagious. I only had two days left in the Islamic heartland now, and anticipating the finish line, I was experiencing a last burst of energy. Despite Reza's repeated phone calls, however, Jaffar had remained elusive quarry, flicking in and out of the reportorial underbrush with a variety of excuses, until he was finally reduced to one he thought perhaps even a bule journalist would understand—he said he was under a writing deadline for a magazine article. When that didn't put Reza off the trail, Jaffar got blunt: "Look," he'd said, "we have no time for you or your friend."

Ever the warrior at heart, Norman instantly brightened at my suggested itinerary, and raced off to arrange a car and driver. And so a few hours later I found myself in a clapped-out van rattling north through Jogja for the suburbs where Jaffar had his boarding school.

The day was bright and sunny, and feeling relaxed, I decided to devote our car time to piercing that other nagging mystery about Indonesia, the one involving Norman's movie career. In America, if a complete stranger doesn't fess up with a reasonable summary of his entire life story in the first five minutes, we think there's something seriously wrong with him; in Asia, some areas are still properly considered off limits. Having known Norman for four years now, and under some authentically trying circumstances, however, I was pretty sure it wasn't modesty alone that was causing him to hold back on the details. Yet all he had ever been willing to tell me about his film debut was the oeuvre's intriguingly poetic title, *Moon Pierced by the Wild Grass,* and that it had been shot against the backdrop of the sunan's palace in crumbling, romantic old Solo in its halcyon days before the city acquired its reputation as home to Terror, Incorporated.

"So it's a porno movie?" I said, hoping to provoke an irascible spilling of the beans, as the clang and clutter of the main thoroughfare in central Jogja merged with the new four-lane highway out of town.

Norman sighed. Then, in the ironic tone of a man who is ready to take his medicine, he said, "I guess you could call it a sort of a porno-erotic Javanese thriller."

"There was sex in the movie?"

"Sex?"

"You know, when people take off their clothes."

"Well, in manner of speaking, Boss," said Norman coyly. To his credit, he did then attempt to explain the plot to me—something complicated about a young man with a traffic-stopping oedipal complex who can only relate to women by touching their breasts.

"And let me guess," I said. "You were that young man."

Norman nodded, involuntarily beaming: "It's good to be me."

In keeping with the traditions of local politics, however, the shooting of the movie had not gone smoothly. Artistic differences inevitably arose between leading man Norman and the talented young director. "He was trying to do the Tarentino thing and the Altman thing at the same time," said Norman cryptically.

"He was winging it?" I said.

Everybody was winging it, said Norman. But when Norman felt obliged to offer what he considered some gimcrack suggestions for improving the story line, the director, like directors everywhere, proved unsurprisingly unsympathetic. Norman had been stripped of his duties as leading man, and his speaking parts were excised from the final cut.

"Well, the whole thing sounds decadent and Western to me, and I'm sure Jaffar would not approve," I said, clucking my tongue as I gazed out the window. The highway reminded me of Florida—flat and straight as an arrow, it was lined with fast-food restaurants, and acres of green vegetation that looked suspiciously like kudzu.

"By the way," I said, "do we have any idea where we're going?"

From the way the driver was swiveling his head from side to side, as if searching for an elusive landmark, the answer seemed pretty obvious, when Norman exclaimed, "Jeez, I thought Rez gave the guy directions." Why Reza would have bothered to orient a driver he did not know while on his way to catch an early-morning flight to Jakarta was a question the maintenance of sanity prevented me from pursuing.

"Let me make a radical suggestion," I said. "Let's stop and ask somebody." Norman folded his arms and shook his head emphatically. "Why on earth not?" I cried.

"The locals might get suspicious, Boss," said Norman, receding into his theatrical James Bond mode. I tried explaining to him that movies were after all really different from real life (though in fact I secretly have my doubts anymore), but Norman stuck to his theory, which, if I understood him correctly, was that protective locals might suspect the government was deploying intelligence operatives to case Jaffar's joint, and so by asking after Jaffar's whereabouts we would ourselves become objects of suspicion.

"So what?" I said, now exploring the brave new world beyond exasperation.

"We will be directed to the wrong place," said Norman, as if I had just asked him for help in finding the nose on my face.

"For godsakes, Norman," I fumed, "aren't we being just a little overly cautious?" But I knew it was hopeless. When Norman was in the thrall of one of his blessed vibes, there was no arguing with him. (And then of course there was the minor detail to consider that nine times out of ten he turned out to be right.) So with Norman determined to make a pageant of it, I sat back to enjoy the show.

At Norman's direction, we turned left off the highway and barreled purposefully along a lush, ferny side road with more of that wild grass boiling from the margins. We charged up a hill, turned around, and charged down again, only to turn up another blind alley. We had repeated this maneuver maybe a half-dozen times when Norman observed, philosophically, "I don't think we're going to find Jaffar today, Boss."

"What a surprise," I said.

"I'll call Reza tonight and check the whereabouts, and we can try again in the morning."

"You do that," I said, with what for me was a surprisingly even keel, though I was in fact just too exhausted to blow my top. All I really wanted now was to go back to the hotel for a quiet dinner and an early night. No sooner had we settled in at the restaurant, however, than the grand staircase leading down from the main lobby filled with dozens of elderly Swiss tourists. Spry and gabbling, they proceeded to descend on every last table in the vast room like a flock of geese zeroing in on a ripe cornfield.

I sat there watching in stunned silence as the energetic seniors, all sharp, happy elbows, attacked the buffet table without quarter, while Norman observed pithily, "Guess their local travel agent didn't fill them in about the Islamic radicals, Boss."

• • •

The next morning dawned bright and clear, and feeling refreshed after a good night's sleep, I was all revved up, looking forward to our midday meeting with the sultan. Norman, despite his worsening eye infection, was in top spirits, too, and over breakfast reported on a phone conversation he'd had with his mother in Jakarta the previous evening. "She gave me the phone number for the sultan's veterinarian," he said portentously.

"Yes?"

"The veterinarian who takes care of the sultan's white monkey," said Norman, as if perplexed over why I was proving particularly slow on the uptake this morning.

"Ah, that one," I said, nodding sagely. In fact even I knew that the white monkey was one of those important Javanese symbols whose vitality was considered barometer of the overall health of the sultan's realm.

"That's very sweet of your mom," I said, "and we'll have to think seriously about the white monkey, but first things first."

"You mean Jaffar?"

"No, I mean my package to New York." I had a batch of notebooks and other research materials I wanted to ship home for safekeeping, which is a sacred weekly ritual with me when I am on the road and it cannot, under any circumstances short of delirium or snakebite, be overlooked. Also, despite a remedial geographical skull session on the phone with Reza, Norman still seemed unsure of exactly where to find the scourge of the Moluccas. Eager to avoid another wild goose chase, I said, "You go ahead and look for Jaffar, Norman, and leave the mailman to me."

As Norman zoomed off to grab his video camera, I thought smugly: Knock yourself out, pal. But as soon as he'd left the dining room, I got a funny feeling—as if I knew exactly what was going to happen, which as it turned out is exactly what did happen.

Ninety minutes later I was in my room when the phone rang. It was Norman and he was in a state of high excitement. "Hey, Boss, you'll never guess what happened!"

"You met Jaffar . . ." I said.

"Hey, how did you know?" he said, sounding deflated.

"Bule intuition," I said. "Tell me about it."

"Well, Boss, it was like this: We were going up one of those little side roads in the same area as yesterday and suddenly I spotted this freshly painted sign for the boarding school. That's how I knew I was in the right place."

"Nice deduction," I said.

"Thank you, Boss. Anyhow, I told the driver to pull into the courtyard and after going a few meters I saw this stocky guy in a turban." From my experiences on the *Bukit Siguntang* I pictured two striding legs pounding the turf.

"The driver got very excited, Boss. He started yelling, 'That's him! That's Jaffar!' "

"That was a nice experience for the driver then."

"Yes, Boss. Anyway, it *was* Jaffar, and I jumped out of the van and called to the guy, 'Sir! You are Jaffar Umar Thalib, aren't you?' "

The man had turned and given Norman a startled look, but he answered with a polite smile. "Yes, I am," he said. "Who are you?"

Norman couldn't believe it. After all this time, and the dangers of our voyage into the far Moluccas, here he was standing in the lush and peaceful countryside talking as calmly to Jaffar as if they'd been discussing the pleasant intricacies of lawn care. "I'm Norman," said Norman, reminding Jaffar that they'd been shipmates on the good ship *Bukit Siguntang* in the spring of 2000.

"Oh yes, I remember now," said Jaffar affably but with suspicion. "What do you want?"

Norman told him that an American writer was staying in Jogja and very much wanted to talk with him. Jaffar stiffened at the word *American*.

"This isn't a good time," said Jaffar politely. "Maybe later."

But Norman pressed: "The American is leaving soon."

"No," said Jaffar. "Don't push me."

At that point, figuring there was nothing to lose, Norman whipped out his video camera, which he'd been concealing behind his back the whole time. He asked if he might take a souvenir shot, and then started filming before Jaffar could say yes or no. Looking suddenly alarmed, the avenger of Ambon, the bearer of Allah's torch, the man on whose orders villages had reportedly boiled with flame, held his hand up to his face and scurried away.

"At that point, Boss, the young guys with the goatees were coming around and giving me the dirty looks, so I figured I'd better get out of there fast. I thought somebody might blow a whistle, you know, and promising young filmmaker disappears forever."

"I don't blame you," I said evenly. And if Norman had been roughed up it wouldn't have been the first time an Indonesian journalist had been worked over by Jaffar's men.

"So what do you think, Boss?" said Norman. You could tell he was very excited about his journalistic coup.

Inwardly, what could I do but chuckle? Our long pursuit of Jaffar, having started in high drama, had now, rather poetically, I thought, ended in low farce. I also confess that I felt very proud of Norman just then. He had turned out to be an excellent reporter in every respect, and I really did admire his guts, gumption, and intelligence. But I wasn't about to tell him that.

"Now let me get this straight," I said slowly, feigning indignation. "I let you out of my sight for two minutes, and you wind up scooping me on my own story?!"

"But Boss . . ."

"Norman, I realize our roles are completely reversed now, and that you are really in charge of this operation, but please do me the favor of maintaining the fiction that I'm somehow still involved?"

By this time of course Norman realized that I was pulling his leg. "Sure thing, Boss," he said. "We're still on a strict need-to-know basis, but I'll try and keep you posted."

The day had turned sultry and overcast again when our driver threaded his way through the jostling pedicabs and belching minibuses and slipped behind the walls of the government compound in downtown Jogja. Ushered into the sultan's reception hall,

Norman and I sat down in a small gallery overlooking a formal courtyard, where pairs of turtledoves burbled softly in wicker cages hung from the eaves.

While we waited, Norman began his usual fidgeting with his electronic gear, and was soon doing a videotape study of the caged birds while I was busy remembering my first encounter with the sultan. Invited to join him on an inspection tour of a fish farm in one of Jogja's rural townships in 1999, Norman and I had managed to show up on time but at the wrong fish farm. Maniacally searching the maze of village roads, we'd finally found Hamengku Buwono X at the end of a particularly twisty lane sitting under a green canopy hemmed in gold and calmly puffing on a cigar.

At the time he was being energetically lectured to by an old man in a red baseball cap and a sarong, while laughing villagers looked on from rows of folding chairs. The sultan looked up and smiled when I sat down near him, and I was immediately struck by how little he resembled the frail, insect-nosed panjandrums depicted in the old sepia photos of Jogja. About my own age, he wore a forest green shirt and a wide floral necktie, and with his full, handsome face and warm, slightly exophthalmic eyes, he had the look of a melancholy big-band crooner from the 1930s.

There was nothing nostalgic about the sultan's message, however. Murmuring into his microphone, he had thanked the old man, and said, "We're trying to change our strategy for developing Jogjakarta." He then told the delighted villagers, in down-to-earth terms, how important it was to use the new tools made available through information technology to tie into the markets of the global economy. He struck me at that moment as a man very much determined to project the image of a modern leader who intended to use the past to inform the future without being trapped by it.[1]

But it was three years later now, and Indonesia seemed to have

---

1. One of Hamengku Buwono's claims on local hearts and minds was his decision to forgo the traditional sultanic pleasures of the seraglio for a modern marriage; he lived in a modest modern house outside the ornate palace with a single wife with whom he had raised a small, identifiable number of children.

effectively painted itself into a corner. Promising new laws designed to break Jakarta's chronic headlock on national power and wealth by giving local governments more say over their own affairs had been implemented badly. In the eyes of the critics, decentralization had succeeded only in democratizing corruption, providing a greater number of local power brokers with opportunities to cheat and swindle, and adopt politically popular elements of shariah law in a sort of chaotic, piecemeal Islamicization that, as a prominent pundit in Jakarta had told me, "is a recipe for breaking up Indonesia."

The sultan disagreed. When he and I were at length seated face-to-face in his cool, dimly lighted official parlor, he acknowledged that the road to reform had been a bumpy one. But he insisted decentralization was a boon—"It gives all areas and ethnic groups around the country a chance to build up their own identities," the sultan said, "and in the long run that's got to be seen as an opportunity for building a stronger national identity." Not to do so, he suggested solemnly, was by far the best recipe for disintegration.

The sultan seemed more subdued than I remembered him, but his eyes still conveyed a sense of modesty and centeredness, if perhaps a stronger hint of sadness, too. Apart from a handful of minor bombings attributed to Islamic radicals, however, Jogja had largely been spared the violence that had rocked other areas, and for that the sultan got the credit. Word on the street had it that Hamengku Buwono was no starry-eyed liberal and brooked little mess; there was an informal "telegraph" in Jogja and his office used it to keep dangerous elements in line. But his behavior was by all accounts impeccably democratic and, probably more important for the times, fair. Even Irfan Awwas and other fundamentalists spoke of the sultan with something like affection and respect.

"How have you managed to maintain control over militant Islam, in the wake of Bali and all?" I asked.

The sultan looked at me and puffed thoughtfully on his ever-present cigar. "All religious have their extremists," he said pointedly. "We will punish the criminals," he said, but you couldn't just go around arresting people for what was going on inside their heads—that wasn't democratic.

I thought briefly of the U.S. government's decision after 9/11 to detain terrorism suspects, even American citizens, as "enemy combatants" without due process of the law, and couldn't help wondering how a conversation between the sultan and presiding U.S. Attorney General John Ashcroft might go, when the sultan said Indonesia's real problem, to his mind, was not religious at all—"It's a crisis of civilization."

What did he mean?

"In Europe two hundred years ago you had the Industrial Revolution," he said. "In Japan it was the Meiji Revolution. That's what Indonesia is going through now. People come from a passive agrarian culture where competition is frowned upon because it disrupts social harmony. In an industrial society . . . individuals need to learn they can compete with one another and still live together peacefully."

Islam could certainly provide a moral basis, an anchor, for that sort of necessary learning process, but the real challenge lay in engineering a new system, with reliable courts, trustworthy police, and sturdy economic institutions, so the huge reservoir of human talent in the country could be properly put to use. "Unity diversity," the slogan of the founding fathers, had been a joke under Suharto's regime of forced tolerance, said the sultan. The challenge now—and one Americans might instinctively recognize—was to create a level playing field, "so minority groups feel they're being treated equally."

That was a matter of basic civil and human rights, said Hamengku Buwono, "and the supremacy of the law over politics. Only when people are proud of their ethnic identity can they appreciate the dignity of being Indonesian."

The sultan's use of the word "dignity" reminded me of something Norman had said back at the hotel on the night of the Swiss. We'd taken refuge from the rowdy seniors on a nearby patio, where, in the flickering Javanese candlelight, Norman had turned as serious as I'd ever seen him. "What does every human being want with their dying breath, Boss?" he demanded.

"Dignity, that's what," said Norman, without waiting for my reply. "That's what this country needs now, too—dignity. That's why people have to know that Indonesians aren't just a bunch of terrorists."

Now in the dusky light of the sultan's parlor, Hamengku Buwono, that other loyal son of Java, basically agreed, though in his opinion, he said, "The only thing more disastrous to self-esteem would be to have an inflated sense of dignity." The Bali bombers had proved that point. Inflamed and humiliated, they had been lured into the false romance of radical Islam and sent to Afghanistan for indoctrination—it was the fruition of globalization's darker dream.

"There will always be friction in a big country like this no matter what," said the sultan. "The only way for the government to manage though is through justice." What's more, dignity had to rest on real achievement.

I was now suddenly more impressed than ever with what Jadul and so many others I'd talked to had said about the power of Indonesia's natural social immunity to heal the country, if it were only allowed to work through the medium of good governance—a luxury that Jogjakarta had and, unfortunately, many other areas did not.

So in other words managing Indonesia's future wasn't a big job at all, I said, and won my first royal laugh. Taking a series of short puffs on his cigar, Hamengku Buwono mused, "Well, it will be a long journey, many generations. And my children already think I'm obsolete!"

From my last talk with the sultan, I knew he preferred to downplay what Norman called the "spooky stuff," but I was reminded of my conversation with Prince Joyokusumo about the old teachings of Javanese Islam, and "the battle within," and I felt compelled to say, "Jihad isn't something Americans easily picture. Tell me how you see it."

The sultan quietly put down his cigar. "My obligation as a Muslim is to wage jihad for the prosperity of my people," he said. "It has nothing to do with endangering others. It is developing the willpower to do whatever it takes to reach a goal *without having any personal stake in it.*"

I was wracking my brain to think of an American public servant to whom the same formula could fairly be applied (I know they exist but, oddly, none sprang immediately to mind) when the sultan leaned forward in his chair and said, *"Yakan?*—Do you see?" He then added with emphasis, "Personal involvement in trying to reach prosperity invites corruption, and that is not jihad. That is failure."

When we had talked for over an hour, and our conversation was drawing to a close, I asked the sultan, "What will happen if there's a war in Iraq? People tell me Indonesia will explode."

Hamengku Buwono shook his head. No—there were big anti-American street demonstrations after the U.S. invaded Afghanistan, he said, "But people will act more proportionately this time. Nobody really considers Saddam Hussein a standard-bearer for Islam."

I was frankly disappointed with that part, since it was so much at odds with the more incendiary view taken by nearly everybody else I'd talked to over the weeks. But of course the Commander of the Jihad Akbar had it exactly right—Indonesia did not explode.

I did. That evening we flew to Jakarta and I am ashamed to say I went completely ballistic when Norman informed me on the way in from the airport that we'd been summarily screwed by the appointments secretary to a high-ranking official I'd badly wanted to interview. After we'd spent several weeks repeatedly faxing letters on demand and jumping through all manner of bureaucratic hoops, it turned out that the man had been conning us all along—he knew his boss would be traveling to the U.S. and unavailable.

I was tired and homesick again—plus nothing infuriates me like bureaucratic game-playing. Having no bureaucrat present to personally berate, however, I ranted and raved, and blamed Norman, not so indirectly, I'm afraid, for failing to anticipate the trap. It is a mistake to set the bar too high for oneself, but I couldn't help thinking of the sultan, a contemporary in age, if nothing else, who was so self-contained, quietly determined, and focused on the big picture, while I, now gray with advancing middle age, remained a pathetic creature of fits and tempers, and an utter failure in my private jihad.

My friend Sabam Siagian was waiting for me at the hotel, pacing the lobby, and looking uncharacteristically frail and haggard. Still miffed at the United States government over its imposition of those ham-handed antiterrorism regulations for visitors from Muslim countries, he'd nonetheless risen from a sickbed with a bad dose of the flu and a jackhammer cough to say goodbye, and offer his advice and friendship. I was touched by that, but all through our dinner I felt extremely rotten nonetheless. I'd been a churlish boss and a bad friend to Norman, and after I shook Sabam's hand and went up to my room, I phoned him.

"Norman, I want to apologize to you deeply and without reservation," I said, and I meant every word of it.

"That's okay, Boss," said Norman philosophically. "There are times in this country when you have to blow your cork."

That was nice of him to say, but I could tell from the sound of his voice that he was feeling mangled by travel, fed up, and crestfallen, too. A willing but woefully inadequate jihadi, I went to bed trying to cheer myself with the only thing approaching a religious tenet I've ever consistently observed: Tomorrow, I promised myself, I will try and do better.

EPILOGUE:
Jihad Everlasting

I started this journal by asking who or what we were up against in fighting the war against terrorism, and whether Indonesia, the world's biggest Muslim enclave, might spin into an unremittingly hostile orbit. As I end it, I am happy to report that that big, tantalizing puzzle of a country, as vast and mysterious as our own, is still well within our global compass. But let's not kid ourselves: It also continues a dangerous, long-haul struggle against poverty, crime, and extremism, and the end to that grim business is nowhere in sight.

Unfortunately, the same holds true for terrorism.

On August 5, 2003, after I was safely back home in Manhattan, the carnage Penny Robertson and our other friends feared finally came to Jakarta when a powerful car bomb ripped the face off the J. W. Marriott Hotel, killing a dozen people and injuring 150. The blast catapulted the severed head of a Jemaah Islamiyah operative five floors up into the rubble—further proof of Sidney Jones's dictum that a small number of bad guys can do a lot of damage. Ten days later in neighboring Thailand, local police and CIA agents finally nabbed the JI warlord, Hambali, only to discover that his information was of limited value—a reminder that terror's international circuitry was morphing so fast even its kingpins couldn't keep up with it.

There were a few important symbolic victories: In September and October 2003, judges on Bali brought in guilty verdicts against the three lead nightclub bombers, Imam Samudra, Amrozi, and Ali Imron, and sentenced them to death. During the same period, however, a court in Jakarta acquitted Abu Bakar Bashir of his alleged role in the Christmas Eve 2000 church bombings and assorted acts of subversion. Sentenced to three years in prison on penny-ante immigration violations, and up for release on appeal to Indonesia's Supreme Court in April 2004, only strong behind-the-scenes pressure from U.S. officials encouraged Jakarta to consider hitting the wily emir with further indictments for Bali and other serious crimes.

Meanwhile Indonesian police and their counterparts in the region had managed to curb Jemaah Islamiyah's war-making capabilities by detaining dozens of lower-level actors. By then, however, unrest had broken out in mainly Buddhist Thailand's Islamic south, climaxing in a blazing gun battle with police in which over a hundred Muslim attackers were killed under typically murky circumstances. Western and regional intelligence officials uncovered a new cluster of JI training camps in the southern Philippines. Most chillingly perhaps, fresh leads pointed to the renewed possibly that JI might be contemplating the targeting for assassination of business people, diplomats, and other "high-profile" bule based in Indonesia.

Sidney Jones and other terrorism detectives were also hard at work, amassing evidence indicating that the embattled JI had spun off an even more radical militia, this one based in Central Sulawesi, up island from storied old Makassar, gateway to the Spice Islands, where fighting had also broken out again between Christians and Muslims. While slow to respond to the reports of renewed conflict, the Megawati government in May 2004 nonetheless made one executive decision: Jakarta effectively expelled Sidney Jones from Indonesia for persisting in her courageous work of exposing the country's terrorist networks, and their links with the worldwide Islamic revolution.

At the same time, and for reasons both good and bad, millions of

Indonesians remained convinced the United States government was continuing to exaggerate the threat of international terrorism to further its greedy pursuit of oil in the Middle East—just as those spice-hungry Europeans had once used the cause of advancing "civilization" to justify their lust for Indonesia's succulent nutmeg. Indonesia hadn't exploded, but elective war in Iraq had made America's job of winning new friends and keeping old ones there immeasurably harder.

The good news of course is that Indonesia was and is no Iraq. The country's game, if highly stressed, democracy has risen from within, not been imposed from without, and therefore despite their presently hibernating regard for the United States, many of its Muslim scholars, activists, business people, and politicians have continued, bravely and of their own accord, to argue for the democratic values and the standards of fairness and decency we all share. In April 2004, important parliamentary elections went off with only modest confusion nationwide. Hidayat Nurwahid's Islamist organization, the rechristened Justice *and Prosperity* Party registered a surge in support at the polls but, despite the fears of Indonesian moderates, it did so by stressing bread-and-butter social issues, not shariah, in a balanced, if contentious, field of competitors. The first-ever direct presidential elections scheduled for later in the year promised to be messily democratic but nonetheless democratic.

"We were hit on 9/11 by people who believed in hateful ideas," Tom Friedman wrote in his *New York Times* column. "We cannot win a war of ideas against such people by ourselves"—only fellow Muslims could do that. I wholeheartedly agree. The best news of all, therefore, is that friendship with the world's largest Muslim enclave not only makes sense for America, it is possible—it's just not inevitable. Friendship will require effort and imagination, and coming up with creative solutions to help Indonesia gain momentum over the social and economic problems that threaten its natural grace and integrity—in other words, it requires jihad, in the best and broadest meaning of the word.

None of that will be easy; on the other hand, building bridges, not blowing them up, strengthening countries from within, not destroying their natural defenses, ultimately marks our best lasting defense in the war against terrorism.

"My immune system is completely shot now, Boss," said Norman, looking up from his lunch tray, that microbe-infested right eye of his now an angry red planet. It was my last day in Indonesia, and our long journey had deposited us at Hoka Hoka Bento, a Japanese fast-food joint in the terminal at the Jakarta airport with sticky tabletops and frantic, gobbling travelers.

"You've really got to stop rubbing that eye and wash it out with some proper medicine," I scolded him.

Norman shrugged forlornly, and complained, "What I've really got to do is find a more stable line of work, Boss."

That was true enough, and frankly I felt a little guilty about leaving Norman in the lurch. All I had to do was return home and write a book. Norman, who had quit his day job to baby-sit yet another obstreperous fly-by-night bule, had to stay behind in Indonesia, come up with a new scheme that would secure his financial future, provide for his domestic tranquillity, and engineer a reunion with his beloved little Annie into the bargain. Where would he find his place in the turmoil of his beloved country?

I wanted to help. For lack at a better idea, I said, "Let's not overlook the exciting opportunities to be had in cultivating the elusive kopi luwak."

I was referring here to a true oddity of Indonesia's vast coffee-growing industry. The luwak, or Paradoxurus hermaphroditus, is a tree-dwelling civet cat, which roams the Indonesian hills, where it consumes coffee beans as an aid to digestion, not unlike the way a chicken ingests bits of gravel. But for the discerning luwak only the enzymes contained in the ripest, sweetest-tasting beans will do. According to Norman's intelligence, beans harvested from luwak scat were so highly prized by the coffee cognoscenti they marketed, when available at all, at three hundred dollars a pound. If we could only harness the kopi cat's gustatory oddities, Norman had theorized, we'd be rich men, just like the old-time spice chasers.

"But we still need a business plan," he said, scratching his jaw, his streaky red eye fixing me expectantly.

"That's easy," I said. "We run the thing the way the big corporations do those giant poultry farms. You put the luwak in little wire cages and then force-feed them so many beans a day—sort of a bean consumption quota."

Norman looked appalled. "But, Boss, the whole idea is for the cats to be free to roam around so they choose only the best beans."

"You're speaking now of the free-range luwak, I believe," I said, playing the role of the crass corporate strategist. "Not cost-effective, Norman. You have to cage them and feed them—that's the only way to make it pay."

Norman laughed skeptically, suggesting my idea for overworking the poor coffee cat was not unlike my attitude toward interpreter-guides, but I could tell he was hooked.

"Look, you just industrialize the process, and then you market a kopi luwak *blend,* you know, maybe ten or twenty percent of the real stuff. That way you capitalize on the lore, the misty plantations of Old Java and all that, while minimizing the use of the expensive beans."

"That's okay?"

"Nobody outside Indonesia will ever know the difference. Starbucks and the other big outfits will eat it up. We'll be the toast of Manhattan."

"We could bring in Reza as a partner," said Norman enthusiastically.

"You bet," I said. "Always room for a good anarchist."

I looked at my watch, and said, "Oh Christ." It was time to go. We'd have to put our dreams of commercial success on hold, for a little while anyway. Two weary soldiers, Norman and I rose and saluted one another over the scattered chopsticks and discarded juice boxes.

"Nice knowing you, Norman."

"Same here, Boss."

I then walked into the security area where a balky conveyor belt pulled my battered shoulder bag through the X-ray machine, and by the time I turned to wave goodbye, Norman had vanished into the crowd of strangers pressing the other side of the thick glass wall.

When I arrived in prosperous, disciplined Singapore that evening, the palmy thoroughfares looking like an immaculate conception of Beverly Hills, my jolly, overfed taxi driver said very pleasantly, "Indonesia?! Thank God you're out of there, and safe and sound now."

I knew exactly what he meant of course—and I must tell you, my friends, I very deeply resented it.

ACKNOWLEDGMENTS

The traveler relies on the kindness of friends and strangers, and I am indebted to many. I would like to thank Bill Allen and the editors at the *National Geographic* for the opportunity to explore Indonesia in the first place, and especially to thank former executive editor Bob Poole for his friendship and guidance. I am also grateful to my friend Ann Judge, who ran the Travel Division at the Geographic Society with skill, enthusiasm, and humor until the morning of September 11, 2001, when she boarded American Flight 77 in Washington and became a victim of the hijacking attack on the Pentagon; the world remains as interesting and endearingly quirky a place as Ann always said it was, though it's no longer nearly so much fun.

While any errors or omissions that have inadvertently crept into this record belong solely to the recorder, approaching the realities of a country as endlessly challenging and complex as Indonesia would have been impossible altogether without the help and forbearance of dozens of Indonesians from many walks of life who took the time (and at times the risk) to try and educate me. I am grateful to them all; whether mentioned by name in this story or not, whether ultimately I saw eye to eye with them or not—the light from their individual torches all helped illuminate our way.

I would like to specifically thank: Sabam Siagian, Aristides Katoppo, Mochtar Buchori, Goenawan Mohamad, and Jusuf Wanandi, for their wise counsel, and Bambang Harymurti of *Tempo* magazine for introducing me to my inimitable guide and friend Norman; my generous colleagues John McBeth, Yuli Ismartono, Tantyo Bangun, Jane Perlez, Raymond Bonner, Desi Anwar, Jason Tedjasukmana, Antonia Soriente, Dennis Heffernan, Alexandra Boulat, Davida Kales, and Greta Morris, and Karl Fritz; experts on Southeast Asia Sidney Jones, Jack Bresnan, Ann Marie Murphy, Peter Drysdale, and Kishore Mahbubani; new and helpful friends Gusky Suarsana and Karen Waddell, Odeck and Tara Ariawan, Iskander Waworuntu, Mohammad Ishom, Adji Damais, and Ardiyanto Pranata; and my old Asia pals, who have taught me much about the territory over the years and nearly everything else I can think of that matters, Susumu Awanohara, Arthur Mitchell, and Robert Delfs.

A book is a journey unto itself of course, and special thanks go to my editor at William Morrow, Henry Ferris, for his direction, insight, and patience, and to my agent, Philip Spitzer, for deftly putting us together.

In life's journey, any traveler is blessed to roam in the company of a few boon companions. My deepest gratitude is reserved for my wife, Toshiko, who has traveled the road for twenty-six years, lovingly and without complaint. In Indonesia, of course, I was lucky enough to cross paths with that remarkable Alwi clan—namely Des, Tanya, and Ramon. And finally, without those excellent men Norman Wibowo and Faisal Reza, there would have been no story to tell at all. I can only hope that in writing about our adventures together I've done some small justice to their dreams for better and more just days ahead.

SUGGESTED READING

Allah's Torch, as I mentioned at the outset, was inspired in part by an article I wrote for *National Geographic* magazine, which appeared in the March 2001 edition under the title, "Indonesia: Living Dangerously." Readers of that original animal will occasionally find its footprints scattered herein, but for those individuals looking to more fully explore the subject matter, I'd recommend turning to the following list of works for an immeasurably greater range of insight and inspiration.

GENERAL

Barber, Benjamin R. *Jihad vs. McWorld: How Globalism and Tribalism Are Reshaping the World.* New York: Times Books, 1995.

Mahbubani, Kishore. *Can Asians Think? Understanding the Divide Between East and West.* Hanover, NH: Steerforth Press, 2002.

ISLAM AND THE WORLD

Armstrong, Karen. *Islam: A Short History.* New York: Random House, 2000.

Berman, Paul. *Terror and Liberalism.* New York: W.W. Norton & Company, 2003.

Buruma, Ian, and Avishai Margalit. *Occidentalism: The West in the Eyes of Its Enemies.* New York: The Penguin Press, 2004.

Friedman, Thomas L. *Longitudes and Attitudes: Exploring the World After September 11.* New York: Farrar, Straus and Giroux, 2002.

Lewis, Bernard. *What Went Wrong? Western Impact and Middle Eastern Response.* New York: Oxford University Press, 2002.

Naipaul, V. S. *Among the Believers: An Islamic Journey.* New York: Alfred A. Knopf, 1981.

———*Beyond Belief: Islamic Excursions Among the Converted Peoples.* New York: Random House, 1998.

TERRORISM

Abuza, Zachary. *Militant Islam in Southeast Asia: Crucible of Terror.* Boulder, CO: Lynne Rienner Publishers, 2003.

Gunaratna, Rohan. *Inside Al Qaeda: Global Network of Terror.* New York: Columbia University Press, 2002.

Ressa, Maria A. *Seeds of Terror: An Eyewitness Account of Al-Qaeda's Newest Center of Operations in Southeast Asia.* New York: Free Press, 2003.

INDONESIA

Hamengku Buwono X, Sultan (patron). *Kraton Jogja: The History and Cultural Heritage.* Jakarta: Karaton Ngayogyakarta Hadiningrat and Indonesia Marketing Association, 2002.

Ricklefs, M. C. *A History of Modern Indonesia Since c. 1300.* Stanford, CA: Stanford University Press, 1993.

Schwarz, Adam. *A Nation in Waiting: Indonesia's Search for Stability.* Boulder, CO: Westview Press, 2000.

Turner, Peter, et al. *Indonesia.* Hawthorn, Australia: Lonely Planet Publications, 1997.

SPICE ISLANDS

Hanna, Willard A. *Indonesian Banda: Colonialism and Its Aftermath in the Nutmeg Islands.* Banda Naira, Moluccas—East Indonesia: Yayasan Warisan dan Budaya, 1991.

Hanna, Willard A., and Des Alwi. *Turbulent Times Past and Present in Ternate and Tidore.* Banda Naira, Moluccas—East Indonesia: Yayasan Warisan dan Budaya, 1990.

Milton, Giles. *Nathaniel's Nutmeg or, The True and Incredible Adventures of the Spice Trader Who Changed the Course of History.* New York: Farrar, Straus and Giroux, 1999.

Muller, Kal. *Spice Islands: Exotic Eastern Indonesia.* Lincolnwood, IL: Passport Books, 1993.

Seabrook, John. "Soldiers and Spice: Why the Dutch Traded Manhattan for a Speck of Rock in the South Pacific." *The New Yorker,* August 13, 2001.

BALI

Pringle, Robert. *A Short History of Bali: Indonesia's Hindu Realm.* Crows Nest, Australia: Allen & Unwin, 2004.

FICTION

Conrad, Joseph. *The Portable Conrad.* New York: Penguin Books, 1985.

Koch, Christopher J. *The Year of Living Dangerously.* New York: Penguin Books, 1983.

Multatuli. *Max Havelaar, Or the Coffee Auctions of a Dutch Trading Company,* trans. Roy Edwards. New York: Penguin Books, 1987.

PAPERS AND REPORTS

Masters, Edward, and the National Commission on U.S.-Indonesian Relations. "Strengthening U.S. Relations with Indonesia: Toward a Partnership for Human Resource Development," Copublished by The National Bureau of Asian Research, Seattle, Washington, et al., 2003, and available online at www.nbr.org.

As noted in the text, various excellent research reports on terrorism in Southeast Asia and the turmoil in the Moluccas are available online from the International Crisis Group at www.icg.org and Human Rights Watch at www.hrw.org.

INDEX